AIRL: INTERVIEW WITH AN ALIEN

Written by

Darryl Harvey

Based on, True Events

94th Place Films
L.A., CA 90047
© 2025 All Rights Reserved

EXT. TOWNHOME - DAY

INSERT CARD: AUGUST 12, 2007, MEATH, IRELAND

The sound of a typewriter is heard over the picturesque view.

INT. TOWNHOME - DAY

Army Achievements Certificates with the name *Matilda O'Donnell MacElroy* sit in picture frames and are prominently displayed on a table.

A dated black and white photo of a youthful *Matilda O'Donnell MacElroy* wearing an Army uniform noticeably stands out on the same table.

An 83-year-old white woman, MATILDA O'DONNELL MACELROY sits at her desk typing away on an old Underwood typewriter.

Matilda pauses momentarily looking over the letter. She continues typing as the sound of the typewriter keys begins to fade and Matilda's voice is heard...

FLASHBACK:

INT. ROOM - DAY

In a very ordinary space, three wooden chairs are butt up against a wall. A cast iron heating radiator sticks out from the same wall, just above that is a window with partially opened flower-patterned curtains.

Squatting in front is MAJOR JESSE MARCEL, a white male age 30. He is wearing a long-sleeved beige khaki shirt with an Air Force patch on the shoulder and metal stripes and bars on his collars.

Flashbulbs are going off, press photographers clamor around Major Jesse Marcel as he holds up the tattered remnants of the weather balloon. The voice of Matilda is heard...

> MATILDA (V.O.)
> Dear, Lawrence, as you know in July 1947, the Roswell Army Airfield (RAAF) issued a press release stating that personnel from the field's 509th Bomb Group had recovered a crashed "flying disc" from a ranch near Roswell, New Mexico, sparking intense media interest.
> (MORE)

> MATILDA (V.O.) (CONT'D)
> Later that same day, the Commanding General of the Eighth Air Force stated that Major Jesse Marcel, who was involved with the original recovery of the debris, had recovered only the tattered remnants of a weather balloon. The facts of the incident have been suppressed by the United States government since then...

Spread out on the hardwood floor in front of Jesse are the tattered metallic debris of what appears to be a weather balloon.

END FLASHBACK.

INT. TOWNHOME - DAY

Matilda is still sitting at the desk and pulls the letter from the old Underwood typewriter. As she peruses the letter, again her voice is heard...

> MATILDA (V.O.)
> You may not know that I was enlisted in the U.S. Women's Army Air Force (WAC) Medical Corp which was a part of the US Army back then. I was assigned to the 509th Bomb Group as a Flight Nurse at the time of the incident. Please accept this material and make it known to as many people as possible. Mankind needs to know the answers to questions that are contained in these documents. Who are we? Where did we come from? What is our purpose on Earth? Is Mankind alone in the universe? If there is intelligent life elsewhere, why have they not contacted us?

Matilda stops scanning the letter with her eyes and takes a breath, she looks up from the letter and ponders...

I/E. JEEP - NIGHT

INSERT CARD: JULY 1947

Driving over rough terrain. A 23-year-old Matilda is accompanying Captain SHERIDAN D. CAVITT, a male white age 40, Chief Counter-Intelligence Corps (CIC) Officer.

EXT. CRASH SITE - NIGHT

Military police have cordoned off the area.

Huge bright lights shine down on what is the obvious uniquely indistinguishable wreckage of an alien spacecraft.

Captain Cavitt dressed in his army uniform and Matilda dressed in her WWII Army Nurse Corps Uniform. As they approach the spacecraft both Captain Cavitt and Matilda look astonished.

                    SHERIDAN D. CAVITT
     Nurse MacElroy render any needed
     emergency medical assistance to any
     survivors, if necessary.

                          MATILDA
     Yes, sir.

Matilda cautiously approaches the spacecraft, she sees three small Alien beings stretched out on the ground, it's apparent they are dead. Matilda is fixated on the dead Alien bodies.

As Matilda looks up, a live ALIEN being wearing a one-piece suit is standing there, surrounded by hostile-looking armed Military personnel including ARMY OFFICER #1, ARMY OFFICER #2, and ARMY OFFICER #3

                       ARMY OFFICER #1
     Can you understand me?

                       ARMY OFFICER #2
     Are you able to speak?

                       ARMY OFFICER #3
        (pointing to his ears)
     Can you hear me?

The Alien just casually stands showing no emotion and is uncommunicative.

The chatter from Army Officer #1, Army Officer #2, and Army Officer #3 goes quiet. Matilda walks through the Military personnel and approaches the live Alien being.

While Matilda examines the Alien being for injuries. Suddenly, the Alien looks straight at Matilda. An explosion of emotions burst into her mind...

INSERT IMAGES:

Quick flashes of Depression, Loneliness, Fear, and Dread.

BACK TO:

Matilda breaks the stare of the Alien and looks shocked.

Captain Sheridan Cavitt has convened with other Military personnel when Matilda approaches.

          MATILDA
Excuse me, Captain Cavitt. May I speak with you?

Captain Sheridan Cavitt and Matilda step away from the Military personnel.

          SHERIDAN D. CAVITT
What is it MacElroy?

          MATILDA
The Alien being.

          SHERIDAN D. CAVITT
Yes.

          MATILDA
It tried to communicate with me. None of the other officers had any success.

          SHERIDAN D. CAVITT
Did it talk to you? What did it say?

          MATILDA
It was non-verbal.

          SHERIDAN D. CAVITT
What do you mean non-verbal?

          MATILDA
Telepathic thoughts.

          SHERIDAN D. CAVITT
MacElroy are you sure?

                    MATILDA
          That's the only way I can describe
          it. None of the other officers
          could perceive these thoughts, and
          the Alien seemed able and willing
          to communicate with me.

                    SHERIDAN D. CAVITT
          Wait here.

Captain Sheridan Cavitt re-convenes with the Military
personnel. It appears they are having a serious
conversation.

Captain Sheridan Cavitt walks away from the Military
personnel and re-approaches Matilda.

                    SHERIDAN D. CAVITT (CONT'D)
          MacElroy.

                    MATILDA
          Yes, sir.

                    SHERIDAN D. CAVITT
          It's been decided, after a brief
          consultation with a senior officer,
          that you will accompany the
          surviving Alien back to the base.
          This is partly due to the fact that
          you're a nurse and can attend to
          the physical needs of the Alien, as
          well as serve as a nonthreatening
          communicator and companion.

EXT. ROSWELL ARMY AIR FORCE BASE - HALLWAY - NIGHT

Matilda is escorted by Military Police up to an office door.
Stenciled on the opaque office door window is the name,
Colonel William H. Blanchard.

Matilda walks in the door and the Military police wait
outside.

INT. ROSWELL ARMY AIR FORCE BASE - OFFICE - NIGHT

Behind a desk dressed in full regalia sits Army Colonel
WILLIAM H. BLANCHARD white male, age 31.

In walks Matilda, she salutes Colonel Blanchard.

MATILDA
Private MacElroy, Nurse, U.S.
Women's Army Air Force reporting.

Colonel Blanchard, with a stoic look on his face, reclines in his chair.

WILLIAM H. BLANCHARD
Relax, MacElroy. -- Do you understand the gravity which your involvement, in this... This unfathomable event is.

MATILDA
I believe so, I've given it some thought.

WILLIAM H. BLANCHARD
Some thought. Would you care to share those thoughts?

MATILDA
I can't quite put it into words, sir.

WILLIAM H. BLANCHARD
Try.

MATILDA
Astonishing, inconceivable, beyond belief, and yet --

WILLIAM H. BLANCHARD
Go, ahead.

MATILDA
It shook my reality. But it was tangible. Mentally disturbing.

WILLIAM H. BLANCHARD
MacElroy, your implication in this situation is life-threatening.

Matilda's face sags and becomes flush.

MATILDA
(threatened)
What do you mean Colonel?

WILLIAM H. BLANCHARD
This is above Top Secret. We will go to any lengths to keep this from the public. Do you understand?

MATILDA
I believe so, yes, sir.

WILLIAM H. BLANCHARD
I'm giving you a new directive.
You are hereby assigned to
permanently serve as a
"companion" to the Alien at all
times. Among your duties is to
communicate with and interview the
Alien and to make a complete report
of all that you discover to command
authorities. You'll be given a
promotion in rank to Senior Master
Sergeant to improve your security
rating and to increase your pay
grade from fifty-four dollars a
month to one hundred thirty-eight
dollars a month. Do you have any
questions?

MATILDA
No, sir.

WILLIAM H. BLANCHARD
You're dismissed.

Matilda with a quizzical look on her face, salutes Colonel Blanchard.

INT. MEDICAL EXAMINATION ROOM - NIGHT

MAN #1 and MAN #2 are wearing biohazard suits they are examining the Alien, and its height and weight measurements are taken. The Alien is completely docile as this takes place.

Man #1 is holding a stethoscope, and he puts it to the Aliens chest -- listening he turns to Man #2.

MAN #1
(muffled voice)
I can't detect a heartbeat.

Man #2 is holding a sphygmomanometer stoops over and places a blood pressure cuff around the Aliens arm.

Man #2 is squeezing the inflation bulb, and the cuff around the Aliens arm inflates. Man #2 turns the valve on the inflation bulb, air can be heard seeping out and he looks at the manometer gauge -- it shows zero.

Man #2 turns to Man #1...

                    MAN #2
               (muffled voice)
          It has no blood pressure.

                    MAN #1
          What do you mean it has no blood
          pressure?

Man #2 holding up the manometer gauge.

                    MAN #2
          Look.

Just then Matilda walks in.

Both Man #1 and Man #2 pause from what they are doing.

                    MATILDA
          I'm Senior Master Sergeant Matilda
          O'Donnell MacElroy. I'm a nurse
          and personal companion to the
          Alien.

Man #2 points to the Alien.

                    MAN #2
          This thing is dead.

The Alien just looks on with ever so slight head movements.

EXT. ROSWELL ARMY AIR FORCE BASE - BUILDING - NIGHT

The area has been transformed into a buzzing hive of
activity. A dozen men are working unloading equipment and
supplies from trucks.

INT. ROSWELL ARMY AIR FORCE BASE - INTERVIEW ROOM - LATER

Military personnel are setting up lights and camera
equipment. A motion picture camera, microphone and tape
recorder are being set up.

A STENOGRAPHER and several people are busy typing on
typewriters.

EXT. MEDICAL EXAMINATION ROOM - HALLWAY - LATER

The doors swing open, and the Alien is carted out in a
wheelchair by Matilda, she is met by Captain Sheridan Cavitt
and the Military police.

SHERIDAN D. CAVITT
Follow me.

As they are walking...

SHERIDAN D. CAVITT (CONT'D)
An expert foreign language
interpreter and a "code breaking"
team have been flown to the base to
assist in efforts to communicate
with the Alien. A professor of
psychology is here to help
formulate questions and "interpret"
the answers.

MATILDA
Yes, sir.

EXT. ROSWELL ARMY AIR FORCE BASE - INTERVIEW ROOM - LATER

The Military police open the door.

It appears that the Alien is strapped in the wheelchair as Matilda pushes it through the door followed by Captain Sheridan Cavitt.

INT. ROSWELL ARMY AIR FORCE BASE - INTERVIEW ROOM

The stenographer, Military and non-military personnel look on with bewilderment.

Matilda with Captain Sheridan Cavitt in tow, parks the wheelchair next to a large recliner.

Matilda carefully unstraps the Alien and assists it into the large recliner. The Alien has no clothes on and no visible signs of genitalia, it doesn't resist and sits calmly.

SHERIDAN D. CAVITT
Alright, everyone clear the room
except for Sergeant MacElroy.

The stenographer, along with military and civilian personnel, exits through the door.

SHERIDAN D. CAVITT (CONT'D)
MacElroy, you will be observed at
all times...
    (pointing)
...through that one-way glass
window.

Captain Sheridan Cavitt hands Matilda some papers.

>   SHERIDAN D. CAVITT (CONT'D)
>   The stenographer will debrief you
>   after each interview.
>
>   MATILDA
>   Yes, sir.

Captain Sheridan Cavitt exits out the door.

EXT. ROSWELL ARMY AIR FORCE BASE - INTERVIEW ROOM

The Military police stand guard at the door.

As Captain Sheridan Cavitt walks out the door he is greeted by Colonel William H. Blanchard.

>   WILLIAM H. BLANCHARD
>   So, what do you think?
>
>   SHERIDAN D. CAVITT
>   She's our only option at the
>   moment.

INT. ROSWELL ARMY AIR FORCE BASE - INTERVIEW ROOM

The Alien sits there in the large recliner showing no emotional sign.

INSERT CARD: TOP SECRET OFFICIAL TRANSCRIPT OF THE U.S. ARMY AIR FORCE ROSWELL ARMY AIR FIELD, 509TH BOMB GROUP SUBJECT: ALIEN INTERVIEW, 9. 7. 1947

Looking at the list in her hand. Matilda sits in a chair directly in front of the Alien being, they look at each other and begin to interface.

>   MATILDA (V.O.)
>   Are you injured?

The Alien answers and its tone is feminine, very similar to Matilda's vocal tone.

>   ALIEN (V.O.)
>   No.
>
>   MATILDA (V.O.)
>   What medical assistance do you
>   require?

ALIEN (V.O.)
None.

MATILDA (V.O.)
Do you need food or water or other sustenance?

ALIEN (V.O.)
No.

MATILDA (V.O.)
Do you have any special environmental needs, such as air temperature, atmospheric chemical content, air pressure, or waste elimination?

ALIEN (V.O.)
No. I am not a biological being.

MATILDA (V.O.)
Does your body or spacecraft carry any germs or contamination that may be harmful to humans or other Earth life forms?

ALIEN (V.O.)
No germs in space.

MATILDA (V.O.)
Does your government know you are here?

ALIEN (V.O.)
Not at this time.

MATILDA (V.O.)
Are others of your kind going to come looking for you?

ALIEN (V.O.)
Yes.

MATILDA (V.O.)
What is the weapons capability of your people?

ALIEN (V.O.)
Very destructive.

INT. ROSWELL ARMY AIR FORCE BASE - INTERROGATION ROOM

While standing, a dim light illuminates Captain Sheridan Cavitt and Colonel William H. Blanchard as Military police stand guard.

A harsh spotlight shines down on Matilda while she sits at a small table.

                    MATILDA
I didn't understand the exact nature of the kind of arms or weapons that they might have, but I didn't feel that there was any malevolent intention in her reply, just a statement of fact.

INT. ROSWELL ARMY AIR FORCE BASE - INTERVIEW ROOM

The Alien still sitting in the large recliner shows no emotion except slight head and torso movement.

Matilda still sits directly in front of the Alien as they continue to interface.

                    MATILDA (V.O.)
Why did your spacecraft crash?

                    ALIEN (V.O.)
It was struck by an electrical discharge from the atmosphere which caused us to lose control.

                    MATILDA (V.O.)
Why was your spacecraft in this area?

                    ALIEN (V.O.)
Investigation of "burning cloud," radiation, explosions.

                    MATILDA (V.O.)
How does your spacecraft fly?

                    ALIEN (V.O.)
It is controlled through "mind." Responds to "thought commands."

INT. ROSWELL ARMY AIR FORCE BASE - INTERROGATION ROOM

Still seated at the small table, a harsh spotlight shines down on Matilda.

Captain Sheridan Cavitt and Colonel William H. Blanchard loom over Matilda as the Military police stand guard.

> MATILDA
> "Mind" or "thought command" are the only English language words I can think of to describe the thought. Their bodies, and I think, the spacecraft, are connected directly to them through some kind of electrical "nervous system" that they control with their own thoughts.

INT. ROSWELL ARMY AIR FORCE BASE - INTERVIEW ROOM

With the list in her hand. Matilda is still seated in front of the Alien, its small child-like body is dwarfed by the large recliner, as they continue to interface...

> MATILDA (V.O.)
> How do your people communicate with each other?

> ALIEN (V.O.)
> Through mind. Thought.

INT. ROSWELL ARMY AIR FORCE BASE - INTERROGATION ROOM

Rigid as a statue. The military police are in silhouette.

Captain Sheridan Cavitt and Colonel William H. Blanchard, barely distinguishable in the dim light, are sitting directly across from Matilda.

Sitting at that small table, under the oppressive heat from the harsh spotlight, Matilda almost seems to wilt.

> MATILDA
> The words "mind" and "thought" combined together are the closest English language words I can think of to describe the idea at this time. However, it was very obvious to me that they communicate directly from the mind, just as she is communicating with me.

INT. ROSWELL ARMY AIR FORCE BASE - INTERVIEW ROOM

The Alien sits in the large recliner, its huge almond-shaped eyes are locked onto Matilda as she sits in front of the being.

          MATILDA (V.O.)
  Do you have a written language or
  symbols for communication?

          ALIEN (V.O.)
  Yes.

          MATILDA (V.O.)
  What planet are you from?

          ALIEN (V.O.)
  The home, birthplace, world of The
  Domain.

INT. ROSWELL ARMY AIR FORCE BASE - INTERROGATION ROOM

The harsh spotlight beams brightly onto Matilda, she appears to be under duress from the intense stares of Captain Sheridan Cavitt and Colonel William H. Blanchard.

          MATILDA
  Since I am not an astronomer, I
  have no way of thinking in terms of
  stars, galaxies, constellations,
  and directions in space. The
  impression I received was of a
  planet in the center of a huge
  cluster of galaxies that is to her
  like "home", or "birthplace". The
  word "domain" is the closest word I
  can think of to describe her
  concept, images, and thoughts about
  where she is from. It could as
  easily be called the "territory" or
  the "realm". However, I am sure
  that it was not just a planet or a
  solar system or a cluster of stars,
  but an enormous number of galaxies!

INT. ROSWELL ARMY AIR FORCE BASE - INTERVIEW ROOM

A solid red tally light is visible on a camera that is set up on a tripod.

An intense interface is happening between the Alien and Matilda.

The Alien sits still in the large recliner as if in a trance. Matilda is locked into the Aliens gaze.

INT. ROSWELL ARMY AIR FORCE BASE - CONTROL ROOM

An AEG Magnetophon reel-to-reel tape recorder is functioning.

A TV monitor displays an image of the Alien and Matilda staring at each other.

Military personnel are seated behind a console turning knobs, pushing buttons, and moving levers.

Looking through the one-way glass window at the Alien and Matilda are Captain Sheridan Cavitt and Colonel William H. Blanchard.

> WILLIAM H. BLANCHARD
> If MacElroy can't extract useful information from the Alien. We may have to take extreme measures.

> SHERIDAN D. CAVITT
> I'm worried that she can be compromised -- And if that happens...

INT. ROSWELL ARMY AIR FORCE BASE - INTERVIEW ROOM

Matilda holding the list looks as if she is hypnotized.

> MATILDA (V.O.)
> Will your government send representatives to meet with our leaders?

The Alien, doll-like in appearance, seated in the large recliner stares into Matilda's eyes.

> ALIEN (V.O.)
> No.

> MATILDA (V.O.)
> What are your intentions concerning Earth?

> ALIEN (V.O.)
> Preserve. Protect property of The Domain.

                    MATILDA (V.O.)
          What have you learned about Earth's
          governments and military
          installations?

                    ALIEN (V.O.)
          Poor. Small. Destroy planet.

                    MATILDA (V.O.)
          Why haven't your people made your
          existence known to the people of
          Earth?

                    ALIEN (V.O.)
          Watch. Observe. No contact.

INT. ROSWELL ARMY AIR FORCE BASE - INTERROGATION ROOM

In the dim light. A cigar smolders as it hangs from the
mouth of Colonel William H. Blanchard.

Captain Sheridan Cavitt with his arms folded sits in front of
Matilda.

                    SHERIDAN D. CAVITT
          Are you sure it's transmitting
          thoughts?

Matilda drops her head in her hands.

                    MATILDA
          Yes.

Colonel William H. Blanchard turns the harsh spotlight onto
Matilda's face, she raises her hand to shield her eyes from
the light.

                    MATILDA (CONT'D)
          Is that necessary?

                    WILLIAM H. BLANCHARD
          Maybe you're being deceptive.
          Trying to deliberately deceive us?

                    MATILDA
          I have no reason to do that.

Captain Sheridan Cavitt looks over a list he's holding.

                    SHERIDAN D. CAVITT
          I don't like the answers it's
          giving you.

MATILDA
I got the impression that contact
with people on Earth was not
permitted, but I could not think of
a word or idea that communicated
the impression I got exactly. They
are just observing us.

INT. ROSWELL ARMY AIR FORCE BASE - INTERVIEW ROOM

The Alien with ever so slight head movement eerily stares at Matilda.

The Alien still in the large recliner and Matilda still sitting in front of the Alien are locked in on each other.

MATILDA (V.O.)
Have your people visited Earth
previously?

ALIEN (V.O.)
Periodic. Repeating observation.

MATILDA (V.O.)
How long have you known about
Earth?

ALIEN (V.O.)
Long before humans.

INT. ROSWELL ARMY AIR FORCE BASE - INTERROGATION ROOM

Captain Sheridan Cavitt sits at the small table in front of Matilda.

Puffing on the cigar, Colonel William H. Blanchard paces back and forth.

WILLIAM H. BLANCHARD
You're forming opinions based on
the Alien's answers. I can't rely
on opinions. Just facts.

MATILDA
I am not sure if the word
"prehistoric" would be more
accurate, but it was definitely a
very long period of time before
human beings evolved.

INT. ROSWELL ARMY AIR FORCE BASE - CONTROL ROOM

The analog magnetic reel-to-reel tape on the AEG Magnetophon slowly turns.

Military personnel are sitting at the console adjusting knobs, pushing buttons, and moving levers.

The Alien and Matilda can be seen through the one-way glass window.

INT. ROSWELL ARMY AIR FORCE BASE - INTERVIEW ROOM

In their usual position, the Alien is planted in the large recliner, and Matilda is stationed in her chair.

The Alien and Matilda are locked in a stare as they interface.

          MATILDA (V.O.)
  What do you know about the history
  of civilization on Earth?

          ALIEN (V.O.)
  Small interest. Attention. Small
  time.

INT. ROSWELL ARMY AIR FORCE BASE - INTERROGATION ROOM

The butt of a cigar hits the floor, and a foot steps on it.

Colonel William H. Blanchard blows smoke out of his mouth and pulls up a seat next to Captain Sheridan Cavitt.

Blanchard takes the list from Cavitt's hand and looks at it.

          WILLIAM H. BLANCHARD
     (perplexed)
  Lack of enthusiasm or curiosity,
  limited focus, a constrained amount
  of time available?

          SHERIDAN D. CAVITT
     (looks at Blanchard)
  Is that an analytical
  interpretation or something?

Scratching his head, Blanchard stares at Cavitt...

          WILLIAM H. BLANCHARD
  I'm just thinking out loud.

Matilda seated at the small table across from Colonel William H. Blanchard and Captain Sheridan Cavitt.

> **MATILDA**
> The answer to that question seemed very vague to me. However, I perceived that her interest in Earth's history was not very strong or that she did not pay much attention to it. Or, maybe, ...I don't know. I didn't get an answer to the question.

INT. ROSWELL ARMY AIR FORCE BASE - INTERVIEW ROOM

Still sitting down interfacing, the Alien and Matilda are riveted on each other.

> **MATILDA (V.O.)**
> Can you describe your home world to me?

> **ALIEN (V.O.)**
> Place of civilization. Culture. History. Large planet. Wealth. Resources always. Order. Power. Knowledge. Wisdom. Two stars. Three moons.

> **MATILDA (V.O.)**
> What is the state of development of your civilization?

> **ALIEN (V.O.)**
> Ancient. Trillions of years. Always. Above all others. Plan. Schedule. Progress. Win. High goals. Ideas.

INT. ROSWELL ARMY AIR FORCE BASE - INTERROGATION ROOM

Standing in the dim light, the Military police are still on post.

Colonel William H. Blanchard and Captain Sheridan Cavitt are still sitting across from Matilda.

> **MATILDA**
> I use the number "trillions" because I am sure that the meaning is a number larger than many billions.
> (MORE)

MATILDA (CONT'D)
The idea of the length of time she communicated is beyond me. It's closer to the idea of "infinity" in terms of Earth years.

SHERIDAN D. CAVITT
It conveys its complete superiority over the human race.

WILLIAM H. BLANCHARD
The ultimate goal is to conquer Earth.

INT. ROSWELL ARMY AIR FORCE BASE - INTERVIEW ROOM

The huge almond-shaped eyes of the Alien penetrate the blank gaze of Matilda.

MATILDA (V.O.)
Do you believe in God?

ALIEN (V.O.)
We Think. It is. Make it continue. Always.

INT. ROSWELL ARMY AIR FORCE BASE - INTERROGATION ROOM

The spotlight shines down on Matilda as she sits at the small table. Both Colonel William H. Blanchard and Captain Sheridan Cavitt, now standing, glare at Matilda.

MATILDA
I am sure that the Alien being does not understand the concept of "god" or "worship" as we do. I assume that the people in her civilization were all atheists. My impression is that they think very highly of themselves and are very prideful, indeed!

SHERIDAN D. CAVITT
MacElroy. I don't appreciate your psychoanalysis.

WILLIAM H. BLANCHARD
You're a nurse, not a psychologist. Remember that.

INT. ROSWELL ARMY AIR FORCE BASE - INTERVIEW ROOM

The slight movements of the Alien are the only signs that it's animated. It stares at Matilda who sits there with an empty expression on her face.

              MATILDA (V.O.)
     What type of society do you have?

              ALIEN (V.O.)
     Order. Power. Future always.
     Control. Grow.

INT. ROSWELL ARMY AIR FORCE BASE - INTERROGATION ROOM

Spotlight still shining on her, Matilda looks a bit frayed as she sits at the small table.

In the dim light, Colonel William H. Blanchard and Captain Sheridan Cavitt stand a few feet away huddled together.

              MATILDA
     These are the closest words I could
     use to describe the idea she had
     about her society or civilization.
     Her "emotion" when communicating
     her response to this question
     became very intense, very bright,
     and emphatic! Her thought was
     filled with an emotion that gave me
     a feeling of jubilation or joy.
     But it made me very nervous also.

Colonel William H. Blanchard and Captain Sheridan Cavitt turn to Matilda.

              WILLIAM H. BLANCHARD
     Well, it's making me nervous too.
     That thing is manipulating you.

              SHERIDAN D. CAVITT
     You can't match wits with it. I'm
     not sure anyone can.

INT. ROSWELL ARMY AIR FORCE BASE - HALLWAY

Military police lead the way as Matilda walks behind them and Colonel William H. Blanchard brings up the rear.

The Military police stop at an office door and open it. Matilda walks in first followed by Colonel Blanchard. The Military police stand guard at the door.

INT. ROSWELL ARMY AIR FORCE BASE - OFFICE

With Colonel William H. Blanchard dutifully observing. The stenographer is taking diction using a stenotype machine.

Matilda sits reading from a list...

                    MATILDA
        Question: Are there other
        intelligent life forms besides
        yourself in the universe? --
        Answer: Everywhere. We are
        greatest. Highest of all.

Matilda looks up from the list.

                  MATILDA (CONT'D)
        This is the conclusion of the first
        interview.

INT. ROSWELL ARMY AIR FORCE BASE - ROOM

Colonel William H. Blanchard walks in holding a list.

He draws the attention of Military officials and other distinguished-looking men wearing suits and lab coats.

                WILLIAM H. BLANCHARD
        Well, gentlemen. Here it is.

Blanchard passes out copies of the list to Military officials, men wearing suits and lab coats. They all light up and are excited.

A MILITARY OFFICIAL wearing a highly decorated army uniform looks over the list.

                  MILITARY OFFICIAL
        I'm surprised she was able to get
        the Alien to say anything!

Military officials, men wearing suits and lab coats peruse the list, they all have perplexed facial expressions.

A GOVERNMENT AGENT wearing a plain grey suit adjusts his dark shades.

                  GOVERNMENT AGENT
        I don't like these answers.

A SCIENTIST wearing a lab coat, lowers the list he's holding and looks irritated.

                    SCIENTIST
          These answers give me pause.

                    MILITARY OFFICIAL
          I'm disappointed she couldn't
          understand the Alien more clearly.

The Military officials, distinguish-looking men wearing
suits, and men wearing lab coats murmur amongst each other.

Colonel William H. Blanchard slack jaw drops his head.

INT. ROSWELL ARMY AIR FORCE BASE - HALLWAY

Military Police officers stand guard at the entrance of an
office door.

Walking at a steady pace, Colonel William H. Blanchard is
approaching the Military police.

INT. ROSWELL ARMY AIR FORCE BASE - OFFICE

An empty chair sits in front of the stenotype machine.

Food tray in front of her, Matilda is sitting on a portable
folding bed. With an unsure look on her face, Matilda picks
over her plate of food, she doesn't look interested in
eating.

The door opens and Colonel William H. Blanchard walks in.

Matilda stands up at attention.

                    WILLIAM H. BLANCHARD
          MacElroy, how are you doing?

                    MATILDA
          I'm ok sir.

                    WILLIAM H. BLANCHARD
          I met with a select group of
          Military officials, government
          officials, and scientists. They
          weren't happy with the answers from
          the interview.

                    MATILDA
          I don't understand sir.

                    WILLIAM H. BLANCHARD
          You are not allowed to continue
          your interview with the Alien.
                    (MORE)

                    WILLIAM H. BLANCHARD (CONT'D)
          You're to be kept here and wait for
          further instructions. You can use
          the restroom facilities as needed.
          Just notify the MPs standing
          outside they will escort you. --
          And get some rest.

                    MATILDA
          Yes, sir.

Colonel William H. Blanchard exits out the door.

INT. ROSWELL ARMY AIR FORCE BASE - ROOM

Chattering, the Military officials, men wearing suits, and men wearing lab coats have convened when Colonel William H. Blanchard walks in.

The chattering subsides and the group's attention turns toward Colonel William H. Blanchard.

Holding a list in his hand, the military official approaches Colonel Blanchard.

The military official extends the list out to Colonel Blanchard, with a quizzical look Blanchard takes the list.

                    WILLIAM H. BLANCHARD
          What's this?

                    MILITARY OFFICIAL
          A new list of questions.

The scientist steps up.

                    SCIENTIST
          We want you to present them to the
          Sergeant.

The government agent steps out from amongst his colleagues.

                    GOVERNMENT AGENT
          We must be in there when the
          Sergeant is questioning the Alien.

INT. ROSWELL ARMY AIR FORCE BASE - OFFICE

There is a nervous calm about Matilda as she sits on the portable folding bed.

The door opens and Colonel William H. Blanchard walks in and he holds a list out to Matilda.

Matilda hesitates and gently takes the list from Colonel Blanchard's hand.

Matilda scans the list with her eyes and looks up at Colonel Blanchard.

          WILLIAM H. BLANCHARD
That's a new set of questions to ask the Alien. Several other people will be in the room with you during the next interview.

INT. ROSWELL ARMY AIR FORCE BASE - INTERVIEW ROOM

Colonel William H. Blanchard, the military official, the scientist, and the government agent look on with fixed facial expressions.

The Alien is sitting in the large recliner, and Matilda sits directly in front of the being.

The Alien's expression is ordinary and difficult to discern. However Matilda's face looks strained, she appears to wince and glares at the Alien.

Matilda, with the list in her hand, turns to Colonel William H. Blanchard, the military official, the scientist, and the government agent.

          MATILDA
I'm not getting anything.

          SCIENTIST
You're not getting anything?

          MATILDA
I'm not receiving thoughts, emotions, or any other perceptible communication.

          GOVERNMENT AGENT
Are you asking it questions from the new list?

          MATILDA
Yes.

The Alien just sits in the large recliner chair without moving.

          MILITARY OFFICIAL
So what? The Alien has shut down?

The military official turns to Colonel Blanchard.

                  MILITARY OFFICIAL (CONT'D)
    Maybe you should let the experts
    handle it. They may get better
    results.

                  WILLIAM H. BLANCHARD
    OK, I need everyone out. That
    includes you, Sergeant MacElroy.

Matilda looks at the Alien and then at Colonel Blanchard.

                  WILLIAM H. BLANCHARD (CONT'D)
    The Alien stays.

The one-way glass window looms large in the background.

EXT. ROSWELL ARMY AIR FORCE BASE - HALLWAY

With the Military police following and Colonel Blanchard leading the way. Matilda looks unsure as she walks with the military official, the scientist, and the government agent.

INT. ROSWELL ARMY AIR FORCE BASE - ROOM

The door opens, and Colonel Blanchard walks in followed by Matilda, the military official, the scientist, and the government agent.

The Military police shut the door.

The military official is agitated, he turns to Matilda, and she is standing at attention.

                  MILITARY OFFICIAL
      (impatient)
    Sergeant MacElroy. I believe
    you're lying or making up the
    answers to the first set of
    questions.

Matilda is taken aback an angry expression shrouds her face.

                  MATILDA
      (perturbed)
    My answers were honest, and as
    accurate as I could make them!

                    MILITARY OFFICIAL
          Bullshit! And watch your tone,
          Sergeant. -- You and that Alien
          have become quite the pair.

                    SCIENTIST
               (ponder)
          Mental telepathy has historically
          been connected to paranormal
          activities and wisdom literature,
          more research on the topic is
          warranted from a psychological and
          scientific perspective.

                    MATILDA
          Empathy. -- The Alien's perception
          of my thoughts and feelings. The
          potential to foster a deeper and
          more direct sense of connection.
          I've become sensitive to the
          requirements and challenges of the
          Alien by sharing in the emotional
          gesture, which may lessen passions
          of loneliness and aloneness.

                    GOVERNMENT AGENT
               (frustrated)
          Hostility causes the Alien to
          withdraw, to shut down. Is that
          what you're telling us?

                    MATILDA
          It's averse to aggression, yes.

                    GOVERNMENT AGENT
               (shout)
          Well, hell. Who isn't?

Matilda is startled and takes a couple of steps back.

                    SCIENTIST
          The questions were completely
          innocuous.

EXT. ROSWELL ARMY AIR FORCE BASE - HALLWAY - OFFICE

Holding two file folders in his hand. Captain Sheridan
Cavitt walks up to a door, stenciled on the opaque office
door window is the name, *Colonel William H. Blanchard*.

Captain Sheridan Cavitt opens the door and walks in.

INT. ROSWELL ARMY AIR FORCE BASE - OFFICE

Colonel William H. Blanchard is sitting behind his desk when Captain Sheridan Cavitt walks in.

Captain Cavitt tosses two file folders onto Colonel Blanchard's desk.

Blanchard picks up one of the file folders and opens it, he sees a photo of a white woman and stares at it.

Blanchard thumbs through some papers in the file folder and begins reading aloud...

          WILLIAM H. BLANCHARD
Gertrude Schmeidler. PhD in psychology from Harvard University. Experimental psychologist and parapsychologist noted for her 'sheep-goat' theory, that experimental subjects' ESP ability, relates to their belief or otherwise in the reality of psychic phenomena.

Colonel Blanchard looks up at Captain Cavitt.

          WILLIAM H. BLANCHARD (CONT'D)
Umm.

Colonel Blanchard tosses the open file folder onto his desk.

Blanchard picks up the other file folder from his desk and opens it. Inside is a photo of an Indian man.

Colonel Blanchard then sees some papers inside the file folder, looking at them, he reads aloud...

          WILLIAM H. BLANCHARD (CONT'D)
Jiddu Krishnamurti. Indian spiritual leader. "If it is accepted that the human brain is evolving under the influence of a super-intelligent life force, then perhaps it is reasonable to view paranormal states of mind such as psychic phenomena as additional, evolving faculties of mind, rather than pathological states, as is commonly done."

Studying the file folder, Colonel Blanchard looks up at Captain Cavitt.

                    WILLIAM H. BLANCHARD (CONT'D)
               Is this the best we can do?

                    SHERIDAN D. CAVITT
               Strange events demand
               introspection, inviting us to
               question the fabric of our reality.

Colonel Blanchard tosses the open file folder onto the desk, and it lands next to the other open file folder displaying both photos of Gertrude and Jiddu.

INT. ROSWELL ARMY AIR FORCE BASE - INTERVIEW ROOM

Conspicuously visible in the background is the one-way glass window.

A chant is heard, *Om... Om... Om... Om...*

Sitting on the floor in the Lotus position, cross-legged, with each foot placed on the opposite thigh is JIDDU KRISHNAMURTI male Indian age 52. He is in deep concentration and his eyes are closed.

                    JIDDU
               Om... Om... Om...

Jiddu slowly opens his eyes and stares straight ahead.

Sitting across from Jiddu in the large recliner chair appearing to be lifeless is the Alien.

A staring match is taking place between Jiddu and the Alien.

INT. ROSWELL ARMY AIR FORCE BASE - CONTROL ROOM

Military personnel are seated at the console turning knobs, pushing buttons, and moving levers.

Colonel William H. Blanchard and Captain Sheridan Cavitt are looking at Jiddu and the Alien through the one-way glass window.

                    WILLIAM H. BLANCHARD
               I don't know what's more strange,
               the Alien or the Indian philosopher
               squatting on the floor -- And what
               the hell is he saying?

                    SHERIDAN D. CAVITT
               It's a chant that's said to be the
               primordial sound from which the
               universe was created.

Colonel Blanchard looks oddly at Captain Cavitt, then turns and looks through the one-way glass window.

                    WILLIAM H. BLANCHARD
               Can you tell if anything is
               happening? I mean if they're
               exchanging thoughts.

                    SHERIDAN D. CAVITT
               Nothing. I can't tell at all.

INT. ROSWELL ARMY AIR FORCE BASE - INTERROGATION ROOM

Colonel William H. Blanchard and Captain Sheridan Cavitt stand shrouded by the dim light.

A harsh spotlight shines down on a small table.

The door opens up and Military police walk in with Jiddu Krishnamurti.

The Military police sit Jiddu down at the small table and walk out shutting the door behind them.

With the harsh spotlight shining down on Jiddu, Colonel Blanchard and Captain Cavitt step out of the dim light.

                    WILLIAM H. BLANCHARD
               Were you able to get it to talk?

                    JIDDU
               It didn't verbalize, at least not
               to me.

Captain Cavitt's hands press down onto the small table and his face penetrates the harsh spotlight with a snarl.

                    SHERIDAN D. CAVITT
               You know what we're talking about.

Jiddu leans back in his chair, with an off-putting look --

                    JIDDU
               I projected my thoughts and mental
               images. It did not reciprocate. I
               meditated, chanted. Not even the
               slightest discernment of
               communication, mentally that is.
                         (MORE)

JIDDU (CONT'D)
I couldn't even detect if the Alien
was even alive.

INT. ROSWELL ARMY AIR FORCE BASE - INTERVIEW ROOM

The door opens and GERTRUDE SCHMEIDLER a white female age 45 walks in.

Gertrude pauses looking at the back of the large recliner chair, she cautiously walks towards it.

As Gertrude gradually walks in front of the large recliner the Alien becomes very apparent.

Gertrude looks unsettled though holding her composure, she gingerly sits down in front of the Alien.

In front of Gertrude is a small table, she produces a set of *Zener cards* that have symbols on them.

Gertrude places five cards face up on the small table, a *hollow circle*, a *plus sign*, *three vertical wavy lines*, a *hollow square*, and a *hollow five-pointed star*.

The *Zener cards* and the small table sit directly in front of the Alien.

-- Gertrude looks at the Alien and picks up the *Zener cards* shuffling them together.

Gertrude holds the back of a *Zener card* up to the Alien for a few seconds. It's the *hollow five-pointed star*. She does this with each *Zener Card*.

Holding the back of the last *Zener card* directly up to the Alien, the *plus sign,* Gertrude looks perplexed.

The Alien just sits in the large recliner, as usual shows no emotion and is unresponsive.

Still holding the *Zener card* in her hand. Gertrude turns her torso in the direction of the one-way glass window.

Gertrude holds the back of the *Zener card* up. She flips the *Zener card* around face side up, exposing the *plus sign.*

INT. ROSWELL ARMY AIR FORCE BASE - INTERROGATION ROOM

An angry Colonel William H. Blanchard holds the *Zener card* with the *plus sign* in the face of Gertrude as the harsh spotlight shines on them both.

                    WILLIAM H. BLANCHARD
               Fucking parlor tricks.

Colonel Blanchard flings the *Zener card*.

                    WILLIAM H. BLANCHARD (CONT'D)
               Miss Schmeidler. What do you think
               this is? A damn séance?

                    GERTRUDE
                 (calm)
               Colonel Blanchard. It was a simple
               clairvoyance test.

                    WILLIAM H. BLANCHARD
               Obviously, it didn't work.

                    GERTRUDE
               I understand your frustration, but
               there are no guarantees.

Captain Cavitt lingers in the dim light.

                    SHERIDAN D. CAVITT
               You have no idea what you're
               dealing with, neither does the US
               Military for that matter. It's
               safe to say that Alien is more
               brilliant than Albert Einstein,
               Nikola Tesla, Enrico Fermi, Niels
               Bohr, Marie Curie, Galileo, and any
               other physicist you can think of...
               All put together.

INT. ROSWELL ARMY AIR FORCE BASE - SOUNDPROOF ROOM

A *Brainwave Synchronizer* emits a *pulsing light*.

Seated in a circle, in a hypnotic state wearing *electroencephalogram headsets on their heads* are Matilda, Gertrude, and Jiddu.

A lone camera is conspicuously mounted on the ceiling.

INT. ROSWELL ARMY AIR FORCE BASE - CCTV ROOM

Military personnel are operating specialized electronic recording and monitoring equipment.

Small black and white monitors display images of Matilda, Gertrude, and Jiddu.

Standing together observing the monitors are Colonel William H. Blanchard, Captain Sheridan Cavitt, and the scientist.

> SCIENTIST
> In experiments dating back to the nineteenth century, scientists have validated two types of telepathy: instinctual, or feeling-based, telepathy and mental, or mind-to-mind, telepathy...

> WILLIAM H. BLANCHARD
> ...And the third?

> SCIENTIST
> According to the wisdom teachings, there is also another, higher type of telepathy called soul-to-soul, or spiritual, telepathy.

> WILLIAM H. BLANCHARD
> I'm concerned about the possible methodological flaws surrounding this experiment.

> SCIENTIST
> You want to determine if the Sergeant has extra-sensory perception abilities, right?

> SHERIDAN D. CAVITT
> We want to know if all three are charlatans.

> SCIENTIST
> Doctor Schmeidler, Mr. Krishnamurti, and Sergeant MacElroy may be selling us quackery.

> SHERIDAN D. CAVITT
> Like this experiment.

INT. ROSWELL ARMY AIR FORCE BASE - SOUNDPROOF ROOM

Still seated in a circle, in a hypnotic state wearing *electroencephalogram headsets* on their heads, images explode from the minds of Matilda, Gertrude, and Jiddu.

MONTAGE:

INT. MATILDA'S MIND

- From the eyes of Matilda emerge vivid pictures of nuclear bombs exploding. War, babies crying, carnage, natural disasters.

INT. GERTRUDE'S MIND

- A piercing light penetrates the mind of Gertrude and pictures blast from her forehead. People in soup lines during the great depression, destitute pea-pickers, the Dust Bowl Dallas South Dakota 1936, crowds of people gather outside the New York Stock Exchange following the crash of 1929.

INT. JIDDU'S MIND

- A barrage of thoughts thrust from the transfixed expression of Jiddu. King George VI signs the Indian Independence Act, a father, and a son pose with volunteer scouts, and Mahatma Gandhi with Annie Besant.

END MONTAGE.

The pulsing light from the *Brainwave Synchronizer* grows bigger and bigger...

INT. ROSWELL ARMY AIR FORCE BASE - HALLWAY

Military police stand guard at the door when Matilda walks out with Gertrude and Jiddu.

They are greeted by Colonel William H. Blanchard.

> WILLIAM H. BLANCHARD
> (ambivalent)
> -- The results from the experiment were inconclusive.

Matilda, Gertrude, and Jiddu remain silent.

> WILLIAM H. BLANCHARD (CONT'D)
> Doctor Schmeidler, Mr Krishnamurti, you're no longer needed.

Colonel Blanchard motions to the Military police and they step forward.

> WILLIAM H. BLANCHARD (CONT'D)
> Go with them.

Gertrude and Jiddu walk off followed by the Military police.

As Colonel Blanchard watches he turns to Matilda...

          WILLIAM H. BLANCHARD (CONT'D)
So, what happened in there?

          MATILDA
I wasn't able to communicate telepathically with either of them.

          WILLIAM H. BLANCHARD
Then you're not psychic?

          MATILDA
         (confused)
No. I'm not sure. I don't think so.

          WILLIAM H. BLANCHARD
Well, which is it, Sergeant?

          MATILDA
It's the Alien sir.

          WILLIAM H. BLANCHARD
         (sarcastic)
So, the Alien is psychic.

          MATILDA
         (frustrated)
Colonel, at this point I'm not certain of anything. All I know is that the Alien communicates with me.

INT. ROSWELL ARMY AIR FORCE BASE - INTERVIEW ROOM

A sense of pleasure emotes from the Alien's face as it sits in the large recliner chair.

INSERT CARD: TOP SECRET OFFICIAL TRANSCRIPT OF THE U.S. ARMY AIR FORCE ROSWELL ARMY AIR FIELD, 509TH BOMB GROUP SUBJECT: ALIEN INTERVIEW, 10. 7. 1947

In the background, the tally light on a lone camera is lit.

A bright countenance emits from Matilda as she sits in front of the Alien holding onto a list.

          MATILDA (V.O.)
Why have you stopped communicating?

                    ALIEN (V.O.)
          No stop. Others. Hidden.
          Covered. Secret fear.

INT. ROSWELL ARMY AIR FORCE BASE - INTERROGATION ROOM

Stepping into the dim light is Colonel William H. Blanchard.

Sitting at the small table under the harsh spotlight is Matilda.

                    MATILDA
          The Alien's communication is
          hindered by human fear and
          distrust; and appears perceptive of
          hidden intentions, displaying no
          fear. The Alien identifies as
          "Airl" by fellow aliens based on
          personality, not physical
          attributes; "Airl" is the closest
          English representation of her
          name...

Colonel Blanchard stands with a stoic look and folded arms.

                    MATILDA (CONT'D)
          ...I sensed her preference for the
          feminine gender; we share a natural
          female empathy. The Alien is
          uncomfortable with male officers'
          combative, self-centered attitude,
          prioritizing personal power over
          discovering the universe's secrets.

INT. ROSWELL ARMY AIR FORCE BASE - INTERVIEW ROOM

The mysterious unseen eyes can almost be felt coming from behind the one-way glass window.

INSERT CARD: TOP SECRET OFFICIAL TRANSCRIPT OF THE U.S. ARMY AIR FORCE ROSWELL ARMY AIR FIELD, 509TH BOMB GROUP SUBJECT: ALIEN INTERVIEW, 11. 7. 1947

A sense of comfort is obvious between the Alien and Matilda as they sit across from each other.

The Alien, sitting in the recliner, shows subtle movements.

Matilda with a confident soft smile sits with her legs crossed and the list dangles from her fingers.

MATILDA (V.O.)
Can you read or write any Earth languages?

ALIEN (V.O.)
No.

MATILDA (V.O.)
Do you understand numbers or mathematics?

ALIEN (V.O.)
Yes. I am officer. Pilot. Engineer.

MATILDA (V.O.)
Can you write or draw symbols or pictures that we may be able to translate into our own language?

ALIEN (V.O.)
Uncertain.

MATILDA (V.O.)
Are there any other signs or means of communication you can use to help us understand your thoughts more clearly?

ALIEN (V.O.)
No.

INT. ROSWELL ARMY AIR FORCE BASE - INTERROGATION ROOM

-- Colonel William H. Blanchard's agitated pace comes to a stop. He adjusts his hat and rubs his face.

Turning to face Matilda Colonel Blanchard lets out a deep breath.

WILLIAM H. BLANCHARD
(exasperated)
Awwww -- What other recourse do we have?

Matilda sits at the small table with the spotlight on her.

MATILDA
I'm certain it wasn't true. Airl
refused written, drawn, or sign
communication, likely following
orders akin to a captured soldier
not to disclose sensitive
information even under duress.
Limited to sharing non-confidential
or personal details, like "name,
rank, and serial number."

INT. ROSWELL ARMY AIR FORCE BASE - INTERVIEW ROOM

Sitting in the usual chair, Matilda looks up from the list of questions that she is holding.

INSERT CARD: TOP SECRET OFFICIAL TRANSCRIPT OF THE U.S. ARMY AIR FORCE ROSWELL ARMY AIR FIELD, 509TH BOMB GROUP SUBJECT: INTERVIEW, 11. 7. 1947, 2ND SESSION

MATILDA (V.O.)
Can you show us from a map of
stars, which star is your home
planet?

-- the Alien with subtle head movement sits still in the large recliner.

ALIEN (V.O.)
No.

INT. ROSWELL ARMY AIR FORCE BASE - INTERROGATION ROOM

Matilda is still sitting at the small table under the relentless beam of the spotlight.

MATILDA
This is not because she does not
know the directions from Earth to
her home planet. She was unwilling
to reveal the location. It was
also due to the fact that the star
system of her home planet does not
exist on any star map on Earth. It
is too far away.

Colonel William H. Blanchard standing in the dim light gives Matilda a hard stare.

WILLIAM H. BLANCHARD
You know that for a fact.

Matilda sighs and places her elbow on the small table, she props her head up with the palm of her hand.

                    MATILDA
    I don't.

                WILLIAM H. BLANCHARD
    MacElroy. I am growing
    increasingly impatient with your
    presumptions.

INT. ROSWELL ARMY AIR FORCE BASE - INTERVIEW ROOM

Sitting in a chair directly in front of the Alien, there is a pleasant countenance on the face of Matilda.

                MATILDA (V.O.)
    How long will it take your people
    to locate you here?

The Alien sits in the large recliner and gives the impression of being lifeless, save for almost imperceptible movements.

                ALIEN (V.O.)
    Unknown.

               MATILDA (V.O.)
    How long would it take your people
    to travel here to rescue you?

                ALIEN (V.O.)
    Minutes or hours.

                MATILDA (V.O.)
    How can we make them understand
    that we do not intend to harm you?

                ALIEN (V.O.)
    Intentions are clear. See in your
    mind. Images. Feeling.

                MATILDA (V.O.)
    If you are not a biological entity,
    why do you refer to yourself as
    feminine?

                ALIEN (V.O.)
    I am a creator. Mother. Source.

Slack-jawed, Matilda looks on with astonishment.

INT. ROSWELL ARMY AIR FORCE BASE - HALLWAY

Walking at a steady pace, Matilda is being escorted by Military police. As they approach a door the Military police open it and Matilda walks in.

The Military police shut the door and stand guard.

INT. ROSWELL ARMY AIR FORCE BASE - ROOM - CONTINUOUS

Matilda walks into a tumult and stops, she has an uncertain expression on her face.

All the attention turns to Matilda. Standing there with straight faces are Colonel William H. Blanchard, Captain Sheridan Cavitt, the military official, the scientist, and the government agent.

The military official looks at a list he is holding, then he looks at Matilda.

                    MILITARY OFFICIAL
Nurse MacElroy. I've gone over the answers you gave the stenographer, well...

                    SCIENTIST
...We're considering taking drastic measures.

                    GOVERNMENT AGENT
None of the answers are considered useful to the military, intelligence agencies, or scientists.

                    MATILDA
I'm sure the Alien is certain of the actual intentions of the people who wrote the questions, she could "read their minds" just as easily as she could read my thoughts and communicate with me telepathically. Because of these intentions, she was unwilling and unable to cooperate with any of you in any way, under any circumstances. I am equally sure that since she is not a biological life form, no kind of torture or coercion would change her mind!

Colonel William H. Blanchard, Captain Sheridan Cavitt, the military official, the scientist, and the government agent murmur amongst each other.

Colonel Blanchard walks over to the door and opens it. The Military police walk in.

                    WILLIAM H. BLANCHARD
        Sergeant, go with them.

As Matilda is walking out the door with the Military police.

                    SHERIDAN D. CAVITT
        What now?

Colonel Blanchard shuts the door and turns to Captain Cavitt.

                    WILLIAM H. BLANCHARD
        She'll continue as the interpreter.

The military official, the scientist, and the government agent all posture and mutter in disgust.

INT. ROSWELL ARMY AIR FORCE BASE - INTERVIEW ROOM

Matilda as usual is sitting in front of the Alien. Her body language is relaxed, and her facial expression is non-threatening.

INSERT CARD: TOP SECRET OFFICIAL TRANSCRIPT OF THE U.S. ARMY AIR FORCE ROSWELL ARMY AIR FIELD, 509TH BOMB GROUP SUBJECT: ALIEN INTERVIEW, 11. 7. 1947, 3RD SESSION

Sitting in the large recliner. The Alien looks mannequinish in appearance, diminutive, and shows minute movements.

                    MATILDA (V.O.)
        What assurance or proof do you
        require from us that will make you
        feel safe enough to answer our
        questions?

                    ALIEN (V.O.)
        Only she speaks. Only she hears.
        Only she questions. No others.
        Must. Know. Understand.

Matilda rubs her temple and sighs deeply, she looks confounded.

INT. ROSWELL ARMY AIR FORCE BASE - ROOM

Sitting in a chair, her head slightly tilted down and her fingers massaging her temple, Matilda lifts her head.

Standing in front of Matilda is the government agent. He has an intimidating stare.

GOVERNMENT AGENT
(impatient)
Surely you can understand my skepticism -- Sergeant! What did the Alien mean by that?

MATILDA
I couldn't really understand what she meant either, but I'm doing the best I can to articulate her telepathic intentions.

The scientist is more reserved as he steps to Matilda.

SCIENTIST
Perhaps your technique is lacking discernment. Deciphering the Alien thoughts is like a code that you have misconstrued.

MATILDA
The communication problem may have to do with my inability to understand the telepathic language of the Alien clearly enough to be satisfactory.

SCIENTIST
Precisely.

The scientist shakes his head. He turns to Colonel Blanchard and Captain Cavitt and just shrugs his shoulders.

The military official blusters and lashes out at Colonel Blanchard.

MILITARY OFFICIAL
We can't continue to wait. There could be an armada heading toward Earth right now. Maybe you ought to let me handle it from here.

WILLIAM H. BLANCHARD
No.

                    MILITARY OFFICIAL
          Shit!

The military official turns away from Colonel Blanchard in frustration.

Matilda sitting in the chair looks completely despondent.

                    GOVERNMENT AGENT
          Use sodium pentothal.

                    WILLIAM H. BLANCHARD
          That may kill it.

                    GOVERNMENT AGENT
          Mind uploading.

                    SHERIDAN D. CAVITT
          You're desperate. We're not
          dealing with the typical prisoner
          here.

                    GOVERNMENT AGENT
          Desperate times call for desperate
          measures. In theory, if the
          information and processes of the
          mind can be disassociated from the
          biological body...

                    MATILDA
          It's not biological.

                    GOVERNMENT AGENT
               (hands on hip)
          -- Aw, fuck it!

The door opens and the Military police walk in following JOHN NEWBLE, a white man in his 40s.

                    JOHN NEWBLE
          Everyone, I may have a solution.

INT. ROSWELL ARMY AIR FORCE BASE - MESS HALL

A plate of *Creamed Chipped Beef on Toast* sits on the table.

The tines of a fork stick into a portion of the *Creamed Chipped Beef on Toast*.

John Newble brings the fork with *Creamed Chipped Beef on Toast* to his mouth and begins eating.

                    JOHN NEWBLE
                (chewing)
            I'm a Navy guy, this was one of my
            favorite foods. The original
            nickname of this dish was called,
            "Shit on a Shingle."

With a sick expression on her face, Matilda sits across from
John Newble.

                    MATILDA
            Argh.

In the background standing guard are the Military police.

John chewing, drinks from a glass.

                    JOHN NEWBLE
            Always good to have something to
            chase this with.

                    MATILDA
            Huh.

                    JOHN NEWBLE
            Sergeant MacElroy, you're a trained
            nurse.

                    MATILDA
            Yes, that's right.

                    JOHN NEWBLE
            I've been briefed on the situation.
            Your interaction with the Alien.
                (eating)
            -- It will only communicate with
            you.

                    MATILDA
            Yes, that's true.

                    JOHN NEWBLE
            I'm a Japanese language specialist.

                    MATILDA
            Oh.

                    JOHN NEWBLE
            First, the problem has very little
            to do with the inability of the
            Alien to communicate. It has more
            to do with its <u>unwillingness</u> to
            communicate with anyone other than
            you.

MATILDA
I see.

                    JOHN NEWBLE
Second, in order for any clear,
comprehensive communication to
happen, both parties need to
understand and communicate through
a common language.

                    MATILDA
Makes sense.

                    JOHN NEWBLE
Words and symbols in language
convey very precise concepts and
meanings. Japanese people have a
lot of homonyms in their language
which causes a lot of confusion in
day-to-day communication. They
solve this problem by using
standard Chinese characters to
write down the exact meanings of
the words they are using. This
clears up the matter for them.

                    MATILDA
Kinda like, "lost in translation."

                    JOHN NEWBLE
Yeah, kinda. Without a defined
nomenclature communication was not
possible beyond the rudimentary
understanding between men and dogs,
or between two small children. The
lack of a common vocabulary of
clearly defined words that all
parties can use fluently was the
limiting factor in communication
between all people, groups, or
nations.

                    MATILDA
              (thinking)
Language barrier. -- What do you
suggest?

John eats another fork full of *Creamed Chipped Beef on Toast*.

                    JOHN NEWBLE
              (chewing)
There are only two choices.
                    (MORE)

JOHN NEWBLE (CONT'D)
You have to learn to speak the
language of the Alien, or the Alien
has to learn to speak English. --
If the Alien is intelligent enough
to communicate with you
telepathically, and fly a
spacecraft across the galaxy, that
it could probably learn to speak a
language as quickly as a 5-year-
old, or faster!

John takes another fork full of food and pauses while
chewing.

JOHN NEWBLE (CONT'D)
Pardon me. I didn't think to ask.
Want some?

Matilda frowns and shakes her head, no.

INT. ROSWELL ARMY AIR FORCE BASE - ROOM

The door is opened by the Military police. John Newble,
holding some books, walks in followed by Matilda.

The Military police shut the door.

John places the books on a table, *McGuffey's Eclectic Reader,
Primer Through Sixth*.

John and Matilda take a seat at the table.

JOHN NEWBLE
The reason I chose these particular
books is that the original eighteen
thirty-six version of these books
were used for three-quarters of a
century to teach about four-fifths
of all American school children how
to read.

MATILDA
Mister Newble, I'm a nurse, not a
teacher.

JOHN NEWBLE
This is an extensive briefing -- a
course that will last the entire
day.

John holds up a book, *McGuffey's Eclectic Primer*.

                    JOHN NEWBLE (CONT'D)
          We'll start with this one. The
          Alien's educational course begins
          in 'The Primer' by presenting the
          letters of the alphabet to be
          memorized, in sequence. Children
          were then taught, step by step, to
          use the building blocks of the
          language to form and pronounce
          words, using the phonics method.
          Which involves teaching children to
          connect sounds with letters.

                    MATILDA
          Learning our alphabet with phonics
          in 'The Primer.' -- Makes me
          ponder the Alien's advanced
          approach to education and our own
          language development.

                    JOHN NEWBLE
          It's a simple approach to teaching
          a far superior species.
                (pointing at a page in the
                 book)
          Now, each lesson begins with a
          study of words used in the reading
          exercise and with markings to show
          the correct pronunciation for each
          word.

INT. ROSWELL ARMY AIR FORCE BASE - INTERVIEW ROOM

Matilda is sitting in the large recliner right next to the Alien.

Matilda opens a book; the cover can be seen. It's the *McGuffey's Eclectic Readers Primer*.

Matilda cradles the open book in her hand. She and the Alien are fixed on a page, it's the *alphabet* in large capital letters.

Matilda points to each letter with her finger.

                    MATILDA
                (slow and deliberate)
          A - B - C - D - E - F - G...

Matilda turns the page, and the Alien is transfixed on the book. The *drawing* of a *cat* looking at a hovering *insect* is on the page.

> MATILDA (CONT'D)
> (pointing at page)
> Cat.

The Alien stares hard at the *drawing* of the *cat*.

Matilda turns the page and there is a *drawing* of a *rat*, above that the font of a lower-case *letter a*, the word *and*, the word *eat*, the word *rat*. Underneath the *drawing* are a few phrases.

The Alien with subtle head movements looks at the page.

Matilda is pointing at the phrases on the page with her finger...

> MATILDA (CONT'D)
> a rat. a cat. A cat. A rat. A cat and A rat. A rat and a cat.

Again, Matilda turns the page, and the Alien looks at the page very closely.

On the page is a *drawing* of a *Boy* wearing a hat and a *Girl* holding a fan as they stand in a pond of water playing with a miniature *sailboat*.

Above the *drawing* are the words Nat, Hat, Fan, Can.

The Alien is focused on the page as Matilda slowly runs her finger over the page.

> MATILDA (CONT'D)
> a fan. a hat. Ann and Nat. Ann has a fan. Nat has a hat. Ann can fan Nat.

Looming large in the background is the one-way glass window.

INT. ROSWELL ARMY AIR FORCE BASE - CONTROL ROOM

The image of Matilda and the Alien sitting on the large recliner is displayed on a black and white TV monitor.

John Newble and Colonel William H. Blanchard are standing together. They are looking at Matilda and the Alien through the one-way glass window.

> WILLIAM H. BLANCHARD
> How do you think she's doing?

JOHN NEWBLE
It's reminiscent of a school
teacher working with a
kindergartener.

WILLIAM H. BLANCHARD
Yeah, but how do you think she's
doing?

JOHN NEWBLE
We're both watching the same thing.
I don't know.

WILLIAM H. BLANCHARD
Care to take a guess?

INT. ROSWELL ARMY AIR FORCE BASE - LIBRARY

There are rows of towering bookshelves and polished wooden floors.

John Newble quietly moves between fiction and reference sections.

Some Military personnel are sitting in chairs and others are in reading nooks.

Seated at a long table, John Newble pours over some English grammar literature books.

A librarian is stationed at an information desk overseeing the exchange of books with Military personnel.

John Newble walks up to the librarian and sets a set of Encyclopedia Britannica books on the countertop.

INT. ROSWELL ARMY AIR FORCE BASE - INTERROGATION ROOM

The harsh light is shining brightly.

Matilda sits at the small desk, sitting directly across from her is Colonel William H. Blanchard.

WILLIAM H. BLANCHARD
We have to accelerate this process,
it's imperative.

MATILDA
I understand that.

WILLIAM H. BLANCHARD
So.

                    MATILDA
          Sir?

                    WILLIAM H. BLANCHARD
          Are the lessons having any effect?

                    MATILDA
          I believe they are.

                    WILLIAM H. BLANCHARD
          You're reading out loud, can the
          Alien even hear you?

                    MATILDA
          I don't know. But Airl's ability
          to discern information from the
          books -- is...

                    WILLIAM H. BLANCHARD
          Yes, sergeant.

                    MATILDA
          ...Perceptible.

                    WILLIAM H. BLANCHARD
          You mean, to you?

                    MATILDA
          Yes.

                    WILLIAM H. BLANCHARD
          Is that supposed to reassure me?

INT. ROSWELL ARMY AIR FORCE BASE - INTERVIEW ROOM

Matilda walks through the door holding a dictionary. After taking a few steps, she pauses.

Sitting in the large recliner chair with the complete set of *McGuffey's* books at its side. The face of the Alien is buried in *McGuffey's Sixth Eclectic Readers*.

Examining the dictionary cover, the Alien speed reads, turning each page quickly.

Matilda looks astonished as she walks over and stands directly in front of the Alien.

The Alien closes the dictionary, sits it on the recliner and looks up at Matilda.

Matilda is locked in a trance-like gaze with the Alien.

                    ALIEN (V.O.)
          I've finished reading the material.

Matilda snaps out of the trance and slowly sits next to the
Alien.

Matilda extends the dictionary to the Alien who carefully
takes it from her hand.

The Alien rapidly speed-reads the dictionary after examining
its cover, turning the pages very quickly.

INT. ROSWELL ARMY AIR FORCE BASE - ROOM

The door opens and in walks Matilda.

Sitting down at a table is John Newble, he stands up from his
chair.

                    JOHN NEWBLE
          Sergeant MacElroy, please have a
          seat.

Matilda sits down next to John.

                    JOHN NEWBLE (CONT'D)
          I paid a visit to the base library.

John pushes a set of Encyclopedia Britannica books to
Matilda.

Matilda picks up an Encyclopedia and looks at the cover.

                    MATILDA
          You want me to give these to Airl?

                    JOHN NEWBLE
          Who is Airl?

                    MATILDA
          The Alien. That's her name.

                    JOHN NEWBLE
          Her?

                    MATILDA
          It's difficult to explain.

                    JOHN NEWBLE
          Yes, well. Give them to -- Airl?

MATILDA
She finished reading the complete
set of McGuffey's Eclectic Readers.

JOHN NEWBLE
With your help of course.

MATILDA
By herself. After reading the
first edition aloud. She scanned
the subsequent editions.

JOHN NEWBLE
You believe it could comprehend the
books?

MATILDA
Yes.

JOHN NEWBLE
How do you know?

MATILDA
Airl communicated it to me
telepathically. She said, "I've
finished reading the material."

John looks mystified.

INT. ROSWELL ARMY AIR FORCE BASE - INTERVIEW ROOM

Face concealed by the Encyclopedia. The long fingers of the
Alien are gripped around the front and back cover of the open
book.

Vivid illustrations stand out on the page of the
Encyclopedia.

The Alien with its long fingers delicately turns the pages,
giving each vivid illustration a long look.

The Alien looks up from the Encyclopedia, staring at Matilda
with laser focus.

ALIEN (V.O.)
I want more books with images. I
can construe and assimilate.

Matilda is standing there looking spellbound.

INT. ROSWELL ARMY AIR FORCE BASE - ROOM

Matilda is standing, looking very attentive and passionate.

MATILDA
It's pointless to continue reading to her.

The government agent stands across from Matilda and looks irritated.

GOVERNMENT AGENT
Her? -- Her?

The government agent quickly turns to Colonel William H. Blanchard.

GOVERNMENT AGENT (CONT'D)
Colonel, what are we doing here? Is the sergeant interviewing, interrogating, or...

The government agent quickly and angrily turns to face Matilda.

GOVERNMENT AGENT (CONT'D)
...Or having a bonding session.

MATILDA
Would you like to give it a try?

GOVERNMENT AGENT
Look here, sergeant. Don't get cheeky with me.

WILLIAM H. BLANCHARD
OK. OK. Relax.

John Newble steps up looking at Colonel Blanchard and the government agent.

JOHN NEWBLE
(pointed)
The sergeant has made significant progress. Let's not deviate from the main objective.

INT. ROSWELL ARMY AIR FORCE BASE - HALLWAY

Accompanied by the Military police, Matilda is pushing a book cart that is carrying a large number of books.

INT. ROSWELL ARMY AIR FORCE BASE - INTERVIEW ROOM

The door opens and Matilda pushes the book cart through, and she stops the book cart next to the large recliner.

Sitting on the large recliner. The Alien looks at the books and reaches to pick one up. The Alien carefully looks at the cover and spine of the book, it's the *Holy Bible*.

Matilda's facial expression goes from relaxed to a hypnotic state.

The Alien holding onto the *Holy Bible* is looking intensely at Matilda.

>   ALIEN (V.O.)
> These will do.

INT. ROSWELL ARMY AIR FORCE BASE - INTERROGATION ROOM

The harsh spotlight shines on Matilda as she sits at the small table.

>   MATILDA
>   (respectful)
> Sir. Does that light have to be
> positioned directly in my face?

Captain Sheridan Cavitt steps up and sits on the edge of the small table.

>   SHERIDAN D. CAVITT
> Sergeant, do you feel you're being
> treated unfairly?

Colonel William H. Blanchard stands stoically in the dim light.

>   WILLIAM H. BLANCHARD (O.C.)
> It's hard to distinguish what's
> happening in that control room.

>   MATILDA
>   (bothered)
> Airl has read through several
> hundred books. She studied every
> subject I could imagine, many very
> technical things I never wanted to
> know anything about. Like
> astronomy, metallurgy, engineering,
> mathematics, various technical
> manuals, and so forth.

INT. ROSWELL ARMY AIR FORCE BASE - INTERVIEW ROOM

The door slowly opens and Matilda steps in, she wavers.

The Alien sitting in the large recliner holds an open book, *One Thousand and One Nights*.

Without looking the Alien can sense Matilda's presence and carefully sits the book down next to several other books.

Matilda composes herself and walks over to the large recliner chair.

The one-way glass window seems to lurk in the background as Matilda stands in front of the Alien.

The Alien looks into Matilda's eyes.

> ALIEN (V.O.)
> Among the books. I prefer Alice's Adventures in Wonderland, Don Quixote de la Mancha, and One Thousand and One Nights.

> MATILDA (V.O.)
> How did you arrive at that conclusion?

> ALIEN (V.O.)
> The authors of these stories showed that it is more important to have great spirit and imagination than great skill or power.

> MATILDA (V.O.)
> I am unable to answer a great deal of the questions you have regarding the material that you have read...

INT. ROSWELL ARMY AIR FORCE BASE - ROOM

Matilda, the scientist, Colonel William H. Blanchard, and Captain Sheridan Cavitt are sitting together at a table.

> MATILDA
> ...Most of Airl's questions had to do with technical and scientific things. A few of her questions were about the humanities. The depth of complex understanding and subtlety of her questions showed that she had a very penetrating intellect.
> (MORE)

> MATILDA (CONT'D)
> Personally, I think she knows a lot more about the culture and history of Earth than she was willing to admit when we started.

> SCIENTIST
> The Alien's mental acuity is beyond cunning.

> WILLIAM H. BLANCHARD
> It's being selectively deceptive.

> SHERIDAN D. CAVITT
> That thing must have an IQ of a thousand.

> SCIENTIST
> Determining the IQ of an alien species is highly speculative. It would depend on the cognitive abilities, problem-solving skills, and intelligence metrics of that particular species.

> MATILDA
> She has exhibited all of those qualities.

> WILLIAM H. BLANCHARD
> The being is ever learning about humans, it's absorbing information like a sponge.

INT. ROSWELL ARMY AIR FORCE BASE - INTERVIEW ROOM

The Alien and Matilda are sitting right next to each other on the large recliner seat.

The Alien closes the last page of a book that it is reading.

Matilda takes a book from the book cart, as she is about to hand it to the Alien...

> ALIEN (V.O.)
> (looking into Matilda's eyes)
> I am ready to speak now.

Matilda looks a little confused as she sits the book down.

INSERT CARD: TOP SECRET OFFICIAL TRANSCRIPT OF THE U.S. ARMY AIR FORCE ROSWELL ARMY AIR FIELD, 509TH BOMB GROUP SUBJECT: ALIEN INTERVIEW, 24. 7. 1947, 1ST SESSION

The eyes of the Alien and Matilda are locked on each other.

> MATILDA (V.O.)
> What would you like to say, Airl?

> ALIEN (V.O.)
> I have been a part of the Domain Expeditionary Force in this sector of space for several thousand years. However, I have not personally interacted with beings on Earth since 5,965 BCE. It is not my primary function to interact with the inhabitants of planets within The Domain. My duties include being an officer, pilot, and engineer. Although I am fluent in 347 other languages within The Domain, I have not been exposed to your English language.

> MATILDA (V.O.)
> Understood. Your experience and expertise are invaluable, regardless of language barriers. We'll find a way to communicate effectively.

INSERT FOOTAGE:

Three flying saucers hover over the Himalayan mountains as the Alien's voice is heard.

> ALIEN (V.O.)
> The last language I was familiar with was Sanskrit of the Vedic Hymns. I was part of a mission sent to investigate the loss of a Domain base in the Himalayan Mountains. The base was destroyed, and an entire battalion of officers, pilots, communications, and administrative personnel went missing.

BACK TO:

Matilda and the Alien sit across from each other lock in a stare.

                    MATILDA (V.O.)
          Your knowledge of Sanskrit could be
          crucial. Let's proceed cautiously
          and investigate further.

INSERT FOOTAGE:

From inside the spacecraft. Aliens are observing the
citizens of Nepal from a highly technical transparent window.

Descending to a remote village. A spacecraft using a tractor
beam abducts citizens of Nepal

Aboard the spacecraft, an Alien interfaces with an abducted
citizen of Nepal, and the Alien's voice is heard.

                    ALIEN (V.O.)
          Millions of years ago, I was
          trained and worked as an
          Investigation, Data Evaluation, and
          Program Development Officer for The
          Domain. My expertise led me to be
          sent to Earth as part of a search
          team. During my time there, I was
          responsible for interrogating the
          human population in the surrounding
          area, as well as investigating
          reports of sightings of "vimanas"
          or spacecraft in the region. Many
          individuals came forward with such
          sightings.

                                              BACK TO:

Matilda is being stared at by the Alien's huge, emotionless
eyes.

                    MATILDA (V.O.)
          Your past experience is invaluable.
          Let's leverage your expertise to
          uncover any relevant information.

The body language and non-verbal cues between Matilda and the
Alien indicates a strong connection.

                    ALIEN (V.O.)
          Based on the logical extension of
          evidence, testimony, and
          observation, as well as the absence
          of certain evidence, I guided my
          team to uncover a startling
          discovery...

59.

INSERT FOOTAGE:

Distinctive starships are stationed in the deep recesses of space. The voice of the Alien is heard.

> ALIEN (V.O.)
> ...We found out that there are still "Old Empire" ships and installations hidden in this solar system. These were previously unknown to us, but we were able to uncover them through our investigation.

BACK TO:

Matilda's gaze is penetrating...

> MATILDA (V.O.)
> Your deduction skills are impressive. Let's proceed with caution as we explore these hidden installations.

> ALIEN (V.O.)
> I apologize for the previous communication breakdown due to my lack of exposure to your language. However, I have now scanned the books and materials you provided me with, and the data has been transmitted to our space station...

INSERT FOOTAGE:

Aliens resembling Airl deftly download binary codes on a digital screen aboard their spacecraft.

The Alien's voice chimes in...

> ALIEN (V.O.)
> ...Our communications officer has processed it through our computers and translated it into my language. I have also gained access to additional information about the English language and Earth civilization from our computer's domain records.

BACK TO:

Matilda's look is very static.

> MATILDA (V.O.)
> No need to apologize. I really appreciate your quick response. Let's use this new info to learn more about the matter.

The Alien's look is also static.

> ALIEN (V.O.)
> I am now ready to share with you certain information that I believe will be of great value to you. I will be truthful in my sharing, although truth may vary from person to person. I will do my best to share my perspective honestly and accurately while staying true to my values and commitments to my organization.

> MATILDA (V.O.)
> OK. Will you answer questions from my superiors now?

The one-way glass window stands out in the background.

INT. ROSWELL ARMY AIR FORCE BASE - CONTROL ROOM

Military personnel sit at the console turning knobs, pushing buttons, and moving levers.

Captain Sheridan Cavitt and Colonel William H. Blanchard observe Matilda and the Alien through the one-way glass window.

INT. ROSWELL ARMY AIR FORCE BASE - INTERVIEW ROOM

Matilda and the Alien still sit across from each other locked in a trance.

> ALIEN (V.O.)
> I will not answer questions. However, I will provide you with information that I believe will be helpful to the well-being of humanity, including the preservation of Earth and all its life forms. It is my mission to ensure the survival and preservation of the planet.

                    MATILDA (V.O.)
          Understood. I appreciate your
          commitment to our planet's well-
          being. Please share any pertinent
          information you deem necessary.

                    ALIEN (V.O.)
          According to my personal belief,
          all living beings, including
          humans, are spiritual entities that
          are immortal. To make things
          easier to understand, I have
          created a term called "IS-BE."
          This term refers to the fundamental
          nature of an immortal being, which
          exists in a timeless state of "is"
          and only exists because it chooses
          to "be."

                    MATILDA (V.O.)
          Your concept of 'IS-BE is
          intriguing. It simplifies the
          understanding of immortal
          existence. Let's explore that
          further.

                    ALIEN (V.O.)
          Regardless of their social status,
          every individual deserves to be
          treated with respect and dignity,
          just like how I would like to be
          treated. Each person living on
          Earth is a spiritual being, whether
          they are aware of this fact or not.

I/E. ROSWELL ARMY AIR FORCE BASE - ROOM

Standing guard on either side of the door entrance are
Military police.

Matilda's calm vocal tone is heard...

                    MATILDA (O.C.)
          I sensed a warm personality in Airl
          during our conversation when she
          referred to 'immortal spiritual
          beings'. It was the first time I
          had considered humans possibly
          being immortal.

At a round table are Matilda, the military official, the
scientist, the government agent, Colonel William H.
Blanchard, and Captain Sheridan Cavitt.

SCIENTIST
The Alien's perspective is thought-provoking. Exploring the concept of human immortality could lead to intriguing insights.

MATILDA
I always believed that status or power was reserved only for The Father, The Son, and The Holy Ghost. Being a devout Catholic, I follow the word of The Lord Jesus and The Holy Father, and I have never considered a woman as an immortal spiritual being, not even the Holy Mother Mary. However, when Airl expressed that thought, I was suddenly and vividly aware that she, and all of us, are immortal spiritual beings.

MILITARY OFFICIAL
(sarcastic)
Well, it seems even devout Catholics can have their beliefs shaken. Who knew?

WILLIAM H. BLANCHARD
MacElroy. We're not interested in a spiritual overview, or being proselytized by an Alien.

MATILDA
Airl noticed that I was confused about something, so she offered to demonstrate to me that I am an immortal spiritual being. She instructed me to "be above my body", and suddenly I realized that I was outside of my body, looking down from the ceiling. I could see my body's head and the room around me, including Airl's body seated next to mine. At that moment, I was struck with the realization that "I" am not just a body.

GOVERNMENT AGENT
This is outrageous! It sounds like what amounts to a séance.

                    MATILDA
               (bright countenance)
          I realized that "I" am "me" -- a
          spiritual being, not just my soul.
          It brought me joy and relief, but
          I'm not sure what 'immortal' means
          since I've always been taught, I'm
          just a spirit.

                    SHERIDAN D. CAVITT
               (mocking)
          Sergeant. Would Epiphany be
          accurate? Like Our Lady of Fátima.

                    MATILDA
          Airl asked me if I had a better
          understanding of the idea.
          Suddenly, I was back inside my body
          again...

INT. ROSWELL ARMY AIR FORCE BASE - INTERVIEW ROOM

Hovering near the ceiling looking down with uncertainty is the ghostly spirit of Matilda.

On the large recliner. Matilda's physical personage, in a trance, is sitting next to the Alien.

Suddenly Matilda's spirit merges back into her body. She snaps out of the trance and looks astonished.

Matilda looks at the Alien with a sense of glee.

                    MATILDA
               (aloud)
          Yes! I see what you mean!

Matilda gets up from the large recliner and momentarily walks around the room, the look of joy radiates her face.

The Alien looks at Matilda as she is trying to calm down.

Matilda, a bit frantic looks at the Alien.

                    MATILDA (CONT'D)
          I need a drink of water.

Matilda hustles off.

EXT. ROSWELL ARMY AIR FORCE BASE - HALLWAY

The door of the interview room flies open. Matilda juts out and comes to an abrupt stop.

The Military police guarding the door react to Matilda's odd behavior.

                   MATILDA
    Everything is OK. Everything is
    fine.

Matilda walks over to the drinking fountain and bends over. She pushes the button and water flows from the spout. As Matilda is drinking water...

INT. ROSWELL ARMY AIR FORCE BASE - BATHROOM

Matilda lifts her head from the face bowl and looks into the mirror. She dries her face with a paper towel, nervously applies lipstick, and straightens her uniform.

INT. ROSWELL ARMY AIR FORCE BASE - ROOM

Still sitting at the round table are Matilda, the military official, the scientist, the government agent, Colonel William H. Blanchard, and Captain Sheridan Cavitt.

                   MATILDA
    I no longer felt like just an
    interpreter for Airl. We are
    kindred spirits. I feel at home,
    safe with a trusted friend. Airl
    sensed my confusion about personal
    immortality and began her first
    lesson.

               MILITARY OFFICIAL
    Well, Colonel. The Sergeant has
    been compromised.

The Colonel puffs on a cigar and blows the smoke from his mouth, he remains silent.

               GOVERNMENT AGENT
    Sergeant, sounds like this Alien
    has become your guru. Youre duty-
    bound to the government of the
    United States. -- Don't forget
    that.

INT. ROSWELL ARMY AIR FORCE BASE - INTERVIEW ROOM

Matilda is sitting in a chair her look is relaxed and calm.

The Alien sits in the large recliner across from Matilda looking directly into her eyes.

INSERT FOOTAGE:

Trinity Nuclear Atomic bomb explosion in New Mexico.

Airl and the Alien beings piloting a spacecraft.

The Alien's voice can be heard...

> ALIEN (V.O.)
> I was sent to Earth to investigate nuclear weapon explosions in New Mexico. My mission was to gather data on radiation and potential harm to the environment. While in the area of the 509th Bomber Squadron, my spacecraft was struck by lightning and crashed.

The Alien spacecraft flying during a thunderstorm is struck by lightning.

BACK TO:

Matilda's eyes are transfixed.

> MATILDA (V.O.)
> Mission details noted. Lightning strike, causing spacecraft crash, understood.

The Alien sitting on the large recliner is transfixed.

> ALIEN (V.O.)
> IS-BEs control spacecraft using "doll bodies" as mechanical tools to operate in the physical world. Officer class IS-BEs and their superiors inhabit these bodies while on duty in space. When off-duty, they can exist without using a body.

The Alien and Matilda sit across from each other with fixated looks.

> MATILDA (V.O.)
> Fascinating insight into IS-BE
> operations. Thank you for sharing.

> ALIEN (V.O.)
> The dolls have synthetic bodies
> with unique electronic wavelengths
> that serve as identification for
> Immortal Spiritual Beings, IS-BEs.
> The doll body acts as a receiver
> for the IS-BE and no two
> frequencies or doll bodies are
> identical.

> MATILDA (V.O.)
> Interesting. Each doll body is
> uniquely coded for its
> corresponding IS-BE. Clever
> design.

INSERT FOOTAGE:

Airl and the Alien beings are plugged into small seats that are molded into the spacecraft.

Within the spacecraft. Airl and the Alien beings shake violently and are dislodged from their small seats.

Airl's voice is heard calm and clear...

> ALIEN (V.O.)
> Each member of the IS-BE crew is
> connected to a nervous system that
> is built into the spacecraft. The
> spacecraft is constructed similarly
> to a doll body, and it is tuned
> specifically to the frequency of
> each IS-BE crew member. This means
> that the craft can be controlled by
> the thoughts or energy emitted by
> the IS-BE. The control system is
> simple and direct, there are no
> complicated controls or navigation
> equipment on board the spacecraft.
> Essentially, the spacecraft
> operates as an extension of the IS-
> BE.

The alien spacecraft crashes to earth, bouncing and coming to rest against an embankment.

BACK TO:

Matilda and the Alien intensely look directly into each other's eyes.

> MATILDA (V.O.)
> Fascinating concept. Direct control via thought is efficient. It's like the spacecraft becomes a part of the IS-BE.

> ALIEN (V.O.)
> When the spacecraft was struck by lightning, a short circuit momentarily disconnected the IS-BEs from the ship's control, resulting in the crash.

INT. ROSWELL ARMY AIR FORCE BASE - INTERROGATION ROOM

Colonel William H. Blanchard steps out from the shadow of the dim light. Holding a paper in his hand, Blanchard looks at it closely.

> WILLIAM H. BLANCHARD
> This is straight out of an H.G. Wells novel.

Spotlight shining on her, Matilda sits at the small table.

> MATILDA
> Airl is part of "The Domain", a space civilization that controls one-fourth of the entire physical universe. Her organization's mission is to expand and secure the territory and resources of The Domain.

> WILLIAM H. BLANCHARD
> Further analysis is required for potential threats due to the Alien's control and expansion objectives.

Matilda sips from a cup of water as Colonel Blanchard stands there looking stoic.

> MATILDA
> Airl pointed out the parallels between their actions and those of European explorers who claimed the New World for their nations and monarchs.
> (MORE)

MATILDA (CONT'D)
While Europe benefited from native lands, the indigenous people were never consulted or given a choice. Soldiers and missionaries acted solely to advance their nations' interests.

WILLIAM H. BLANCHARD
I guess as a species, we're not that much different from them.

MATILDA
Airl mentioned reading in a history book that the Spanish king, fearing divine retribution, asked the Pope to prepare "The Requirement," a statement intended to be read to newly encountered native inhabitants, expressing regret for the brutal treatment by Spanish soldiers.

WILLIAM H. BLANCHARD
That Alien has become quite the historian.

MATILDA
The King aimed to use the statement, whether accepted or rejected by natives, to absolve himself of responsibility for the slaughter and enslavement, justifying land confiscation by soldiers and priests. Allegedly, the Pope felt no guilt or responsibility.

WILLIAM H. BLANCHARD
Who's doing the deducing? You are the Alien?

Colonel Blanchard pulls up a chair, takes a seat, and studies the paper in his hand.

MATILDA
Airl deemed such actions cowardly, unsurprised by Spain's rapid territorial decline. Shortly after, the King's death led to the assimilation of his empire by other nations.

Colonel Blanchard looks up from the paper.

                    WILLIAM H. BLANCHARD
               The end didn't justify the means,
               is that it?

                    MATILDA
               Airl noted that such behavior is
               absent in The Domain, where leaders
               take full responsibility without
               denigrating themselves or fearing
               gods. This aligns with the
               suggestion that Airl and her people
               likely hold atheistic beliefs.

                    WILLIAM H. BLANCHARD
                         (sarcasm)
               The Domain's leaders skip blame
               games, opting for bold ownership.
               No gods, no regrets—just decisive
               leadership.

Matilda pauses, staring at Colonel Blanchard and she takes
another sip of water.

                    MATILDA
               In the case of the acquisition of
               Earth by The Domain, the rulers of
               The Domain have chosen not to
               openly reveal this intention to the
               "native inhabitants" of Earth until
               a later time when it may, or may
               not, suit their interests to reveal
               themselves. For the present time,
               it is not strategically necessary
               to make the presence of The Domain
               Expeditionary Force known to
               Mankind. In fact, until now, it
               has been very aggressively hidden,
               for reasons that will be revealed
               later.

Colonel Blanchard taking notes and writing on the paper looks
up...

                    WILLIAM H. BLANCHARD
               So, the Earth has already been
               conquered? Is that what you're
               telling me, Sergeant?

Matilda is under the spotlight, and beads of sweat appear on
her brow.

MATILDA
The asteroid belt near Earth holds significant value for The Domain in this sector of space. Objects like low-gravity space stations are highly sought after. Their primary interest lies in the low-gravity satellites, including the far side of the moon and the asteroid belt—a remnant of a planet destroyed eons ago. Mars and Venus are also of interest, albeit to a lesser extent. Structures like doom structures made from gypsum or underground bases with electromagnetic force screens serve as easily constructed housing for Domain forces.

Colonel Blanchard sitting in the chair straightens his posture and gives Matilda a pointed look.

WILLIAM H. BLANCHARD
MacElroy. Do you believe you're being programmed?

A bead of sweat rolls down Matilda's temple.

MATILDA
Once under Domain control, any space area is considered Domain property. The Earth's space station is significant as it lies along The Domain's expansion route towards the Milky Way galaxy's center and beyond. However, this knowledge is kept from Earth's inhabitants.

WILLIAM H. BLANCHARD
(suspicious)
The teacher and the teachie.

MATILDA
Sir? I don't get your meaning.

Colonel Blanchard lights a cigar.

WILLIAM H. BLANCHARD
You've become an astute student --
Of the Alien that is.

INT. ROSWELL ARMY AIR FORCE BASE - BATHROOM - SHOWER

Steam rises as water sprays from the shower head.

Water runs down Matilda's face and head.

INT. ROSWELL ARMY AIR FORCE BASE - MESS HALL

A cacophony of chatter resounds as Military personnel sit at tables eating their food.

Sitting all alone at a table, a solemn-looking Matilda takes in a fork full of food.

INT. ROSWELL ARMY AIR FORCE BASE - ROOM

The stenographer is taking diction using a stenotype machine.

Standing in a semi-circle are John Newble, Colonel William H. Blanchard, Captain Sheridan Cavitt, the military official, the scientist, and the government agent.

                    GOVERNMENT AGENT
               (pressing)
        You need to clarify your
        statements.

                    MILITARY OFFICIAL
               (pointed)
        Use your influence to persuade the
        Alien to answer specific questions.

                    SCIENTIST
               (rational)
        Maybe you're not being direct
        enough.

Matilda, sitting in a chair, looks poised.

                    MATILDA
        I've formed a trusted rapport with
        Airl. I will continue to give it
        my best effort.

                    SHERIDAN D. CAVITT
        Is there anything we can do? It's
        imperative, the Alien must answer
        each question directly.

                    MATILDA
          Airl resolutely refused to answer
          any questions that she sensed had
          been posed by or suggested to me by
          my superiors.

The government agent turns to Colonel Blanchard.

                    GOVERNMENT AGENT
          So, the Alien is calling the shots?
          Is that what's happening here, huh?
          I can't believe this shit.

Colonel Blanchard is silent as he puffs on a cigar.

                    MATILDA
          Airl will continue to "instruct" me
          in subject matters of her own
          choice.

                    MILITARY OFFICIAL
          The relationship between you and
          that Alien is trying my patience.

                    MATILDA
          Airl gave me a new list of subject
          matter, about which she wants more
          information.

Matilda produces a folded paper from the pocket of her uniform.

John Newble approaches Matilda.

                    JOHN NEWBLE
          May I see that?

Matilda hands the paper to John Newble and he unfolds it.

John puts on some glasses and looks over the paper.

Colonel Blanchard walks over to John and gently takes the paper from his hand.

                    WILLIAM H. BLANCHARD
                      (reading aloud)
          Several books, some magazines, and
          newspapers... Huh.

INT. ROSWELL ARMY AIR FORCE BASE - INTERVIEW ROOM

The long thin fingers of the Alien are clutching a *newspaper*. It's the *Roswell Daily Record* and the headline reads. *"RAAF Captures Flying Saucer On Ranch in Roswell Region."*

The Alien's huge almond-shaped eyes are fixed on the newspaper.

Matilda sets a stack of books and magazines on the large recliner beside the Alien.

The Alien emotionless, seems to pay no attention to Matilda as it continues scanning the newspaper.

INT. ROSWELL ARMY AIR FORCE BASE - OFFICE

Matilda enters, appearing fatigued, and removes her uniform jacket, draping it over a coat rack.

Matilda sits on the portable folding bed, slips off her shoes and lays down. She pulls a blanket over herself, reaches up to the lamp, and turns off the light.

Matilda lays her head on a pillow and closes her eyes.

INT. ROSWELL ARMY AIR FORCE BASE - INTERVIEW ROOM

The one-way glass window, always watching, stands out in the background.

The large recliner chair dwarfs the tiny body of the Alien.

INSERT CARD: TOP SECRET OFFICIAL TRANSCRIPT OF THE U.S. ARMY AIR FORCE ROSWELL ARMY AIR FIELD, 509TH BOMB GROUP SUBJECT: ALIEN INTERVIEW, 25. 7. 1947, 1ST SESSION

Sitting in a chair across from the Alien is Matilda, she is writing on a notepad.

Matilda looks up from writing and the Alien is locked in on her eyes.

                    ALIEN (V.O.)
     To grasp history, understand time
     as the measure of motion through
     space.

INSERT FOOTAGE:

From a transparent window. The Alien peers from the spacecraft, eyes fixed on the distant stars, navigating through the cosmic expanse of space.

The Alien's voice resonates...

                ALIEN (V.O.)
    Space is relative to an IS-BEs
    viewpoint, defining distance as the
    'space' between observer and
    object.

INSERT FOOTAGE:

Planets revolve around a fixed entity. Mercury, Venus, Earth, Mars, Jupiter, Saturn, Uranus, and Neptune revolve around the sun.

                              BACK TO:

A pen hangs from Matilda's hand.

The Alien and Matilda are locked in a gaze.

                ALIEN (V.O.)
    History isn't just a linear tale;
    it's a subjective observation of
    events occurring interactively and
    concurrently, akin to the body's
    synchronized functions.

INSERT FOOTAGE:

The inner workings of the human body.

A heart pumps blood, while the lungs provide oxygen to the cells.

Green plants and certain other organisms transform light energy into chemical energy.

The liver straining toxic waste from the blood and eliminating it through the bladder and the bowels.

                              BACK TO:

Still sitting across from each other. The Alien and Matilda eyeball each other.

                    ALIEN (V.O.)
          Interactions occur simultaneously,
          forming an interactive whole in
          history and reality. Time,
          perceived as a uniform vibration,
          isn't a linear stream.

INT. ROSWELL ARMY AIR FORCE BASE - INTERROGATION ROOM

Sitting at the small table under the harsh spotlight, Matilda
drinks from a glass of water.

                    MATILDA
          Airl noted that IS-BEs existence
          predates the universe. Termed
          'immortal', spirits perceive
          existence as 'is-will be'. Each
          spirit is unique in identity and
          abilities.

Colonel William H. Blanchard is still sitting in front of
Matilda. He adjusts his hat and rubs his brow.

                    WILLIAM H. BLANCHARD
          Beyond bizarre. This shakes my
          reality to the core.

Captain Sheridan Cavitt standing in the dim light.

                    SHERIDAN D. CAVITT
          It's psychological warfare.

Colonel Blanchard looks at Captain Sheridan.

                    WILLIAM H. BLANCHARD
          Or is it truth?

                    MATILDA
          Airl, unlike most IS-BEs on Earth,
          can freely enter and leave her
          'doll' and perceive selectively
          through matter. IS-BEs like Airl
          can communicate telepathically and
          are not bound by space or time,
          allowing them to traverse vast
          distances instantly.

                    WILLIAM H. BLANCHARD
          Maybe the Alien is a demon.

                    SHERIDAN D. CAVITT
          You're reaching Colonel.

                    WILLIAM H. BLANCHARD
               That thing is supernatural.

                    MATILDA
               They can experience sensations
               intensely without physical sensory
               mechanisms and exclude pain from
               perception. Airl can recall her
               identity for trillions of years.

Colonel Blanchard gets up from his seat and looks closely at a paper.

Captain Cavitt steps out of the dim light.

                    SHERIDAN D. CAVITT
                    (to Blanchard)
               May I see that?

Colonel Blanchard hands Captain Cavitt the paper.

                    SHERIDAN D. CAVITT (CONT'D)
                    (studying paper)
               Well, torture would be completely
               ineffective.

                    WILLIAM H. BLANCHARD
               I'm at my wit's end at this point.

Matilda looks up at Colonel Blanchard from the table.

                    MATILDA
               She says the suns in this vicinity
               have burned for 200 trillion years.
               The physical universe is likely
               over four quadrillion years old.

                    SHERIDAN D. CAVITT
                    (sarcasm)
               Oh, sure, just trying to calculate
               the age of the universe. Easy
               peasy—only a mere quadrillion years
               or so to consider!

INT. ROSWELL ARMY AIR FORCE BASE - CONTROL ROOM

The reels of the videotape recorder turn.

Military personnel are seated behind a console turning knobs, pushing buttons, and moving levers.

Matilda and the Alien can be seen through the one-way glass window.

INT. ROSWELL ARMY AIR FORCE BASE - INTERVIEW ROOM

A solid red tally light is lit on the lone camera.

Matilda in the chair, and the Alien in the large recliner, are locked in a stare.

> ALIEN (V.O.)
> Time is a difficult factor to measure as it depends on the subjective memory of IS-BEs. There is no uniform record of events throughout the physical universe since it began...

INSERT FOOTAGE:

Egyptians, Greeks, and Romans create sundials, water clocks, and other early chronometric tools. The Alien's voice is heard...

> ALIEN (V.O.)
> ...As on Earth, there are many different time measurement systems, defined by various cultures, which use cycles of motion, and points of origin to establish age and duration.

INSERT FOOTAGE:

Planets form around a star condensing in a disc of molecular gas and dust, embedded within a larger molecular cloud.

Condensation increases until it becomes a giant planet.

A supernova occurs, a stellar explosion that briefly outshines an entire galaxy.

Again, the Alien's voice can be heard...

> ALIEN (V.O.)
> The physical universe is the result of merging individual universes created by IS-BEs. These collisions formed our universe, which continues to expand infinitely due to the creation of energy and forms.

BACK TO:

As though they are face-to-face. The Alien and Matilda are still locked in a stare.

> ALIEN (V.O.)
> Before the physical universe formed, there was a vast period of illusionary universes. IS-BEs acted as 'magicians', creating and dissipating illusions at will. Memories of this period linger among IS-BEs on Earth, reflected in tales of magic and mythology.

INSERT FOOTAGE:

In a cosmic panorama, alien fleets converge, their colossal ships eclipsing stars.

With advanced technology and formidable power, Aliens sweep across galaxies, unfurling their banners of conquest.

Planets tremble as civilizations fall under their dominion, and the once-vast expanse of the physical universe becomes a realm subdued by the might of the alien overlords.

BACK TO:

Matilda's eyes are wide open, in a trance she is fixed on the Alien's glare.

> MATILDA (V.O.)
> So, IS-BEs created an illusionary universe before ours, and now we remember that through our myths? Crazy!

> ALIEN (V.O.)
> On Earth, pinpointing when an IS-BE entered the physical universe is tough due to erased memories and arrivals happening over vast spans—some 60 trillion years ago, others just 3 trillion. Every few million years, new IS-BEs take over areas or planets.

INSERT FOOTAGE:

In death, a soul departs one vessel, its ethereal essence floating amidst the cosmic tapestry.

Guided by unseen forces, a soul descends, drawn to the earthly realm. It enters a newborn form, breathing life into tiny lungs.

A new journey begins as the soul experiences the world afresh. The Alien's voice again, chimes in...

                    ALIEN (V.O.)
          At times, they capture other IS-BEs
          as slaves, forcing them into bodies
          for manual labor, mining ores on
          heavy-gravity planets like Earth.

INSERT FOOTAGE:

Alien overlords craft a plan, shaping humanity from the clay
of Earth.

By technological means, the Aliens mold humans into a labor
force, imbuing them with strength and resilience.

Humans are placed upon fertile soil, toil mining precious
minerals.

Thus, humans emerge as a slave species, bound to the will of
their extraterrestrial masters.

                                        BACK TO:

INT. ROSWELL ARMY AIR FORCE BASE - ROOM

Matilda is standing, she looks withdrawn and introspective.

                    MATILDA
          Airl's been in The Domain
          Expeditionary Force for over 625
          million years, starting as a pilot
          for a biological survey mission
          with visits to Earth. She recalls
          her entire career and even longer
          before that.

The military official, the scientist, the government agent,
and Colonel William H. Blanchard are grouped in front of
Matilda.

                    GOVERNMENT AGENT
          So, humans are still under the
          watchful eye of this -- Domain
          Force?

                    MATILDA
          She mentioned Earth scientists lack
          an accurate measuring system to
          gauge the age of matter. They
          erroneously link the deterioration
          of organic matter to all matter,
          but matter doesn't truly
          deteriorate—it can only change
          form.

The scientist looks befuddled, he rubs his jaw.

> SCIENTIST
> Radiocarbon dating is relatively
> new, but it's been found to be
> reliable.

Matilda looks at the scientist and shrugs her shoulders.

> MATILDA
> The Domain has surveyed this galaxy
> sector since it developed space
> travel technologies about 80
> trillion years ago. Changes on
> Earth, like shifting continents and
> changing landscapes, occur, but the
> basic material remains constant.
> It's always the same.

The military official turns to Colonel Blanchard.

> MILITARY OFFICIAL
> Colonel. The Earth is under siege.
> These beings have been on a
> continual reconnaissance mission.

Matilda turns to Colonel Blanchard as if trying to reason with him.

> MATILDA
> It's mind-boggling to imagine the
> advancements a civilization could
> achieve over trillions of years!
> Just look at how far we've come in
> only 150 years. Just a few
> generations ago, our daily life was
> so different. Transportation on
> foot, reading by candlelight,
> heating, and cooking over a
> fireplace. No indoor plumbing!

Colonel Blanchard looking unmoved lights up a cigar.

INT. DOMAIN SPACECRAFT

A holographic display flickers to life in the command center. A commanding officer gestures to a communications officer, who swiftly accesses the vast archives of information stored within The Domain's "files".

With deft movements, the communications officer navigates through the data, selecting pertinent information about Earth's history.

81.

Airl, a seasoned member of The Domain Expeditionary Force, stands nearby, her gaze focused on the unfolding display.

As the information is "fed" to her, Airl processes the data, her expression thoughtful.

With clarity, Airl relays to the officer, and in turn Matilda, the observations and insights gleaned from The Domain's records.

The scene is one of efficiency and collaboration, as The Domain's knowledge illuminates the history of Earth and its place within the cosmos.

INT. ROSWELL ARMY AIR FORCE BASE - INTERVIEW ROOM

A strange interaction is taking place. The Alien and Matilda are mannequin-like.

Sitting across from each other the Alien and Matilda show but the slightest of movement.

                      MATILDA (V.O.)
Did we... you... Experience some sort of download?

                      ALIEN (V.O.)
My communications officer accessed The Domain's files of Earth's history and relayed the information to me telepathically. Upon receiving the data, I will provide a condensed history lesson. The Domain Expeditionary Force entered the Milky Way galaxy around 10,000 years ago. Our initial objective was to conquer the home planets of the "Old Empire" in the Big Dipper constellation's tail, which served as the central government's seat.

                      MATILDA (V.O.)
What is the Old Empire?

                      ALIEN (V.O.)
A conquered civilization by The Domain Forces that served as the seat of central government for this galaxy, and other adjoining regions of space.

FLASHBACK:

EXT. HIMALAYA MOUNTAINS - DAY

A towering peak stands against the backdrop of a vast, rugged landscape.

Within its craggy confines, hidden from view, lies a secret installation of The Domain Expeditionary Force.

Massive ships, sleek and advanced, are nestled within the hollowed-out mountain, their presence concealed by an intricate electronic illusion projected onto the surrounding terrain.

A force screen shrouds the entrance, allowing ships to come and go unnoticed by the unsuspecting humans below.

However, the tranquility is shattered as an unexpected attack erupts...

EXT. MARS - NIGHT

A flotilla of spaceships emerges from a hidden underground base operated by the "Old Empire" forces.

INT. HIMALAYA MOUNTAINS - DAY

The Domain base is engulfed in chaos as "Old Empire" forces descend upon them, overwhelming their defenses.

Amid the chaos, the IS-BEs of The Domain Expeditionary Force are captured, their fate hanging in the balance amidst the clash of intergalactic powers.

INT. ROSWELL ARMY AIR FORCE BASE - INTERVIEW ROOM

Intense eye contact is happening between the Alien and Matilda as they sit across from each other.

EXT. DEEP SPACE

Spacecraft bearing The Domain's insignia streak towards Earth.

The voice of the Alien is heard...

> ALIEN (V.O.)
> The Domain was very upset about losing such a large force of officers and crew, so they sent other crews to Earth to look for them.

As The Domain spacecraft approaches the Earth's atmosphere, they are met with hostility. The "Old Empire forces strike swiftly, launching a relentless assault on The Domain's crews, thwarting their rescue mission.

> ALIEN (V.O.)
> On Earth's surface, a shadowy operation unfolds...

INT. OLD EMPIRE SPACECRAFT

Captured IS-BEs from The Domain Forces undergo a multi-step procedure to erase their original memories and identities.

Advanced neurotechnological methods aimed at accessing and manipulating neural networks within the brain are performed on captured IS-BEs from The Domain Forces.

Again, the voice of the Alien is heard...

> ALIEN (V.O.)
> These captured IS-BEs from The Domain Forces, now implanted with false memories and hypnotic commands, were sent to Earth to inhabit human bodies, where they remain today.

EXT. DEEP SPACE

The imposing ships of The Domain Forces and the formidable vessels of the Old Empire emerge from the depths of the cosmic void.

As the tension between the two factions reaches its zenith, a fierce confrontation ensues, marked by the brilliant bursts of energy weapons and the thunderous roar of ship engines.

Again, the voice of the Alien is heard...

                    ALIEN (V.O.)
          After an exhaustive investigation
          into their lost crews, The Domain
          uncovered a long-concealed base of
          operations belonging to the "Old
          Empire" in this galaxy sector,
          operating for millions of years.

The Domain Forces, launch a relentless assault on the hidden
base of the Old Empire, their ships weaving through the
cosmic battlefield with precision and purpose.

The Old Empire's vessels shrouded in darkness and secrecy,
retaliate with equal ferocity, their advanced weaponry
unleashing devastation upon their adversaries.

Amidst the chaos of battle explosions illuminate the darkness
of space as ships clash and maneuver in a deadly dance of
combat. The clash between The Domain Forces and the Old
Empire rages on, each side fighting fiercely for dominance
over the vast expanse of the galaxy.

END FLASHBACK.

INT. ROSWELL ARMY AIR FORCE BASE - INTERROGATION ROOM

Colonel William H. Blanchard, perplexed look, pulls a
smoldering cigar from his mouth.

                    WILLIAM H. BLANCHARD
          And humans are their ponds, some of
          which are hybrids.

Matilda's elbow on the table, her head propped up by hand,
glances up at Colonel Blanchard.

                    MATILDA
          Airl mentioned a lengthy conflict
          between the "Old Empire" and The
          Domain, which ended around 1235 AD
          when The Domain destroyed the last
          of the "Old Empire" spacecraft in
          the area, albeit at the cost of
          many Domain ships.

                    WILLIAM H. BLANCHARD
          So, If, I'm supposed to believe
          this, all the Military might in the
          world can't stop them.

MATILDA
In 1914 AD, the "Old Empire" base was unintentionally discovered when an officer of The Domain Expeditionary Force took control of the body of the Archduke of Austria during a routine Earth reconnaissance mission.

A cigar is mashed out in an ashtray.

Colonel Blanchard takes a seat in front of Matilda, and he exhales.

WILLIAM H. BLANCHARD
An Alien possessed the Archduke of Austria?

MATILDA
An IS-BE.

Colonel Blanchard pushes his hat back, rubbing his face as he ponders.

MATILDA (CONT'D)
The aim was to infiltrate human society for intelligence gathering by using the body as a disguise. The officer, being an IS-BE with superior power, simply displaced the inhabitant and took control.

WILLIAM H. BLANCHARD
(facetious)
Are you possessed? Am I possessed?

MATILDA
Are memories of past lives erased?

WILLIAM H. BLANCHARD
So, you're buying into that rubbish?

MATILDA
Colonel Blanchard. You've seen Airl, she is real.

WILLIAM H. BLANCHARD
Yeah, but is what the Alien telling you real?

> MATILDA
> The officer, unaware of the Hapsburgs' unpopularity, was taken by surprise when the Archduke's body was assassinated by a Bosnian student. Consequently, the officer, or IS-BE, was forcefully ejected from the body upon its demise. Disoriented, the IS-BE inadvertently breached an "amnesia force screen" and was captured.

> WILLIAM H. BLANCHARD
> What the hell is an "amnesia force screen?"

FLASHBACK:

EXT. DEEP SPACE

A shimmering electronic force field extends across the region, spanning galaxies and enveloping celestial bodies. Within this force field, intricate webs of energy form a network, pulsating with power.

The voice of Matilda is heard...

> MATILDA (V.O.)
> The Domain found that a vast space area is overseen by an "electronic force field" governing all IS-BEs in this galaxy section, Earth included.

Suddenly, an IS-BE ventures too close to the force field, triggering a response from the electronic barrier. Bolts of energy surge forth, encasing the IS-BE in a glowing net of electricity. The IS-BE struggles against the overwhelming force but to no avail.

The captured IS-BE is ensnared within the electronic net and subjected to a relentless barrage of electrical shocks. The intense energy courses through their being, erasing memories and identities with each jolt.

The once-vibrant consciousness of the IS-BE is gradually subdued, succumbing to the invasive brainwashing treatment.

The electronic force field stands as a sentinel, enforcing its control over all IS-BEs within its reach, including those on Earth.

I/E. EARTH - LABORATORY

Surrounded by complex machinery and ominous apparatus, a solitary figure lies strapped to a table. The room hums with an eerie energy, crackling with anticipation.

The voice of Matilda resonates...

> MATILDA (V.O.)
> On Earth, this "therapy" uses mere hundreds of volts, but the "Old Empire" employs billions of volts against IS-BEs.

A technician adjusts dials and monitors, preparing for the procedure ahead. Thick cables snake from imposing machines, ready to deliver their payload of power.

With a flick of a switch, the room is bathed in blinding light as an immense surge of electricity courses through the equipment. The voltage meters soar into the billions, dwarfing any earthly measure.

The figure on the table convulses violently as the electrical current surges through their body. Their form trembles with the intensity of the shock, every fiber resonating with the overwhelming force.

As the volts of electricity continue to surge, a profound transformation occurs. Memories fade, identities dissolve, and the essence of the IS-BE is obliterated by the relentless power of the electrical onslaught.

In the wake of the electrical storm, the figure lies motionless, stripped bare of all memory and identity. The echoes of an infinite past are silenced, leaving only a blank slate in their wake.

END FLASHBACK.

INT. ROSWELL ARMY AIR FORCE BASE - INTERROGATION ROOM

With the harsh spotlight shining down...

Colonel William H. Blanchard is still sitting in front of Matilda.

> MATILDA
> The shock erases the IS-BEs' identity, memories, skills, and spiritual awareness, rendering them a mindless, robotic entity.

INT. ROSWELL ARMY AIR FORCE BASE - INTERVIEW ROOM

The emotionless Alien sits in the large recliner chair staring.

Sitting across from the Alien. Matilda, a blank stare on her face, looks at the Alien.

> ALIEN (V.O.)
> After the shock, post-hypnotic suggestions implant false memories and time orientation, commanding the IS-BE to "return" to the base upon death for repeated shock and hypnosis sessions indefinitely, while also inducing forgetfulness.

> MATILDA (V.O.)
> Spellbinding...

> ALIEN (V.O.)
> The Domain discovered that the "Old Empire" has used Earth as a "prison planet" for an unknown, possibly millions of years.

> MATILDA (V.O.)
> Intriguing... What else did they find out?

> ALIEN (V.O.)
> When the IS-BEs' body dies, they're captured by the force screen and ordered to "return to the light." This concept of "heaven" and the "afterlife" is part of the hypnotic suggestion that manipulates them.

> MATILDA (V.O.)
> So, what happens to them after they "return to the light"?

> ALIEN (V.O.)
> After the IS-BE is shocked and hypnotized to erase their memory, they're ordered to "report" back to Earth and inhabit a new body, believing they have a special purpose there...

INT. ROSWELL ARMY AIR FORCE BASE - INTERROGATION ROOM

Both Colonel William H. Blanchard and Matilda are still sitting across from each other.

Hand on his brow, Colonel Blanchard has an unsure expression on his face.

Captain Sheridan Cavitt slowly shuts the door behind him. The voice of Matilda is heard...

                    MATILDA (O.C.)
         But, of course, there is no purpose
         for being in a prison -- at least
         not for the prisoner.

                    SHERIDAN D. CAVITT
         Wait, what?

Matilda, looking up at Captain Sheridan.

                    MATILDA
         Undesirable IS-BEs sent to Earth by
         the "Old Empire" were labeled as
         "untouchable", including those
         deemed irredeemable criminals or
         unproductive individuals.

                    SHERIDAN D. CAVITT
         Untouchable? What could make
         someone untouchable to an empire?

                    MATILDA
         "Untouchables" on Earth encompass
         IS-BEs considered political
         dissidents, rebels, and those with
         a history of opposition against the
         "Old Empire."

                    WILLIAM H. BLANCHARD
         Hmm, so who exactly are these
         'untouchables' then?

                    MATILDA
         Earth boasts the highest
         concentration of artists per capita
         in the "Old Empire," including
         painters, singers, musicians,
         writers, actors, and performers of
         various kinds.

INT. ROSWELL ARMY AIR FORCE BASE - INTERVIEW ROOM

Seemingly face to face. Matilda and the Alien are telepathically locked in on each other.

> ALIEN (V.O.)
> "Untouchables" also encompass intellectuals, inventors, and geniuses in diverse fields. With all valuable creations already existing for trillions of years, the "Old Empire" deems them unnecessary. Skilled managers are similarly deemed superfluous in a society of compliant, robotic citizens.

> MATILDA (V.O.)
> Really? That's... quite shocking.

> ALIEN (V.O.)
> Those who resist conformity to the oppressive system of the 'Old Empire' are "untouchable" and face memory wipeout and imprisonment on Earth.

> MATILDA (V.O.)
> Wait, they do what to those who resist?

The diminutive Alien sits in the large recliner. Matilda sits in her chair. Both show no emotion as if having an out-of-body experience.

> ALIEN (V.O.)
> IS-BEs are trapped, lost in a fog of false identities and memories, unable to find their way back to themselves.

> MATILDA (V.O.)
> Wow, that's... beyond belief.

> ALIEN (V.O.)
> The Domain officer who was "assassinated" while in the body of Archduke of Austria was, likewise, captured by the "Old Empire" force.

INSERT FOOTAGE:

A luminous being, representing the Domain officer, is forcefully pulled from the physical body of the Archduke of Austria.

The luminous being is then captured by shadowy figures, representing the Old Empire forces, and transported through space.

BACK TO:

The huge almond-shaped eyes of the Alien seem to speak to Matilda.

                ALIEN (V.O.)
     The Domain officer was able to
     escape from an underground base
     after 27 years in captivity on
     Mars.

FLASHBACK:

I/E. MARS

The Domain officer, depicted as a radiant figure, breaks free from the confines of the electronic prison cell.

With determination, the officer flees the underground base, navigating through dimly lit corridors and evading patrolling guards.

EXT. ASTEROID BELT

A sleek battle cruiser, representing the Domain's forces, speeds towards Mars, its engines glowing brightly against the backdrop of space.

As the cruiser approaches Mars, it unleashes a barrage of powerful energy beams, targeting the hidden base in the Cydonia region.

Explosions erupt across the Martian landscape as the base is obliterated, leaving behind a trail of destruction.

END FLASHBACK.

INT. ROSWELL ARMY AIR FORCE BASE - INTERVIEW ROOM

The Alien and Matilda are still sitting across from each other locked in a trance.

> ALIEN (V.O.)
> The Domain officer's escape and strike against the Old Empire's Martian stronghold marked a triumphant victory.

> MATILDA (V.O.)
> Interesting! What were the repercussions of that strike?

> ALIEN (V.O.)
> Despite the destruction of the "Old Empire" base, the IS-BE force screens and mind control machinery continue to operate from undiscovered locations, as the main control center remains elusive, perpetuating its influences.

Matilda from her chair is engaged in a full-on gaze with the Alien.

> MATILDA (V.O.)
> So, the battle might be far from over?

> ALIEN (V.O.)
> Since the destruction of the "Old Empire" space forces, Earth has become a dumping ground for "untouchable" IS-BEs from across multiple galaxies.

INT. ROSWELL ARMY AIR FORCE BASE - ROOM

Sitting at the conference table holding a transcript is Colonel William H. Blanchard.

Also seated at the conference table are Captain Sheridan Cavitt, the military official, the scientist, and the government agent.

Colonel Blanchard puts on his glasses and reads from the transcript.

> WILLIAM H. BLANCHARD
> This, in part, explains the very unusual mix of races, cultures, languages, moral codes, religious and political influences among the IS-BE population on Earth.
> (MORE)

                    WILLIAM H. BLANCHARD (CONT'D)
          The number and variety of
          heterogeneous societies on Earth
          are extremely unusual on a normal
          planet. Most "Sun Type 12, Class
          7" planets are inhabited by only
          one humanoid body type or race, if
          any.

                    MILITARY OFFICIAL
          Oh, fantastic! Earth is just the
          cosmic equivalent of a dumping
          ground sale, where everyone's
          unwanted IS-BEs get tossed in for a
          cultural mishmash! How quaint.
          Who needs homogeneity when you can
          have chaos, right?

Colonel Blanchard pulls his glasses down from his face.

                    SCIENTIST
          Earth's diverse mix of cultures and
          influences provides opportunities
          for rich exchanges of ideas and
          perspectives, fostering greater
          understanding and cooperation among
          its inhabitants.

                    MILITARY OFFICIAL
          Oh, yeah. That's just something a
          scientist would say.

Colonel Blanchard puts his glasses back on and continues to
read from the transcript.

                    WILLIAM H. BLANCHARD
          Ancient civilizations and events on
          Earth have been significantly
          shaped by the covert operations of
          the "Old Empire" base. However,
          the exact location and operators of
          this operation remain elusive due
          to extensive protection measures.

Colonel Blanchard pauses as he is interrupted by the
government agent.

                    GOVERNMENT AGENT
          Oh, so the "Old Empire" is like
          some shadowy puppet master pulling
          the strings behind our history?
          And no one's been able to figure it
          out? Sounds like a convenient
          scapegoat for explaining away the
          mysteries of the past.

                    SHERIDAN D. CAVITT
          And GOD said let us make man in our
          image. It seems that the aliens
          are our god.

Colonel Blanchard continues reading.

                    WILLIAM H. BLANCHARD
          Until the ancient network of
          electronics creating the force
          screens is found and destroyed, we
          can't stop the "Old Empire" from
          continuing their electric shock,
          hypnosis, and remote thought
          control on Earth.

                    GOVERNMENT AGENT
          Does anyone sitting here really
          believe that they are an, an... IS-
          BE?

                    MILITARY OFFICIAL
          If any of this is real. Militarily
          we are at a disadvantage. And,
          and... We've been here before.

                    SCIENTIST
          Scientifically speaking, it is a
          probability. Past lives that is.

                    GOVERNMENT AGENT
          Even if it were true. Past lives.
          All memories, according to the
          Alien, has been wiped out.

                    WILLIAM H. BLANCHARD
          May I continue?
              (reading)
          -- All Domain Expeditionary Force
          members are now aware of this
          phenomena to avoid detection and
          capture by "Old Empire" traps while
          operating in this solar system.

INT. ROSWELL ARMY AIR FORCE BASE - INTERVIEW ROOM

Like a silent witness the one-way glass window lurks in the
background.

The camera with its red tally light is on constant watch.

95.

INSERT CARD: TOP SECRET OFFICIAL TRANSCRIPT OF THE U.S. ARMY AIR FORCE ROSWELL ARMY AIR FIELD, 509TH BOMB GROUP SUBJECT: ALIEN INTERVIEW, 26. 7. 1947, 1ST SESSION

As if a patient is under a doctor's care. The diminutive Alien sits in the large recliner chair.

In her usual place, Matilda sits in front of the Alien and the interface continues between them.

> ALIEN (V.O.)
> Since 1150 AD, The Domain Expeditionary Force has noticed a revival in Western science and culture after the remnants of the "Old Empire" space fleet in this solar system were wiped out. Though the influence of remote control hypnosis has lessened, it still holds sway.

> MATILDA (V.O.)
> Hmm, so the "Old Empire" remnants were wiped out, yet their influence still lingers? Quite intriguing how these ancient forces continue to shape our present-day world.

> ALIEN (V.O.)
> Damage to the "Old Empire" control operation caused a slight decrease in its power, allowing IS-BEs to start recalling their previous knowledge. This led to the decline of the "Dark Ages" in Europe.

> MATILDA (V.O.)
> Riveting! So, a slight hiccup in the control system led to a resurgence of knowledge? That's quite an unexpected turn of events.

INT. ROSWELL ARMY AIR FORCE BASE CONTROL ROOM

The Alien and Matilda, facing each other, are seen through the one-way glass window.

Military personnel are stationed behind a console, deftly adjusting knobs, pressing buttons, and maneuvering levers.

INT. ROSWELL ARMY AIR FORCE BASE - INTERVIEW ROOM

A notepad and pen sit in Matilda's lap.

Sitting across from each other, face to face. The Alien and Matilda are locked in an intense stare.

Though looking directly into the Alien's eye, Matilda is performing psychography, automatic writing.

> ALIEN (V.O.)
> Since then, knowledge of physics and electricity has revolutionized Earth's culture almost overnight. Many geniuses among the IS-BE population regained partial access to suppressed technology after 1150 AD. Sir Isaac Newton exemplifies this, reinventing major scientific and mathematical disciplines in just a few decades.

> MATILDA (V.O.)
> Wow, so Newton was like a one-man scientific revolution!

> ALIEN (V.O.)
> The men who "remembered" these sciences already knew them before they were sent to Earth. It's extraordinary how much they've advanced in science and mathematics, topics that typically take civilizations billions of years to develop.

Written words flow from Matilda's pen onto the notepad.

> MATILDA (V.O.)
> Oh, so they're like walking encyclopedias of knowledge? Imagine having access to centuries of wisdom in just one lifetime!

> ALIEN (V.O.)
> IS-BEs on Earth are just starting to recall bits of the vast array of technologies across the universe. If the amnesia mechanisms were completely shattered, they could potentially recover all their memory!

                    MATILDA (V.O.)
          Huh. It's quite intriguing to
          consider the vastness of knowledge
          waiting to be unlocked within us.

                    ALIEN (V.O.)
          Humanities have not advanced
          similarly; Earth's IS-BEs still
          exhibit negative behavior,
          influenced by "hypnotic commands"
          between lifetimes.

The Alien and Matilda are locked in a psychic exchange. Spiritual energy pulsates and flows between the two.

The pen in Matilda's hand vibrates rapidly and the written words on the notepad become sketchy.

INSERT FOOTAGE:

In a dimly lit, crowded prison yard, a diverse group of individuals interacts. In one corner, criminals huddle together, exchanging whispers and glances.

Nearby, artists work on intricate sketches, their creative minds focused despite the chaos.

Revolutionaries engage in heated debates, their voices rising above the din.

Meanwhile, intellectuals sit apart, deep in thought, pondering the mysteries of the universe.

Suddenly, alarms blare, and guards rush in, activating electronic force screens that separate the inmates.

...The voice of the Alien is heard.

                    ALIEN (V.O.)
          The purpose of the prison planet is
          to keep IS-BEs on Earth, forever.

As the chaos subsides, the prison population remains divided, trapped behind invisible barriers, symbolizing their eternal confinement.

                                        BACK TO:

Matilda is shaken out of the trance and collects herself -- she looks at the notepad displaying lengthy notes.

Matilda looks up from the notepad and again she locks onto the Alien with her eyes.

INT. ROSWELL ARMY AIR FORCE BASE CONTROL ROOM - DAY

Matilda and the Alien can be seen through the one-way glass window.

Staring in amazement are the military official, the scientist, and the government agent.

>   GOVERNMENT AGENT
>   What the hell are we witnessing?

>   MILITARY OFFICIAL
>   -- I don't know.

Colonel William H. Blanchard steps through the door, shutting it behind him --

>   SCIENTIST
>   Amazing.

INT. ROSWELL ARMY AIR FORCE BASE - INTERVIEW ROOM - DAY

Matilda staring straight ahead, the pen operating independently, continues the automatic writing on the notepad.

The emotionless Alien sits in the large recliner staring back at Matilda.

>   ALIEN (V.O.)
>   IS-BEs from across galaxies,
>   including Sirius, Aldebaron, the
>   Pleiades, and more, have been
>   deposited on Earth. They represent
>   diverse races, cultures, and belief
>   systems, each with its own language
>   and history.

FLASHBACK:

EXT. DEEP SPACE

Various star systems and galaxies twinkle in the distance.

Suddenly, a series of bright lights streak across the screen, representing spacecraft arriving from different corners of the universe.

As the bright lights converge on Earth...

EXT. EARTH

A bustling cityscape filled with diverse characters of different shapes, sizes, and appearances. These beings interact with each other, speaking different languages and practicing unique customs and rituals.

Amid the bustling crowd, groups of IS-BEs from various planets and civilizations can be seen, each distinguished by their distinct features and attire. Some have humanoid forms, while others exhibit exotic and otherworldly appearances. Despite their differences, they coexist in this melting pot of diversity, sharing their knowledge, stories, and experiences.

Different clusters of IS-BEs, highlighting their interactions and exchanges. They engage in animated conversations, showcasing the richness of their cultural backgrounds and the depth of their histories.

The voice of the Alien is heard...

> ALIEN (V.O.)
> Despite the vastness of space that separates their homeworlds, they find common ground on Earth, forming a vibrant tapestry of intergalactic diversity.

The world now embodies an eclectic array of IS-BEs, all co-mingling, who have made the planet their home.

END FLASHBACK.

INT. ROSWELL ARMY AIR FORCE BASE - INTERVIEW ROOM

The Alien, eyes glazed over, is perched on the large recliner.

> ALIEN (V.O.)
> The IS-BEs from Atlantis and Lemuria, originating from another star system over 400,000 years ago, mingled with Earth's earlier inhabitants. These civilizations were wiped out by a planetary "polar shift" long before the arrival of the current population on Earth, contributing to the origins of the original oriental races from Australia.

Sitting in the chair. Matilda reading from her notepad glances at the Alien her gaze becomes focused.

                  MATILDA (V.O.)
Huh, so Earth's past is like a galactic reunion, mixing ancient civilizations with newer arrivals. Intriguing!

                  ALIEN (V.O.)
On the other hand, the civilizations set up on Earth by the "Old Empire" prison system were very different from the civilization of the "Old Empire" itself, which is an electronic space opera, atomic powered conglomeration of earlier civilizations that were conquered with nuclear weapons and colonized by IS-BEs from another galaxy.

                  MATILDA (V.O.)
Riveting! Earth's civilizations from the "Old Empire" prison system differ greatly from the high-tech conglomerate of conquered galaxies it originates from.

                  ALIEN (V.O.)
The "Old Empire" was governed by a rigid hierarchy of planetary governments under a monarchic figurehead from an ancient space opera society.

                  MATILDA (V.O.)
Quite a dystopian setup, isn't it?

                  ALIEN (V.O.)
This type of government often arises when citizens relinquish personal responsibility for self-regulation. They surrender their freedom to paranoid IS-BEs who view everyone as enemies to be controlled or destroyed, even their closest allies whom they claim to cherish.

FLASHBACK:

EXT. THE DOMAIN

A vast technologically advanced cityscape belonging to The Domain contrasts with the desolate ruins of the former governing planet of the "Old Empire" in the background.

The citizens of The Domain are shown engaged in various activities, working together harmoniously and with purpose. There's a sense of unity and camaraderie among them as they go about their daily lives.

In the distance, we can see the remnants of the once powerful "Old Empire", now reduced to rubble and chaos.

The strength and resilience of The Domain's civilization symbolize their victory over the oppressive regime of the past.

END FLASHBACK.

INT. ROSWELL ARMY AIR FORCE BASE - INTERVIEW ROOM

The automatic writing of Matilda comes to an abrupt stop. The face-off continues, and Matilda seems eye to eye with the Alien.

> ALIEN (V.O.)
> The German totalitarian state on Earth resembled the "Old Empire" but was far less brutal and weaker. Many IS-BEs on Earth oppose totalitarianism or are too violent to be controlled by it. As a result, Earth's population has a high proportion of such beings, leading to conflicting cultural and ethical norms among them.

> MATILDA (V.O.)
> So, Earth became a refuge for those who couldn't fit into the oppressive mold of the Old Empire. It's no wonder our world is a melting pot of conflicting ideologies and moral codes.

Like fighters in opposite corners. The Alien and Matilda glare at each other.

The pen in Matilda's hand starts to write, automatically jotting on the notepad in her lap.

                    ALIEN (V.O.)
          The Domain conquered the core "Old
          Empire" planets using electronic
          weapons. These planets are filled
          with a degraded society of enslaved
          workers, engaging in cannibalism
          and violent entertainment like
          deadly racing and bloody
          spectacles.

                    MATILDA (V.O.)
          That's quite a grim picture. It's
          hard to fathom a society so steeped
          in degradation and brutality.

                    ALIEN (V.O.)
          The Domain avoids using atomic
          weapons on the planets of the "Old
          Empire" to preserve their
          resources, regardless of any
          justifications for their use.

                    MATILDA (V.O.)
          That's commendable. It shows a
          level of restraint and respect for
          the environment and resources of
          those planets, even in the face of
          conflict.

                    ALIEN (V.O.)
          The current U.S. civilization is
          adopting elements of the "Old
          Empire" civilization, seen in the
          design of transportation and
          architecture.

INT. ROSWELL ARMY AIR FORCE BASE - CONTROL ROOM

The electronic sensor lights up. Technical equipment hums
and vibrates.

Military personnel seated behind the console turn knobs, push
buttons and move levers.

Looking through the one-way glass window at the Alien and
Matilda are Captain Sheridan Cavitt and Colonel William H.
Blanchard.

                    WILLIAM H. BLANCHARD
          What do you think is going on in
          there?

                    SHERIDAN D. CAVITT
          I have no idea.

Colonel Blanchard gives Captain Sheridan an off-putting look.

                    WILLIAM H. BLANCHARD
          Well, you should. You're the
          communications officer.

INT. ROSWELL ARMY AIR FORCE BASE - INTERVIEW ROOM

Matilda's automatic writing suddenly stops, she breaks eye contact with the Alien.

The Alien sitting across from Matilda in the large recliner shows no emotion.

Matilda looks over at the one-way glass window for a moment, then turns and looks at the Alien.

Matilda's gaze at the Alien becomes intense.

                    ALIEN (V.O.)
          The former "Old Empire" government,
          akin to the Axis powers, displayed
          similar intelligence and behavior.
          Their exile to Earth mirrored their
          treatment of other IS-BEs,
          underscoring the cycle of kindness
          and cruelty. Effective prevention
          of brutality demands both force and
          wisdom, but also remarkable
          understanding and courage to resist
          its corrosive influence.

                    MATILDA (V.O.)
          It's a sobering reminder of the
          profound impact our actions can
          have on others, and how patterns of
          behavior can echo through time and
          space. It underscores the
          importance of empathy, restraint,
          and courage in shaping a better
          future for all beings.

                    ALIEN (V.O.)
          Such a government's twisted "logic"
          would advocate for erasing the
          memory of every artist, genius,
          manager, and inventor, and
          imprisoning them with criminals and
          the marginalized from across the
          galaxy.

>   MATILDA (V.O.)
>   A grim testament to the lengths
>   tyrannical regimes will go,
>   sacrificing creativity,
>   intelligence, and diversity for
>   their own ends.

INSERT FOOTAGE:

A surreal setting where ethereal beings are stripped of their memories and placed into human bodies.

A conveyor belt moves them through a process where their consciousness is altered, and false memories are implanted.

As they emerge from the process, they find themselves in human form, completely unaware of their true origins.

Meanwhile, intricate illusions of diverse civilizations materialize around them, designed to mask the reality of their existence.

                                        BACK TO:

The Alien and Matilda sit across from each other in a fixated trance.

INSERT FOOTAGE:

A cosmic view of various civilizations from different time periods and regions flashing across the screen in rapid succession.

Each civilization is represented by iconic landmarks, architectural styles, and cultural symbols.

As civilizations transition, we see ethereal beings guiding the construction of temples, pyramids, cities, and monuments using advanced technology and intricate blueprints.

These beings communicate and collaborate with human populations, subtly influencing their development and shaping the cultural elements of each society.

Finally, a vast cosmic tapestry of civilizations spanning the universe, all interconnected by the guiding influence of the IS-BEs.

                                        BACK TO:

Matilda appears to be in a catatonic state, her hand furiously jotting information on the notepad.

The doll like Alien sits in the large recliner in a focused gaze.

> ALIEN (V.O.)
> The IS-BEs sent to Earth were initially located in India, then spread to Mesopotamia, Egypt, Mesoamerica, Greece, Rome, Medieval Europe, and the New World. They were hypnotically guided by the "Old Empire" to adopt the patterns of each civilization, masking their true origins. This strategy, with distinct languages, costumes, and cultures, reinforces amnesia and prevents recollection of their original home planets.

> MATILDA (V.O.)
> Fascinating how deeply ingrained the deception goes.

> ALIEN (V.O.)
> On the very far back-track of time...

FLASHBACK:

INT. TIME-LAPSE VISION - VARIOUS ERAS

Different civilizations emerge over time, from ancient Mesopotamia to classical Greece to medieval Europe.

Each civilization bears striking similarities in architecture, clothing, language, and customs, hinting at a repetitive pattern dictated by the IS-BEs.

END FLASHBACK.

INT. ROSWELL ARMY AIR FORCE BASE - INTERVIEW ROOM

The almond-shaped eyes of the Alien penetrate the fixed-glazed expression of Matilda.

> ALIEN (V.O.)
> ...The gradual evolution of civilizations underscores the recurring themes and structures that persist across different time periods and geographical locations.

MATILDA (V.O.)
Sounds like civilizations on repeat, sticking to what works.

EXT. VAST EXPANSE OF SPACE

Stars twinkling in the distance.

The Alien's calm gentle voice is heard...

ALIEN (V.O.)
A "Sun Type 12, Class 7" planet is the designation given to a planet inhabited by carbon-oxygen-based life forms.

A specific star, revealing a bright, yellow planet comes into view, orbiting the star at a precise distance.

Again, the Alien's voice is heard...

ALIEN (V.O.)
This planet is labeled as "Class 7."

A cross-section of the planet shows its layers and composition.

The Alien's voice chimes in.

ALIEN (V.O.)
The size and radiation intensity of the star, along with the planet's orbit and characteristics, determine its class.

MONTAGE:

EXT. VARIOUS LANDSCAPES - DAY

- Diverse environments.

- Lush forests.

- Deserts.

- Oceans.

- Planet's inhabitants - carbon-oxygen-based life forms.

- Alien creatures roam the landscapes, while colorful flora decorates the surroundings.

- Various species uniquely adapted to their environment, reflecting the planet's classification.

- The planet in its entirety, bathed in the warm glow of its sun.

END MONTAGE.

INT. ROSWELL ARMY AIR FORCE BASE - INTERVIEW ROOM

Matilda stares deeply into the Alien's huge eyes.

              ALIEN (V.O.)
     The interconnectedness of the star
     type, planet class, and the life
     forms that call it home.

EXT. SOLAR SYSTEM

Various stars of different sizes and intensities are scattered across the cosmic landscape. Each star emits a unique glow, illuminating the space around it.

One particular star becomes the focus.

The Alien's voice comes in...

              ALIEN (V.O.)
     The planet's class is determined by
     the star's size, radiation,
     planetary orbit, as well as the
     planet's size, density, gravity,
     and composition.

Graphics overlay depicting equations and diagrams illustration.

Planets orbit their respective stars. Each planet is labeled with its class designation.

EXT. PLANET SURFACE

Diverse flora and fauna thrive.

The voice of the Alien is heard.

              ALIEN (V.O.)
     Flora and fauna are designated and
     identified according to the star
     type and class of planet they
     inhabit.

Alien landscapes come to life, featuring exotic plants, creatures, and ecosystems unique to each world.

                    ALIEN (V.O.)
     Life forms are intricately
     connected to the planet's
     classification, adapting to its
     specific conditions.

EXT. SOLAR SYSTEM

Stars orbit planets.

The Alien's voice is heard...

                    ALIEN (V.O.)
     The cosmos supports life forms on
     planets based on their class and
     the type of star they orbit.

INT. ROSWELL ARMY AIR FORCE BASE - MESS HALL

Chatter echoes loudly...

Uniformed soldiers and army officers are sitting at tables eating and carousing.

Captain Sheridan Cavitt and Colonel William H. Blanchard are seated at a table drinking cups of coffee.

                WILLIAM H. BLANCHARD
     The president has to be briefed
     personally.

                SHERIDAN D. CAVITT
     I prepared the report for you.

Captain Sheridan pushes a folder to Colonel Blanchard.

Colonel Blanchard suspiciously looks around and opens the folder. He glances and sees a piece of paper that has *Above Top Secret* stamped on it.

Blanchard closes the folder --

              SHERIDAN D. CAVITT (CONT'D)
     Aren't you gonna read it?

                WILLIAM H. BLANCHARD
     Not here. This has to be given to
     General Ramey immediately.

                    SHERIDAN D. CAVITT
               Will he be the person briefing
               President Truman?

Colonel Blanchard sips from the cup and nods his head in acknowledgment.

INT. ROSWELL ARMY AIR FORCE BASE - INTERVIEW ROOM

Jotting on the notepad, Matilda looks fatigued, she wipes her brow and lifts her head.

Sitting across from Matilda in the large recliner, staring, showing no emotion is the Alien.

                    ALIEN (V.O.)
               Most planets in the physical
               universe lack a breathable
               atmosphere. Only a small
               percentage, like Earth, have an
               atmosphere with a chemical
               composition that sustains plant
               life and other organisms.

                    MATILDA (V.O.)
               It's intriguing that only a few
               planets have an atmosphere that can
               sustain life, with Earth being one
               of the rare exceptions.

                    ALIEN (V.O.)
               The Vedic Hymns were introduced to
               the Himalayas region 8,200 years
               ago by the Domain Force, coinciding
               with the Aryan invasion and
               conquest of India, where existing
               human societies were present.

MONTAGE:

EXT. HIMALAYAS - ANCIENT TIMES - SUNSET

- a group of ancient scholars sitting in a circle. They are dressed in simple robes, meditating and reciting the Vedas.

- Various groups throughout the years, showing how the knowledge is passed down orally from one generation to the next.

- An elder sage, his voice resonating as he recites the hymns to a group of young disciples. Their eyes are closed, absorbing each word.

- Through the generations, showing the dedication to memorizing the Vedas.

- The first scripts, where ancient scholars carefully write the Vedas on palm leaves and parchment. The focus is on their meticulous work, demonstrating the commitment to preserving the knowledge in written form.

- An officer of The Domain Expeditionary Force being incarnated on Earth as "Vishnu." He is depicted with a majestic aura, his eyes intense and full of determination.

- The "Vishnu" fights against the forces of the "Old Empire" in dramatic battle sequences.

- Epic battles where "Vishnu" leads the charge against the "Old Empire" forces.

- Warriors, chariots, and weapons clashing in a grand display of combat. Vishnu's combat prowess is highlighted as he moves through the battlefield with precision and strength.

- The reverence of Vishnu in the Rig-Veda. Statues, temples, and worshippers paying homage to his legacy.

- The enduring influence of Vishnu is conveyed through the grandeur of the temples and the devotion of his followers.

- A serene image of Vishnu as he transitions from Earth, being reassigned to other duties in The Domain.

END MONTAGE.

Matilda sits in the chair, her body quakes ever so slightly, and her glare is glazed over.

The Alien, though emotionless, has a gleam in its eyes.

          ALIEN (V.O.)
This orchestrated episode was a revolt against the Egyptian pantheon installed by "Old Empire" administrators, aimed at freeing humankind from false civilization elements. It was part of mental manipulation to conceal criminal actions against Earth's IS-BEs.

Matilda breaks eye contact with the Alien, still jotting on the notepad.

          MATILDA (V.O.)
     (looking up)
Got it.

Sitting in the large recliner. The piercing eyes of the diminutive Alien stare out at Matilda.

                    ALIEN (V.O.)
The priesthood enforced the belief that individuals, as Immortal Spiritual Beings, are mere bodies without identity, past lives, or power, while the gods controlled everything through the priests, who wielded authority with threats of eternal punishment.

Matilda's pen jots on the notepad, but her eyes remain steadfast on the Alien.

                    ALIEN (V.O.)
On a prison planet where everyone has amnesia, even the priests, what else could be expected? The Domain Force's intervention on Earth has been hindered by the ongoing secret mind-control operation of the "Old Empire."

FLASHBACK:

EXT. ANCIENT BATTLE - DAY

INSERT CARD: BETWEEN 1500 BCE AND ABOUT 1200 BCE...

A fierce battle rages between the "Old Empire" forces and The Domain. Swords clash, arrows fly, and the air is thick with the sounds of war.

Amid the chaos, members of The Domain Forces attempt to impart a profound teaching to influential beings on Earth. They strive to convey the concept of an individual as an Immortal Spiritual Being, amidst the tumult of religious conquest.

The clash of ideologies and swords echoes through the ancient battlefield, as the struggle for spiritual liberation unfolds against the backdrop of war.

END FLASHBACK.

INT. OFFICE OF ROGER M. RAMEY - DAY

Sitting at a desk wearing a decorated Lieutenant General Air Force uniform and hat is ROGER M. RAMEY, male white 42. The phone on his desk buzzes and Ramey picks it up.

> ROGER M. RAMEY
> Yes, send him in.

A uniformed officer walks in with a briefcase handcuffed to his wrist.

A folder sits on Ramey's desk, and he flips it open. *Above Top Secret* prominently stands out on the paper.

Ramey scans the paper with his eyes and picks up the phone.

> ROGER M. RAMEY (CONT'D)
> Get me the President.

INT. ROSWELL ARMY AIR FORCE BASE - INTERVIEW ROOM

The lone camera stands out in the background, its red tally light shines bright.

The faceoff continues, the Alien and Matilda sit across from each other locked in a staring contest.

> ALIEN (V.O.)
> The concept was tragically twisted to suggest there's only one IS-BE, rather than recognizing everyone as an IS-BE. It was a profound misunderstanding and a refusal to acknowledge individual power.

Matilda holding the pen, her eyes locked onto the Alien, rapidly writes on the notepad.

> MATILDA (V.O.)
> Quite a twist on the truth, wasn't it?

> ALIEN (V.O.)
> The "Old Empire" priests distorted the concept of individual immortality into the belief in a singular, omnipotent IS-BE, denying others their inherent identity as IS-BEs. This manipulation stems from the "Old Empire" amnesia operation.

Matilda breaks eye contact with the Alien and writes on the notepad.

-- Matilda looks up from the notepad making eye contact with the Alien.

MATILDA (V.O.)
Understood.

ALIEN (V.O.)
It's simple to teach this warped idea to those who refuse to take responsibility for their own lives. Slaves are such people. If someone shifts responsibility for creation, existence, and personal accountability to others, they remain a slave.

MATILDA (V.O.)
That perspective sure keeps people stuck in their chains.

ALIEN (V.O.)
The idea of a single monotheistic "god" emerged, propagated by prophets like Moses, who was raised in the Egyptian royal household of Amenhotep III, Akhenaten, Nefertiti, and Tutankhamen.

MATILDA (V.O.)
Interesting twist, especially with the Egyptian royal connection.

The Alien's huge hypnotic eyes seem to speak to Matilda.

ALIEN (V.O.)
The effort to reveal to certain Earthlings that they are IS-BEs aimed to undermine the fictional gods created by the "Old Empire" mystery cult, "The Brothers of The Serpent," known in Egypt as the Priests of Amun. This secret society was a key part of the "Old Empire."

Matilda looks at the notepad and writes, she looks back at the Alien, staring at its huge eyes.

MATILDA (V.O.)
That's quite the secret society backstory.

ALIEN (V.O.)
Akhenaten, driven by ambition, distorted the concept of the individual spiritual being into worshiping the sun god Aten.
(MORE)

114.

>   ALIEN (V.O.) (CONT'D)
>   His reign ended when he was
>   assassinated by Maya and
>   Parennefer, Priests of Amun, who
>   served the "Old Empire."

FLASHBACK:

EXT. EGYPTIAN TEMPLE - NIGHT

The moon casts shadows across the massive stone walls. Two figures, MAYA and PARENNEFER, both cloaked in dark robes, move stealthily through the temple corridors, avoiding the patrols of the palace guards.

INT. AKHENATEN'S CHAMBER - NIGHT

Inside a lavishly decorated room, Pharaoh AKHENATEN stands in front of a towering golden idol of the sun god, Aten. He stretches his arms wide, soaking in the dim light of flickering torches, a look of self-glorification on his face.

The door creaks open, and Maya and Parennefer slip in. Akhenaten turns, startled. His expression shifts from shock to anger as he recognizes them, but it's too late.

Maya and Parennefer strike quickly and silently, their movements swift and deliberate. Akhenaten collapses, his eyes fading to emptiness as his body hits the cold stone floor.

Maya and Parennefer exchange glances before disappearing into the darkness, leaving the pharaoh's lifeless form behind.

END FLASHBACK.

INT. ROSWELL ARMY AIR FORCE BASE - INTERVIEW ROOM

The Alien sits in the large recliner, its focused gaze locked on Matilda.

>   MATILDA (V.O.)
>   Whoa, that took a dramatic turn!
>   Akhenaten's downfall is
>   intense—assassinated by his own
>   priests!

ALIEN (V.O.)
The Hebrew leader Moses, during his time in Egypt, spread the idea of "One God." After leaving Egypt with the Jewish slaves, Moses was intercepted near Mt. Sinai by an "Old Empire" operative. Using hypnosis and other tricks, the operative convinced Moses that he was the one true God. Since then, the Jewish people have worshiped a single god named "Yahweh," based on Moses's experience.

MATILDA (V.O.)
That's a dramatic twist on the origins of monotheism.

Matilda breaks eye contact with the Alien and writes on the notepad. She looks up from the notepad and into the eyes of the Alien.

ALIEN (V.O.)
"Yahweh" means "anonymous," since the IS-BE who dealt with Moses couldn't reveal his identity without compromising the secrecy of the prison system. The covert operation relies on staying hidden to prevent prisoners from regaining their memories.

MATILDA (V.O.)
No way! They kept their identity secret just to maintain the cover of the entire operation. That's wild!

The diminutive Alien stares at Matilda from the large recliner.

ALIEN (V.O.)
This is the reason that all traces of physical encounters between operatives of space civilizations and humans are very carefully hidden, disguised, covered up, denied, or misdirected.

FLASHBACK:

EXT. DESERT MOUNTAIN TOP - NIGHT

The moon casts a silver glow over the rocky terrain, shrouded in an eerie silence. The silhouette of a solitary figure, MOSES, is barely visible against the starlit sky. He stands at the summit, his face filled with awe as he gazes at a strange, luminous light emanating from behind a jagged boulder.

A low, commanding VOICE emanates from the glowing light, its tone both seductive and intimidating.

                VOICE
           (booming and deep)
  Moses! Listen carefully, for I am
  the One who commands all things.
  Take these words and deliver them
  to your people

MOSES' eyes glaze over as he listens, his body rigid as if frozen by the power of the voice.

                MOSES
  Who are you? What should I call
  you?

The commands grow in intensity, the light pulsing in sync with each word.

                VOICE
  I am that I am. I am the force
  that binds, the will that controls.
  There are none but me. Write these
  commands and ensure that they are
  followed without question.

A subtle wind sweeps across the mountain, swirling Moses' robes, adding to the sense of otherworldly presence.

                MOSES
           (awed)
  What would you have me do?

As the voice intones a list of strict commandments, each word seems to hang in the air, heavy with authority. The words throb with hypnotic force, compelling obedience.

                VOICE
  You shall have no other gods before
  me. You shall not make for
  yourself an idol. You shall not
  take my name in vain.
                (MORE)

                    VOICE (CONT'D)
          These commands and more I give to
          you, and you shall inscribe them on
          stone. Disobey at your peril.
          Share these with your people, and
          do not stray from my will.

In rapid succession, vivid imagery flashes: tablets with
engraved commandments, glowing symbols, and harsh landscapes
that echo the commands' rigid tone. The commands
reverberate, their energy seeping into the very fabric of the
mountain as if binding Moses to them.

The light dims, leaving Moses standing alone, his face etched
with a newfound sense of purpose, yet clouded by an unseen
force.

                    MOSES
          Yes, my Lord. I will obey. I will
          do as you command. What else must
          I do?

                    VOICE
          Lead your people, Moses. Guide
          them with these words, and they
          will find their way. But remember,
          I am the one and only voice you
          should heed. Disregard my
          commands, and you will know my
          wrath. Now go! And ensure my
          words are obeyed for all time.

The hypnotic commands have taken hold, and their influence
stretches far into the future, reaching millions of IS-BEs
through the ages.

END FLASHBACK.

INT. ROSWELL ARMY AIR FORCE BASE - INTERVIEW ROOM

The one-way glass window looms large giving off the feeling
of someone watching.

The camera with its red tally light stands as the lone
sentry.

Resembling two fighters standing in the middle of the ring
before the contest. The Alien and Matilda are fixed on each
other.

INT. ROSWELL ARMY AIR FORCE BASE - CONTROL ROOM

Amid electronic equipment functioning and Military personnel performing technical duties, stands Colonel William H. Blanchard. He stares intently, looking at the Alien and Matilda through the one-way glass window.

INT. ROSWELL ARMY AIR FORCE BASE - INTERVIEW ROOM

Unemotional, the perception of life from the Alien is undetectable.

Matilda, with a blank face stare, sits in front of the Alien.

> MATILDA (V.O.)
> Incredible! It's like the birth of an entire belief system right before our eyes, with that kind of hypnotic grip shaping centuries of thought.

> ALIEN (V.O.)
> The so-called "Yahweh" not only gave Moses the "Ten Hypnotic Commands," but also wrote and programmed the Torah, ensuring that its literal and decoded interpretations contained a significant amount of misleading information.

> MATILDA (V.O.)
> No way! So, the entire Torah could be part of their control scheme?

Matilda snaps out of the trance; she shakes herself and looks to the one-way glass window as if wanting to say something.

Matilda jots on the notepad, she turns, looking back at the Alien and immediately resumes the blank face stare.

> ALIEN (V.O.)
> The Vedic Hymns inspired most Eastern religions, shaping the philosophies of Buddha, Laozi, and Zoroaster. Their teachings gradually replaced the "Old Empire" religions' brutality, introducing kindness and compassion.

> MATILDA (V.O.)
> How did these philosophies manage to shift entire civilizations away from violent idol worship to principles of compassion and understanding?

> ALIEN (V.O.)
> You asked me earlier why The Domain and other space civilizations do not land on Earth or make their presence known. We would have to be insane! It's a prison planet with an unstable, violent population. No IS-BE is completely safe from getting trapped, as happened to our Domain Expeditionary Force in the Himalayas 8,200 years ago.

> MATILDA (V.O.)
> That's intense! No wonder space civilizations steer clear.

> ALIEN (V.O.)
> The Domain isn't currently taking full control of the space around Earth. The plan is to do so in about 5,000 years, so for now, transports from other planets and galaxies can still drop IS-BEs into the amnesia force screen. This will eventually change.

INT. ROSWELL ARMY AIR FORCE BASE - THEATER

The whirring sound of the movie projector fills the air, while the bulb's warm light illuminates the dusk.

The seating area is sparsely filled with military soldiers who are scattered around.

The movie "*Flash Gordon Conquers the Universe*" is shown on the screen.

Seated next to each other watching the movie and eating popcorn are the government agent and the military official.

> GOVERNMENT AGENT
> Truman is forming a new government agency. He's scrapping the OSS.

MILITARY OFFICIAL
I've been informed.

GOVERNMENT AGENT
Rumor is that it will be called the
Central Intelligence Agency.

MILITARY OFFICIAL
Out with the old in with the new.
So where do you fit in?

GOVERNMENT AGENT
Covert operations as usual.

MILITARY OFFICIAL
Military brass objected to OSS
officials anyway. They slept
through Pearl Harbor.

GOVERNMENT AGENT
Yeah, well. The current situation
is one we're working together on.

MILITARY OFFICIAL
And it's bigger than Pearl Harbor.

GOVERNMENT AGENT
Indeed. The Soviet Union is being
used as a cover.

Light from the movie screen reflects on the faces of the
government agent and the military official.

MILITARY OFFICIAL
Many within the OSS are determined
to keep it intact.

The military official holding a drink sip from a straw.

GOVERNMENT AGENT
It doesn't matter. Truman is going
to sign a National Security Act.
It's now necessary for the US
government to undertake a
comprehensive reorganization of its
foreign policy and military
institutions.

MILITARY OFFICIAL
Let me guess. It's a guise to
cover up the saucer crash.

                    GOVERNMENT AGENT
                (chewing popcorn)
            It's deeper than that. The Air
            Force will be an independent
            service, USAF.

                    MILITARY OFFICIAL
            And Russia will be our eternal
            enemy. -- Is the President
            preparing for war?

                    GOVERNMENT AGENT
            Wars will be perpetual. The
            President wants to be prepared for
            the ultimate war. An
            interplanetary war.

                    MILITARY OFFICIAL
            He knows then --

INT. ALIEN SPACESHIP - NIGHT

In the dimly lit control room, a single ALIEN PILOT sits at
the helm, looking out at the dark expanse of space.

Scattered across the console are various gauges and screens,
some blinking, others static. The Alien's eyes scan the
readouts, seemingly deep in thought.

The ethereal voice of the Alien, Airl, is heard...

                    ALIEN (V.O.)
            The continental land masses of
            Earth float on a sea of molten
            lava, causing them to crack and
            drift. The planet's core is
            volatile, making Earth prone to
            earthquakes and volcanic eruptions.
            The magnetic poles shift every
            20,000 years, leading to tidal
            waves and drastic climate changes.

EXT. EARTH'S LANDSCAPE - NIGHT

INSERT CARD. DISTANT PAST

Volcanic eruptions light up the sky, while cracks spread
across the ground.

Massive earthquakes shake the land, sending debris cascading
into the oceans.

Again, the diaphanous voice of the Alien, Airl, is heard...

                ALIEN (V.O.)
    Earth's distance from the galaxy's
    center and its isolation make it
    unsuitable for anything more than a
    pit stop. The moon and asteroids
    are more suitable, with their lower
    gravity. Earth's heavy gravity,
    metallic soil, and dense atmosphere
    create navigational challenges.

INT. ALIEN SPACESHIP - NIGHT

In the control room. The single Alien pilot adjusts the controls, his expression shows signs of concern.

The mysterious voice of the Alien, Airl, reverberates...

                ALIEN (V.O.)
    My presence here, due to an in-
    flight accident, shows the risks of
    landing on Earth, even with
    advanced technology and piloting
    expertise. There are approximately
    sixty billion Earth-like planets in
    the Milky Way galaxy alone, not to
    mention the vast territories in The
    Domain. It's hard to justify
    investing resources on Earth when
    there's so little to gain.

The Alien pilot continues to work the controls.

EXT. EARTH'S LANDSCAPE - NIGHT

The hovering alien spaceship ascends upward, leaving behind the distant rumbling of Earth's shifting continents and the faint echoes of volcanic eruptions.

INT. WHITE HOUSE - OVAL OFFICE - DAY

A white man sits behind a desk, his legs are crossed. He looks dejected, his elbow resting on the arm of the chair.

The man's chin is tucked in, resting in the palm of his hand.

The man lifts his head and rubs his chin with his fingers. This is HARRY S. TRUMAN age 63.

INSERT CARD. HARRY S. TRUMAN 33RD PRESIDENT OF THE UNITED STATES

                    HARRY S. TRUMAN
I will assemble a committee of top military officials and scientists. They will be tasked with investigating these matters and report to me.

Sitting in front of Truman dressed in full military regalia is General Roger M. Ramey.

                    ROGER M. RAMEY
Mr. President. How do you want to proceed with the being?

An open folder sits on Truman's desk and inside is a paper that reads *Above Top Secret*.

Truman picks up the paper and adjusts his rimmed glasses. He scans the paper with his eyes.

Truman sets the paper down on his desk leans back in his chair letting out a deep breath... Truman's silence is deafening.

INT. ROSWELL ARMY AIR FORCE BASE - INTERVIEW ROOM

The eye of the camera's invasive obtrusiveness is noticeable. The red tally light on the camera has an alarming feel to it.

Matilda sits in her chair writing on the notepad, and she looks up...

Showing subtle head movement. The Alien sits in the large recliner chair staring at Matilda.

                    ALIEN (V.O.)
IS-BEs have been waging war since time immemorial to establish domination over one another. Because IS-BEs can't be killed, the goal has been to capture and immobilize them, often using different types of "traps."

                    MATILDA (V.O.)
Traps? What do you mean by traps?

ALIEN (V.O.)
IS-BE traps, used by various invading societies like the "Old Empire" since sixty-four trillion years ago, are typically set in the target's territory. They often employ electronic waves of "beauty" to attract IS-BEs, using structures like beautiful buildings or music. When the IS-BE approaches, the trap is activated by its energy.

MATILDA (V.O.)
Wait, so they use beauty to lure IS-BEs into traps? That's a clever yet disturbing strategy.

ALIEN (V.O.)
A common trap mechanism uses an IS-BE's thought energy. When the IS-BE tries to fight back, their energy activates the trap, making it stronger. The more they resist, the tighter the trap's hold.

Matilda's face crinkles yet her gaze is intense.

MATILDA (V.O.)
Amazing!

INT. MILITARY COMMAND CENTER - NIGHT

The surroundings are futuristic. A massive holographic display shows a detailed map of a galaxy. The display highlights various regions with different colors, indicating territorial boundaries.

The voice of the Alien, Airl, chimes in...

ALIEN (V.O.)
Throughout the entire history of this physical universe, vast areas of space have been taken over and colonized by IS-BE societies who invade and take over new areas in this fashion. In the past, these invasions have always shared common elements.

ALIEN COMMANDERS monitor the display, preparing for an imminent invasion.

EXT. OUTER SPACE - NIGHT

A fleet of massive alien ships, equipped with advanced weapons. They move swiftly through the cosmos, heading toward a distant planet. As they approach, the fleet unleashes a barrage of nuclear and electronic weapons, causing massive explosions and wreaking havoc on the planet's surface.

INT. LABORATORY - NIGHT

IS-BEs are subjected to intense electroshock therapy. Their bodies convulse as drugs are injected into them. Hypnotic waves wash over the room, erasing their memories and implanting false information designed to keep them subdued.

EXT. MINING FACILITY - DAY

A vast mining facility, where enslaved IS-BEs are forced to extract valuable resources under harsh conditions.

Guards with electronic weapons patrol the area, ensuring compliance. The IS-BEs work tirelessly, but their will is broken by invasive mind control.

EXT. SLAVE MARKET - DAY

Bustling with activity, IS-BEs are bought and sold. Political, economic, and social structures are in place to keep them in check, reinforcing the invading IS-BEs' control over the local population.

Again, the voice of the Alien, Airl, chimes in...

          ALIEN (V.O.)
  These oppressive tactics are used
  to subjugate and enslave new
  territories in the universe.

INT. ROSWELL ARMY AIR FORCE BASE - INTERVIEW ROOM

Matilda's meticulous automatic writing on the notepad comes to a stop. She stares at the Alien sitting across from her.

          MATILDA (V.O.)
  The ruthless tactics of
  intergalactic conquest. It's
  intense and unsettling to see how
  IS-BEs are controlled and
  exploited.

The Alien sitting in the large recliner with its huge eyes stares back at Matilda.

                    ALIEN (V.O.)
These activities are still happening. Every IS-BE on Earth has been part of these conflicts- either as invaders or the invaded. There are no "saints"; almost everyone has been involved in IS-BE warfare at some point.

                    MATILDA (V.O.)
It's sobering to think that everyone on Earth has been part of these conflicts, and no one is truly innocent.

                    ALIEN (V.O.)
IS-BEs on Earth are still victims of the "Old Empire" traps, which use between-lives amnesia to keep them from escaping.

                    MATILDA (V.O.)
It's disheartening that the system keeps IS-BEs trapped like this.

The eye of the camera surveils Matilda. She breaks eye contact with the Alien and jots on the notepad.

Matilda looks up from the notepad and into the Aliens' eyes...

                    ALIEN (V.O.)
A rogue secret police force from the "Old Empire" manages this operation, using false provocation to hide their activities from their own government, The Domain, and their victims. Their tactics are mind-control methods developed by government psychiatrists.

Matilda's pen stands erect and very still in her hand. Her stare is blank Matilda looks directly at the Alien.

                    MATILDA (V.O.)
That's a dark layer of deception. A completely unscrupulous method.

> ALIEN (V.O.)
> Earth is a "ghetto" planet. It is
> the result of an intergalactic
> "Holocaust". IS-BEs have been
> sentenced to Earth either
> because...

INT. DARK LABORATORY - NIGHT

The place is grim, shadowy, and filled with strange machinery.

Electronic devices hum ominously as sparks fly from exposed wires.

IS-BEs, disoriented and restrained, are forced into biological bodies by masked operatives. They struggle against the restraints, but their efforts are futile.

INT. OLD EMPIRE COURTROOM - DAY

The place is lavish but oppressive with an austere JUDGE presiding over a trial.

The accused IS-BEs are paraded before the judge...

The mystifying voice of the Alien, Airl is heard.

> ALIEN (V.O.)
> These "untouchables" were either
> too insane, perverse, or
> revolutionary to be allowed in the
> "Old Empire."

The judge's gavel slams, sealing their fate.

EXT. PRISON TRANSPORT - DAY

IS-BEs are shackled and loaded into a transport vehicle. It lifts off, heading towards Earth.

The cryptic voice of the Alien, Airl, is heard.

> ALIEN (V.O.)
> They are condemned to live as
> biological bodies, the lowest order
> in the "Old Empire" caste system.

The IS-BEs look through the small windows, despair etched on their faces.

INT. EARTH PRISON CAMP - NIGHT

The transport vehicle lands, and the surroundings are dour.

The IS-BEs wearing basic clothing are marched out into a harsh environment, surrounded by barbed wire and armed guards.

The ominous voice of the Alien, Airl, sounds off...

> ALIEN (V.O.)
> Operatives from the "Old Empire" forcibly erase the identity and memory of IS-BEs while providing them with minimal resources.

EXT. EARTH LANDSCAPE - DAY

The vast prison camp, where IS-BEs are forced to labor and live under strict surveillance. The guards watch them closely, ready to enforce the rules with brutal force.

The eerie and gripping voice of the Alien, Airl, is heard...

> ALIEN (V.O.)
> In the 'Old Empire,' biological bodies are designed as the lowest order of the caste system. Being sent to Earth is a double imprisonment—trapped in a biological body and isolated from the rest of the universe. This 'final solution' was conceived by psychopathic criminals to rid the 'Old Empire' of these 'untouchables.'

A sweeping view of the prison camp, emphasizes the bleakness of the IS-BEs' fate.

INT. ROSWELL ARMY AIR FORCE BASE - INTERVIEW ROOM

Matilda's reflection is seen in the Alien's huge almond-shaped eyes.

> ALIEN (V.O.)
> The mass extermination of "untouchables" and prison camps in World War II Germany were recently exposed.
> (MORE)

ALIEN (V.O.) (CONT'D)
Similarly, Earth's IS-BEs suffer spiritual eradication and eternal slavery in frail biological bodies, driven by the same craven hatred as the "Old Empire."

The pen in Matilda's hand activates and begins writing on the notepad.

Matilda's blank stare is fixed on the Alien.

MATILDA (V.O.)
It's chilling to think how similar the cruelty is, from the "Old Empire" to World War II. The hatred driving such brutal acts seems universal.

ALIEN (V.O.)
The kind and creative inmates of Earth are tormented by brutal and insane minions controlled by the "Old Empire." Earth's so-called "civilizations," from ancient pyramids to nuclear holocaust, represent a massive waste of resources, a distortion of intelligence, and blatant oppression of every IS-BE's spiritual essence.

MATILDA (V.O.)
It's tragic how much human potential is squandered under oppressive regimes. The cycle of cruelty seems relentless.

Matilda's hand seems to be separate from her body. The pen she is holding writes furiously on the notepad.

ALIEN (V.O.)
If The Domain sought "Hell" across the universe, they could find it on Earth. There's no greater brutality than erasing one's spiritual awareness, identity, ability, and memory—the core of who they are.

MATILDA (V.O.)
It's hard to imagine a more severe form of savagery. Erasing someone's essence is like condemning them to a living hell.

130.

The Alien sits in the large recliner chair across from Matilda. Save for tenuous movement, signs of life in the being are almost undetectable.

INT. SECRET COMMAND CENTER - NIGHT

Amid high-tech technology, a group of DOMAIN OFFICERS stands before a massive screen displaying Earth.

They examine a complex network of glowing points representing the 3,000 IS-BEs from the Expeditionary Force Battalion scattered across the globe.

The voice of the Alien, Airl, bellows...

           ALIEN (V.O.)
    The Domain has been unable to
    rescue the 3,000 IS-BEs from the
    Expeditionary Force Battalion,
    forced to inhabit biological bodies
    on Earth for the past 8,000 years.
    We can track their locations, but
    communication is nearly impossible.

FLASHBACK:

EXT. VARIOUS PERIODS OF EARTH'S HISTORY - DAY

IS-BEs in various periods of Earth's history, living ordinary human lives. They walk through ancient cities, work in medieval workshops, and move through bustling modern streets. Yet their expressions reveal a sense of loss as if they know something is missing.

INT. SECRET COMMAND CENTER - CONTINUOUS

One DOMAIN OFFICER attempts to make contact with an IS-BE by sending a signal, but the IS-BE seems oblivious, lost in their current life. The domain officer shakes his head in frustration.

The voice of the Alien, Airl, speaks out...

           ALIEN (V.O.)
    Despite our efforts to communicate,
    they cannot remember their true
    identity. The amnesia and the
    constraints of their biological
    bodies are too strong.

Domain officers, illuminated by the dim glow of the tracking screen, their expressions a mix of determination and sorrow.

END FLASHBACK.

INT. ROSWELL ARMY AIR FORCE BASE - INTERVIEW ROOM

Matilda rocks back in the chair, her body trembles and she exhales. Matilda catches her breath and visually reengages with the Alien.

> ALIEN (V.O.)
> Most lost members of The Domain force have followed the trajectory of Western civilization, moving from India to the Middle East, through Chaldea and Babylon, then to Egypt, Achaia, Greece, Rome, Europe, the Western Hemisphere, and ultimately worldwide.

> MATILDA (V.O.)
> That's quite a journey, tracing the spread of Western civilization across continents and eras.

> ALIEN (V.O.)
> The lost Battalion members and many other IS-BEs on Earth could be valuable to The Domain, excluding criminals and perverts. Unfortunately, there's no effective method to free the IS-BEs from Earth.

> MATILDA (V.O.)
> So, there's no way to free them from Earth? That's shocking.

INT. ROSWELL ARMY AIR FORCE BASE - ROOM

The stenographer takes diction using a stenotype machine.

Matilda, seated next to the stenographer, reads aloud from the notepad.

                    MATILDA
          Thus, as a logical and official
          policy, The Domain avoids contact
          with Earth's IS-BEs until resources
          are available to destroy the "Old
          Empire" force screen and amnesia
          machinery and develop a method to
          restore IS-BE memories.

The stenographer takes the transcript from the stenotype
machine handing it to Colonel William H. Blanchard.

INT. ROSWELL ARMY AIR FORCE BASE - INTERROGATION ROOM

Sitting at the table under the intense gleam of the spotlight
Matilda looks haggard.

                    MATILDA
          I took written notes because Airl
          gave me a lot of dates and names
          that I couldn't possibly remember
          without writing them down.

Stepping out of the shadow of the dim light, Colonel William
H. Blanchard takes a gnawed-on cigar from his mouth, spitting
out bits of tobacco.

                    WILLIAM H. BLANCHARD
          Why do you need to write it down?
          Trying to keep track of something
          you're not supposed to know?

                    MATILDA
          I don't usually take notes, but I
          felt it was important to record the
          information accurately during this
          lesson. However, I found that note-
          taking made it difficult to focus
          on Airl's communication.

Colonel Blanchard looks irritated as he shoves the cigar in
his mouth.

                    WILLIAM H. BLANCHARD
          Why take notes now? What's so
          crucial that you're jotting it
          down? You're up to something.

                    MATILDA
          As I mentioned, I was inundated
          with so much information. I have
          no ulterior motive.

Captain Sheridan Cavitt sits in an adjacent chair, his legs crossed, listening attentively.

> MATILDA (CONT'D)
> Airl stayed in touch with the Communications Officer on the asteroid belt space station, from whom she got much of this information. As she is an officer/pilot/engineer, not a historian, Airl relied on records from other Domain Expeditionary Force officers' reconnaissance missions.

> SHERIDAN D. CAVITT
> Should we be preparing for something?
>   (looking at Blanchard)
> This doesn't sound good at all.

INT. ROSWELL ARMY AIR FORCE BASE - HALLWAY

A Military police officer walks beside Matilda. They stop at a door guarded by another Military police officer.

INT. ROSWELL ARMY AIR FORCE BASE - INTERVIEW ROOM

The Alien with its lifeless doll-like body sits in the large recliner chair.

Matilda walks in the door holding a notepad and pen, her eyes locked onto the Alien, she sits across from the being.

INSERT CARD: TOP SECRET OFFICIAL TRANSCRIPT OF THE U.S. ARMY AIR FORCE ROSWELL ARMY AIR FIELD, 509TH BOMB GROUP SUBJECT: ALIEN INTERVIEW, 27. 7. 1947, 1ST SESSION

The Alien's body shutters slightly as it stares at Matilda.

> ALIEN (V.O.)
> Earth's history is extremely bizarre, filled with missing information, nonsensical relics, and arbitrary mythology. The Earth's volatile nature further obscures evidence by cyclically covering, drowning, and shredding it.

                    MATILDA (V.O.)
          A deliberate cover-up laced with
          existential confusion.

                    ALIEN (V.O.)
          Amnesia, hypnosis, and covert
          manipulation make Earth's true
          history nearly impossible to
          reconstruct. Investigators face a
          maze of inconclusive assumptions
          and perpetual mystery.

                    MATILDA (V.O.)
          All of this is incomprehensible.

Matilda breaks eye contact with the Alien and jots on the
notepad. Matilda looks up, right into the eyes of the Alien.

                    ALIEN (V.O.)
          The Domain, with its memory and
          perspective, can clarify Earth's
          history.

The Alien makes subtle robotic movements, its stare becomes
magnified.

                    ALIEN (V.O.)
          These dates, often omitted, reveal
          the influence of the "Old Empire"
          and The Domain on Earth.

Matilda stares, her head and body tremble slightly.

                    MATILDA (V.O.)
          The "Old Empire" is the axis of
          evil. "The Domain" are the Allied
          powers, both battling for universal
          dominance.

The camera's red tally light and the one-way glass window are
seemingly living witnesses.

                    ALIEN (V.O.)
          I'll primarily use data from
          records captured after we invaded
          the "Old Empire" planetary
          headquarters, supplemented by
          briefings from mission control, to
          inform you about Earth's recent
          history.

The pen in Matilda's hand automatically writes on the
notepad, *The Domain Force history of Earth*.

                    ALIEN (V.O.)
          While The Domain isn't directly
          concerned with Earth or its
          inhabitants, we intervene
          occasionally to protect Earth's
          resources. Some officers have been
          sent on reconnaissance missions to
          gather information. The dates and
          events I'll discuss are
          extrapolated from our data files.

FLASHBACK:

EXT. COSMIC SPACE URSA MAJOR CONSTELLATION

INSERT CARD: 208,000 BCE

A vast expanse of stars twinkles against the dark backdrop of space. In the center of the constellation, near one of its "tail stars," lies the imposing headquarters of the "Old Empire."

Suddenly, bursts of intense light erupt as nuclear explosions ravage the region, signaling the conquest by the "Old Empire" invasion force. As the chaos subsides, a sense of desolation hangs in the air, but soon, signs of life emerge as the radioactivity dissipates, and cleanup efforts commence.

Amidst the ruins of the "Old Empire" headquarters. A procession of beings from another galaxy arrives. With determination, they set about rebuilding and establishing a society, their presence breathing life into the once-devastated landscape.

The voice of the Alien, Airl, seeps in...

                    ALIEN (V.O.)
          For millennia, this civilization
          thrived under the influence of the
          "Old Empire" until a shift
          occurred. About 10,000 years ago,
          a new force emerged- The Domain.
          With their arrival, the balance of
          power shifted, and the once-
          dominant influence of the "Old
          Empire" began to wane.

There is an ebb and flow of cosmic civilizations. Empires rise and fall against the vast canvas of the universe.

END FLASHBACK.

INT. ROSWELL ARMY AIR FORCE BASE - INTERVIEW ROOM

The Alien and Matilda sit across from each other locked in a forceful gaze.

>   ALIEN (V.O.)
> Earth's civilization now bears striking resemblances to that of the "Old Empire," having slipped from its direct influence. This is evident in transportation technologies like planes, trains, ships, and automobiles, as well as in the architectural styles of modern cities, echoing those of the "Old Empire."

FLASHBACK:

INT. DOMAIN ARCHIVE ROOM - DAY

INSERT CARD: BEFORE 75,000 BCE

Dimly lit, filled with rows of ancient-looking consoles and holographic displays, a lone DOMAIN ARCHIVIST sifts through digital records projected before them.

The Archivist pauses, their expression piqued as they access a particular set of files labeled "Atlantis" and "Lemuria." They navigate through the data, scanning text and images that flicker to life before them.

As they delve deeper, the Archivist's brows furrow with intrigue. They find snippets of information, snippets of advanced civilizations that once thrived on the continents of Atlantis and Lemuria. The records are scant, but they reveal that these societies coexisted on Earth, shrouded in mystery and enigma.

A holographic display depicts bustling cities with towering spires and intricate architecture, and bustling streets filled with diverse beings engaged in trade and discourse.

The Archivist leans closer to the holographic display, absorbing every morsel of information, their curiosity ignited by the remnants of these ancient cultures.

The voice of the Alien, Airl, chimes in...

> ALIEN (V.O.)
> Despite their efforts, much about Atlantis and Lemuria remains elusive, their origins and fates veiled in the shadows of time.

END FLASHBACK.

INT. ROSWELL ARMY AIR FORCE BASE - INTERVIEW ROOM

Matilda's fixed blank stare is disconcerting.

> MATILDA (V.O.)
> Every myth is rooted in reality.

The Alien's eyes loom intrusively large, its head movement is ever so slight.

> ALIEN (V.O.)
> The Domain suspects that the "Old Empire" enforced a strict ban on unauthorized planet colonization, suggesting their destruction may have been carried out by authorities pursuing the colonists as criminals. Despite this theory, no concrete evidence exists to explain the total annihilation of two advanced civilizations.

The pen in Matilda's hand rapidly writes on the notepad, her sights locked on the Alien.

> MATILDA (V.O.)
> The "Old Empire" is tyrannical and capable of anything.

> ALIEN (V.O.)
> Another possibility is that...

FLASHBACK:

INT. SPACE STATION - THE DOMAIN COMMAND CENTER

A large screen displays a 3D holographic map of Earth. Scientists and officers analyze the data.

INSERT: MAP OF EARTH

ZOOM IN on the region of Lake Toba, Sumatra, and Mt. Krakatoa, Java.

EXT. LEMURIAN CITY - DAY

A bustling Lemurian city with advanced technology: flying vehicles, sleek buildings, and electronic devices. The city is vibrant and full of life.

EXT. MOUNT KRAKATOA - DAY

RUMBLING SOUND grows as the ground shakes violently. A massive volcanic eruption explodes from Mt. Krakatoa. Lava and ash spew into the sky.

EXT. LAKE TOBA - DAY

A massive eruption from Lake Toba causes a colossal tsunami. Water crashes over the land, submerging everything in its path.

EXT. LEMURIAN CITY - DAY

Panic spreads through the Lemurian city. People flee as water and lava consume the land. Buildings collapse, and the city is overwhelmed by the disaster.

EXT. OCEAN - DAY

The floodwaters rise, covering even the highest mountains. The Lemurian civilization is swallowed by the sea.

EXT. AUSTRALIA - DAY

Survivors struggle to reach the shores of Australia. They look around, finding themselves in a new, desolate land. They begin to rebuild.

EXT. ORIENTAL LANDSCAPE - DAY

Scenes of early Chinese ancestors, descendants of Lemurians, establishing new settlements and developing their unique culture.

INT. SPACE STATION - THE DOMAIN COMMAND CENTER

The map zooms out showing the entire globe. Officers nod, taking notes on the possible causes of Lemuria's destruction.

INSERT: DATA SCREEN

Data about the Lemurian civilization's technology and culture flash across the screen: electronics, flight, and space opera technologies.

EXT. AUSTRALIA AND OCEAN AREAS - DAY

Images of ancient Australia and surrounding ocean areas as the center of the Lemurian civilization. Early Oriental races emerge from the remnants of Lemuria.

END FLASHBACK.

INT. ROSWELL ARMY AIR FORCE BASE - INTERVIEW ROOM

As if about to have a showdown. The Alien and Matilda sit across from each other in a face-to-face stare.

> ALIEN (V.O.)
> The volcanic eruption expelled so much molten rock that a vacuum beneath the Earth's crust caused large land areas to sink below the oceans. These continents were covered with volcanic matter and submerged, leaving little evidence except for global flood legends and survivors who became the ancestors of oriental races and cultures.

> MATILDA (V.O.)
> The global flood is not just a legend. I believe it to be true.

> ALIEN (V.O.)
> Such a colossal volcanic explosion fills the stratosphere with toxic gases, causing rain for "40 days and 40 nights," global cooling, an ice age, extinctions, and long-term changes lasting thousands of years.

> MATILDA (V.O.)
> Then, it's true. The global flood that is.

Matilda's pen stops writing and she breaks her stare with the Alien. She glances over at the one-way glass window and looks back at the Alien. Matilda instantly has a frozen expression on her face.

                    ALIEN (V.O.)
          Due to natural and IS-BE-induced
          global cataclysms, Earth is
          unsuitable for habitation by IS-
          BEs. Events like the one that
          destroyed the dinosaurs over 70
          million years ago, caused by
          intergalactic warfare and atomic
          weapons, have rendered many planets
          in this galaxy uninhabitable
          deserts.

                    MATILDA (V.O.)
          IS-BEs seem to be the masterminds
          of chaos.

                    ALIEN (V.O.)
          Earth is undesirable due to heavy
          gravity, dense atmosphere, floods,
          earthquakes, volcanoes, polar
          shifts, continental drift, meteor
          impacts, and climatic changes. No
          sophisticated culture could sustain
          a lasting civilization in such
          conditions.

                    MATILDA (V.O.)
          And, yet The Domain Force and the
          "Old Empire," continue to dual over
          the Earth and its inhabitants.

                    ALIEN (V.O.)
          Earth is a small, isolated planet
          on the galaxy's rim, far from
          concentrated civilizations. This
          makes it suitable only as a
          zoological or botanical garden, or
          as a prison, but not much else.

                    MATILDA
          Completely nonsensical. An utter
          contradiction.

INT. ROSWELL ARMY AIR FORCE BASE - ROOM

The air is filled with cigarette smoke, and a smoldering
cigar sits in an ashtray. On the table are beer cans, liquor
bottles, and half-filled cocktail glasses.

A card game is taking place, money sits in the middle of the
table. Colonel William H. Blanchard, Captain Sheridan
Cavitt, the government agent, the scientist, and the military
official are holding cards.

Colonel Blanchard is holding two cards, an ace, and a queen.

> WILLIAM H. BLANCHARD
> I'll raise you forty.

Colonel Blanchard tosses money to the middle of the table.

The government agent is holding two aces...

> GOVERNMENT AGENT
> Call. -- How long is MacElroy going to be in there with that thing?

The government agent pushes money to the middle of the table.

> WILLIAM H. BLANCHARD
> Until I'm told to end the interview.

The scientist is holding two sevens. He tosses money to the middle of the table.

> SCIENTIST
> I'm all in. -- That _thing_, may be reading our minds right now.

The government agent tosses more money to the middle of the table.

> GOVERNMENT AGENT
> I'll re-raise you. If that's the case, it's too dangerous to contain.

Captain Cavitt has the remaining deck of playing cards in his hand.

The military official studies his playing cards.

> SHERIDAN D. CAVITT
> What are you suggesting?

> MILITARY OFFICIAL
> If it's what I think it is. There may be no choice.

> SCIENTIST
> Speaking as a scientist. The Alien is far too valuable to terminate.

The government agent pushes money to the middle of the table.

                    GOVERNMENT AGENT
          Calling...

Colonel Blanchard studies his playing cards.

                    WILLIAM H. BLANCHARD
          All in...

Captain Cavitt lays out some playing cards face up, an eight of spades, a five of hearts, and a five of clubs.

Colonel Blanchard, the government agent, and the scientist, watches Captain Cavitt closely.

Captain Cavitt draws a card from the deck, a three of diamonds. He lays it face up on the table.

-- Captain Cavitt lays an eight of diamonds face up on the table.

The scientist purses his lips.

FLASHBACK:

INT. SPACEPORT - OLD EMPIRE PRISON SHIP - NIGHT

A massive prison ship hovers ominously above Earth.

Inside, ALIEN GUARDS escort rows of shackled IS-BEs (Immortal Spiritual Beings) through dimly lit corridors.

EXT. PLANETARY SURFACE - NIGHT

INSERT CARD: BEFORE 30,000 BCE

An IS-BE is ensnared by an ELECTRONIC TRAP, struggling futilely against the glowing energy net.

INT. PRISON SHIP - CONTAINMENT CHAMBER - NIGHT

The IS-BE is encapsulated in a high-tech pod, a translucent barrier sealing them inside.

INT. PRISON SHIP - CARGO HOLD - NIGHT

Rows of encapsulated IS-BEs are stacked like cargo. The ship hums with a low, eerie vibration.

143.

EXT. PLANET EARTH - NIGHT

The ship descends through the atmosphere, casting an eerie glow on the landscape below.

INT. MARS - UNDERGROUND FACILITY - NIGHT

ALIEN TECHNICIANS construct an underground facility, machines whirring and flashing with ominous lights.

EXT. RWENZORI MOUNTAINS, AFRICA - NIGHT

The station is hidden beneath a rugged mountain range, alien architecture blending with natural rock formations.

EXT. PYRENEES MOUNTAINS, PORTUGAL - NIGHT

Another facility is embedded deep within the mountains, high-tech equipment is visible through narrow rock openings.

EXT. STEPPES OF MONGOLIA - NIGHT

The final station is concealed beneath vast, windswept plains, only a small, inconspicuous entrance indicating its presence.

INT. RWENZORI AMNESIA STATION - CONTROL ROOM - NIGHT

Alien Operators monitor screens displaying the encapsulated IS-BEs. A LEAD OPERATOR presses a button, initiating the amnesia process.

The display screen shows an IS-BE's memory being erased, vibrant images, and emotions fading away.

EXT. RWENZORI MOUNTAINS - NIGHT

The station is buried deep within the mountain, a small, glowing beacon amidst the vast darkness of the Earth's night.

END FLASHBACK.

INT. ROSWELL ARMY AIR FORCE BASE - INTERVIEW ROOM

Matilda subtly shakes her head and shuts her eyes. When Matilda opens her eyes, the Alien is sitting across from her.

The Alien's large eyes stare out at Matilda.

> **ALIEN (V.O.)**
> These electronic monitoring points create force screens to capture IS-BEs at death, using extreme electronic force to brainwash them and maintain Earth's population in perpetual amnesia. Long-range electronic thought control mechanisms further enforce population control. These stations are still operational and are difficult to attack or destroy, even for The Domain, which won't deploy a significant military force in this area until later.

> **MATILDA (V.O.)**
> It seems like a vicious cycle that can't be broken.

> **ALIEN (V.O.)**
> The pyramid civilizations were created as part of the IS-BE prison system on Earth. Although pyramids symbolize "wisdom," this "wisdom" of the "Old Empire" serves the amnesia trap of MASS, MEANING, and MYSTERY. This contrasts with Immortal Spiritual Beings, which have no mass or meaning and exist solely because they think they "are."

> **MATILDA (V.O.)**
> The pyramids are an enigma. I don't think that will ever change.

> **ALIEN (V.O.)**
> MASS represents the physical universe: stars, planets, gases, liquids, energy particles, and objects like tea cups. The Pyramids, and other structures of the "Old Empire," were heavy and solid, creating the illusion of eternity. Entombed bodies with possessions and symbols suggest eternal life. However, physical symbols are the opposite of an IS-BE, which has no mass or time. Objects don't last forever; an IS-BE does.

Matilda breaks her gaze from the Alien, she jots on the notepad. Looking up from the notepad Matilda stares into the Alien's Eyes.

                  ALIEN (V.O.)
MEANING: False meanings obscure truth. The pyramid cultures are fabricated illusions, created by the "Old Empire" cult, Brothers of the Serpent. These false civilizations reinforce the amnesia mechanism in Earth's prison system.

                  MATILDA (V.O.)
Confusion -- deceit. To what end?

                  ALIEN (V.O.)
MYSTERY is built on lies and half-truths. Lies persist by altering facts. When the exact truth is known, the mystery vanishes.

A glowing gaze beams from Matilda's eyes.

                  MATILDA (V.O.)
Evil personified.

                  ALIEN (V.O.)
All pyramid civilizations were built on layers of lies mixed with some truths. The "Old Empire" priest cult used advanced math, technology, and symbolic theatrics to create appealing yet fabricated truths.

                  MATILDA (V.O.)
A controlled conned game.

                  ALIEN (V.O.)
The rituals, astronomical alignments, secret rites, monuments, architecture, hieroglyphs, and man-animal "gods" were all designed to mystify the IS-BE prison population on Earth, diverting them from the truth of their capture, amnesia, and imprisonment far from home.

                  MATILDA (V.O.)
Far from home? Where is home?

The pen that Matilda is holding swiftly writes on the notepad.

> ALIEN (V.O.)
> Every IS-BE on Earth came from another planetary system; no one is a native inhabitant. Humans did not evolve on Earth.

Matilda's head quivers ever so slightly, she stares deep into the eyes of the Alien.

> MATILDA (V.O.)
> If not Earth, then where?

> ALIEN (V.O.)
> In the past...

FLASHBACK:

EXT. ANCIENT EGYPTIAN CITY - DAY

The bustling city is dominated by the grand pyramid and the imposing statue of a Pharaoh. Priests in ornate robes oversee laborers building monuments. The Pharaoh, in his chariot, is surrounded by priests, directing his every move.

INT. EGYPTIAN TREASURY - DAY

Priests meticulously count gold and resources, keeping the wealth tightly controlled. The Pharaoh observes, signing decrees under the priests' watchful eyes.

EXT. MODERN CITY - DAY

Skyscrapers and modern buildings dominate the skyline. Business suits replace the robes of priests. Corporate leaders and politicians move through the city, making decisions under the influence of unseen advisors.

INT. CORPORATE OFFICE - DAY

A high-rise office filled with executives, led by a powerful CEO. Advisors whisper into the CEO's ear, guiding his choices. They, too, are chained by the system, just like the Pharaohs of old.

END FLASHBACK.

INT. ROSWELL ARMY AIR FORCE BASE - INTERVIEW ROOM

The diminutive Alien sits in the large recliner staring out at Matilda.

Matilda sits across from the Alien; they are completely in sync telepathically.

The camera with its noticeably red tally light and the one-way glass window loom large in the background.

> MATILDA (V.O.)
> That does not answer my question. Where did humans evolve?

> ALIEN (V.O.)
> Mystery reinforces the prison. The "Old Empire" priesthood's primary function is to prevent IS-BEs on Earth from remembering their true origins.

> MATILDA (V.O.)
> "It's a riddle wrapped in a mystery inside an enigma" ...

> ALIEN (V.O.)
> The "Old Empire" operators of the prison system, and their superiors, do not want IS-BEs to remember who murdered them, captured them, stole all of their possessions, sent them to Earth, gave them amnesia, and condemned them to eternal imprisonment!

Matilda sits in her chair staring straight ahead, the pen she holds writes automatically on the notepad.

Sitting directly across from Matilda. The doll like Alien with its huge eyes and subtle body gestures, stare back at her.

> ALIEN (V.O.)
> Imagine if all the inmates suddenly remembered their right to be free and realized they were falsely imprisoned, rising up together against the guards!

Matilda looks like an automaton, using the pen she writes furiously on the notepad never breaking her stare at the Alien.

> MATILDA (V.O.)
> Revolution. All be it highly
> improbable.

> ALIEN (V.O.)
> They fear revealing anything
> resembling the inmates' home
> civilizations, as even a body,
> piece of clothing, symbol,
> spaceship, or device could rekindle
> memories.

> MATILDA (V.O.)
> The human spirit is subjected to
> this ploy, caught between two
> opposing factions. What's the end
> game?

> ALIEN (V.O.)
> The "Old Empire" used advanced
> technologies to create a false
> façade for the Earth prison,
> integrating every piece into the
> system all at once.

> MATILDA (V.O.)
> The epitome of evil personified.

INT. ROSWELL ARMY AIR FORCE BASE - CONTROL ROOM

Dimly lit and filled with military personnel in crisp uniforms. The walls are lined with large, bulky monitors showing black-and-white screens displaying live broadcasts and static. Banks of switches, dials, and knobs cover the control panels.

TECHNICIANS in headsets are adjusting controls and communicating through radios.

Colonel William H. Blanchard stands overseeing the operation, clipboard in hand, barking orders.

> WILLIAM H. BLANCHARD
> Johnson, adjust the signal
> frequency immediately. Anderson,
> report on the radar sweep status.
> Keep the channel clear. We can't
> afford any disruptions. Signal
> locked? Good. Begin the
> transmission now. Stay focused,
> everyone. No room for errors.

A large wall clock ticks ominously, marking the passage of time.

On the main monitor, Matilda and the Alien are seen locked in a telepathic stare.

The room hums with the sound of equipment and the low murmur of coordinated activity. The atmosphere is tense and focused, reflecting the gravity of the wartime broadcast.

INT. ROSWELL ARMY AIR FORCE BASE - INTERVIEW ROOM

Like two fighters in neutral corners, the Alien and Matilda are locked in a glaring gaze.

> ALIEN (V.O.)
> Every pyramid civilization uses mumbo-jumbo religion to control the population through force, fear, and ignorance. Irrelevant information, geometric designs, mathematical calculations, and astronomical alignments create a false spirituality based on solid objects to confuse and disorient IS-BEs on Earth.

> MATILDA (V.O.)
> Spirituality is deliberately suppressed, and corporate structure has replaced the pyramids.

> ALIEN (V.O.)
> When a person died, they were buried with their possessions and their body wrapped in linen to sustain their "soul" or "Ka." An IS-BE does not "have" a soul; an IS-BE is a soul.

Matilda's body posture is mannequin-ish, her hand, a separate entity continues the fluid writing on the notepad.

> ALIEN (V.O.)
> On an IS-BE's home planet, possessions could be reclaimed after death. However, with amnesia, the IS-BE forgets their possessions, allowing governments, insurers, bankers, and families to claim them without fear of retribution.

Matilda sitting erect stares out at the Alien before her.

> MATILDA (V.O.)
> That's the same thing that happens here on Earth. Greed and treachery.

> ALIEN (V.O.)
> The false meanings are meant to convince IS-BEs they are physical objects, not spirits. This lie traps IS-BEs. People waste endless hours trying to solve the unsolvable puzzles of Egypt and other "Old Empire" civilizations. The answer to the mystery of these cultures is simply: mystery.

> MATILDA (V.O.)
> You're being redundant. You still haven't explained where the IS-BE's home planet is located.

FLASHBACK:

EXT. ANDES MOUNTAINS, TIWANAKU - DAY

INSERT CARD: CIRCA 15,000 BCE

A breathtaking view of the Andes Mountains with the serene waters of Lake Titicaca in the distance.

EXT. TIWANAKU CONSTRUCTION SITE - DAY

A vast expanse where hydraulic mining operations are in full swing. Beings, human and alien, labor under the supervision of "Old Empire" forces, working together to carve massive stone blocks.

EXT. KALASASAYA COMPLEX - DAY

Giant stone buildings take shape, their surfaces intricately carved with symbols and figures. Workers meticulously position the colossal stones, assembling the structures with incredible precision.

EXT. GATE OF THE SUN - DAY

The grand "Gate of the Sun" stands tall at the center of the complex, its imposing presence commanding attention.

Beams of sunlight pierce through its openings, casting intricate shadows on the ground.

EXT. ANDES MOUNTAINS - HIGH ALTITUDE - DAY

At nearly 14,000 feet elevation, the scale and ambition of the construction are awe-inspiring. The camera pans out, capturing the enormity of the project against the stunning backdrop of snow-capped peaks and clear blue skies.

EXT. LAKE TITICACA - SUNSET

As the day ends, the hydraulic mining operations continue tirelessly, illuminated by the setting sun, casting a golden hue over the entire scene.

END FLASHBACK.

INT. MILITARY BRIEFING ROOM - DAY

Army Sergeant Matilda O'Donnell MacElroy stands at a table covered with maps and documents. Colonel William H. Blanchard enters, glancing at the materials.

          WILLIAM H. BLANCHARD
Sergeant MacElroy, what do you have for me?

          MATILDA
Sir, according to Airl. Around 11,600 BCE, the Polar Axis of Earth shifted dramatically. This led to the end of the last Ice Age.

          WILLIAM H. BLANCHARD
How significant was this shift?

          MATILDA
Very significant, sir. The polar ice caps melted rapidly, causing ocean levels to rise and submerge large sections of the land masses.

          WILLIAM H. BLANCHARD
What about Atlantis and Lemuria?

          MATILDA
The remaining vestiges of both were covered by water, sir.

                    WILLIAM H. BLANCHARD
               Any other impacts?

                    MATILDA
               Yes, sir. Massive extinctions of
               animals occurred across the
               Americas, Australia, and the Arctic
               Regions due to the pole shift.

                    WILLIAM H. BLANCHARD
               Understood. Thank you, Sergeant.

FLASHBACK:

EXT. GIZA PLATEAU - DAY

INSERT CARD: 10,450 BCE

THOTH, an imposing figure dressed in ornate robes, stands atop a sandy ridge, overlooking the vast desert landscape of Giza. He holds a scroll with intricate designs and celestial maps. Surrounding him are a group of architects and laborers, all dressed in simple linen garments, eagerly awaiting his instructions.

Thoth gestures grandly towards the sky, pointing to the key stars of the constellation Orion. The architects nod in understanding, referencing their star charts and making precise measurements on the ground.

Laborers begin marking out the base of the Great Pyramid on the desert floor, using ropes and stakes to define the massive structure's dimensions. The sun beats down, casting long shadows over their diligent work.

As the day progresses, the workers tirelessly move enormous limestone blocks into place, each piece meticulously aligned. The air is filled with the sounds of chiseling stone and the grunts of effort.

Evening falls, and the architects pause to observe the sky. The stars of Orion begin to emerge, perfectly aligned with the air shafts they've planned. They exchange satisfied glances, knowing their calculations are correct.

The view reveals the early stages of the Great Pyramid's construction, a testament to the precision and ambition of Thoth and his team. The Nile River flows gently nearby, reflecting the stars of the Milky Way above, mirroring the grand design laid out by the "Old Empire".

END FLASHBACK.

INT. MILITARY BRIEFING ROOM - DAY

Army Sergeant Matilda O'Donnell MacElroy and Colonel William H. Blanchard sit across from each other at a table, documents spread out before them.

Captain Sheridan Cavitt stands near the door, silently observing the interaction.

                WILLIAM H. BLANCHARD
According to Herodotus, records from Atlantis were buried beneath the Sphinx. Electronic technology and other advanced devices of that society are supposedly hidden in a vault.

                MATILDA
The Priests of Anu in Heliopolis shared this with him. But would the "Old Empire" allow any electronic traces to remain?

                WILLIAM H. BLANCHARD
Highly unlikely. The prison system administrators would have erased any evidence of such technology.

Captain Sheridan Cavitt shifts slightly, his eyes narrowing as he takes in the information, but remains silent, his presence adding weight to the discussion.

                MATILDA
So, any hope of finding intact remnants of an electronic civilization on Earth is slim to none?

                WILLIAM H. BLANCHARD
Exactly. The "Old Empire" wouldn't risk leaving any clues behind.

MacElroy nods thoughtfully, jotting down notes while Cavitt continues to observe, his expression unreadable.

                SHERIDAN D. CAVITT
Rubbish. Colonel, don't tell me you're buying into that Alien's guff.

FLASHBACK:

INT. ANCIENT TEMPLE - DAY

Priests dressed in simple robes sit in a circle within the dimly lit temple, reciting the Vedic hymns. Their voices rise and fall in unison, echoing off the stone walls. Candles flicker around them, casting a warm glow on the ancient texts they hold.

EXT. VARIOUS LANDSCAPES - DAY

Generations of people, from children to elders, sit around fires in different environments - lush forests, arid deserts, and bustling villages. They listen intently as elders recite the hymns, their faces reflecting a mix of reverence and understanding. Young disciples repeat the verses, committing them to memory.

EXT. MOUNTAIN VILLAGE - DUSK

An elder sage stands on a hillside overlooking a village, his voice strong and clear as he recites "The Hymn to the Dawn Child." Villagers gather around, watching the sunset, absorbing the teachings about the cycle of the physical universe.

INT. ANCIENT TEMPLE - NIGHT

The priests now chant the "theory of evolution" hymn, their expressions intense and focused. Symbols of creation, growth, and decay are depicted in intricate carvings on the temple walls around them.

EXT. RIVERBANK - DAY

Villagers along a riverbank practice rituals associated with the hymns. They pour water, light incense, and offer flowers, all while chanting verses. The cycle of nature and time is illustrated in their actions and the changing landscape around them.

INT. ANCIENT TEMPLE - NIGHT

Priests finish their recitation and close the ancient texts, placing them carefully back into their protective coverings. They look around at each other with a mix of pride and weariness, knowing the knowledge they guard is both powerful and perilous.

EXT. TEMPLE RUINS - DAY

Centuries later, the once grand temple lies in ruins. Overgrown with vines and partially buried, it stands as a testament to the passage of time. A group of modern archaeologists examines the remnants, piecing together the forgotten wisdom, unaware of the traps laid within the ancient texts.

END FLASHBACK.

INT. MILITARY BRIEFING ROOM - DAY

The room remains tense. Colonel Blanchard adjusts his posture, the weight of the information settling on his shoulders. Army Sergeant Matilda O'Donnell MacElroy continues her report with an air of authority. Captain Sheridan Cavitt stands to the side, his expression a mix of skepticism and ambivalence.

> MATILDA
> In 8,050 BCE, the home planet government of the 'Old Empire' in this galaxy was destroyed. This marked the end of the 'Old Empire' as a political entity. However, given its vast size, it will take many thousands of years for The Domain to conquer it completely.

> WILLIAM H. BLANCHARD
> So, the 'Old Empire' is essentially a ghost of its former self, but its influence persists?

> MATILDA
> Correct, sir. The inertia of its political, economic, and cultural systems will remain in place for some time.

> SHERIDAN D. CAVITT
> (ambivalent)
> Interesting. But how reliable is this information? We're talking about events that happened thousands of years ago. The inertia you speak of... it's hard to believe it's still relevant.

> MATILDA
> Captain, the evidence suggests these systems are deeply entrenched. The Domain has confirmed that the remnants of the 'Old Empire' still influence various sectors.

> WILLIAM H. BLANCHARD
> Cavitt, whether we fully understand it or not, we need to consider the implications. If the 'Old Empire' structures are still in place, we might be dealing with more than just a decaying relic.

> SHERIDAN D. CAVITT
> (ambivalent)
> Understood, Colonel. But let's not get carried away with ancient history. We need actionable intel that affects us now.

The room falls silent as they absorb the gravity of the situation, each officer lost in thought about the remnants of a long-gone empire and its lasting impact.

Colonel Blanchard finally nods, signaling an end to the briefing. The officers begin to gather their notes and prepare to leave the room, each with a mix of concern and determination on their faces.

FLASHBACK:

EXT. SPACE ABOVE EARTH - NIGHT

INSERT CARD: 1,230 AD

The vastness of space is dotted with stars. A colossal battle rages. The remnants of the "Old Empire" space fleet engage in a fierce conflict with the advanced ships of The Domain Forces. Explosions light up the darkness, debris scattering in all directions.

EXT. SPACE NEAR EARTH - CONTINUOUS

The last of the "Old Empire" ships are obliterated. The Domain Forces' ships begin to pull back, their mission accomplished. Silence returns to the void.

EXT. EARTH ORBIT - CONTINUOUS

A few battered ships manage to slip through the chaos, heading towards Earth. They land in remote areas, hidden from sight.

EXT. EARTH - VARIOUS LOCATIONS - CONTINUOUS

Renegade beings from the "Old Empire" disembark from their ships. They survey the unfamiliar landscapes of Earth, each with a different intent. Some mine precious minerals from mountains, while others establish clandestine outposts. Shady merchants and entrepreneurs exchange goods in secret dealings, exploiting Earth's resources.

EXT. EARTH - ABANDONED CITY - NIGHT

A shadowy figure, a military renegade, sets up a base of operations. Weapons and contraband are unloaded, ready for illicit activities.

EXT. EARTH - DENSE FOREST - NIGHT

A group of space pirates stealthily move through the trees, searching for hidden treasures and resources to plunder.

EXT. EARTH - MINING SITE - NIGHT

Miners, clad in advanced exosuits, drill into the ground, extracting valuable materials. The site is a hub of activity, with equipment and vehicles scattered around.

EXT. EARTH - HIDDEN COVE - NIGHT

A merchant ship docks in a secluded cove. Exotic goods are unloaded, and deals are made in the shadows.

EXT. EARTH - VARIOUS LOCATIONS - CONTINUOUS

The presence of these beings begins to influence the local populations. Villagers trade with mysterious merchants, unaware of their origins.

EXT. EARTH - NIGHT

A view across the different scenes, highlighting the diverse activities of the "Old Empire" remnants now scattered across Earth, each driven by their nefarious reasons.

END FLASHBACK.

INT. ROSWELL ARMY AIR FORCE BASE - INTERVIEW ROOM

The door opens and Matilda walks in looking a bit tired. She takes her usual position and sits down in front of the Alien.

The Alien showing subtle head and body gestures is seated in the large recliner chair.

The telepathy session resumes Matilda and the Alien sync up by making eye contact with each other.

> ALIEN (V.O.)
> ...The history of Earth, according to the Jewish people, describes the "Nephilim". Chapter 6 of The Book of Genesis, describes the origin of the "Nephilim"

The pen in Matilda's hand cryptically jots on the notepad.

> ALIEN (V.O.)
> The ancient Jewish people who wrote the Old Testament were slaves, herders, and gatherers. To them, any modern technology, even a flashlight, would seem miraculous, attributed to a "god". This is common among IS-BEs with amnesia, who forget their experiences, training, technology, personality, and identity.

Matilda looks stoic showing no emotion, staring straight ahead at the Alien.

> ALIEN (V.O.)
> Obviously, if these were men who mated with Earth women, they were not "sons of god" but IS-BEs in biological bodies. They took advantage of the "Old Empire" political situation or indulged in physical sensations, setting up colonies on Earth beyond police and tax authorities' reach.

                    MATILDA (V.O.)
                (deep gaze)
            According to the bible, they were
            referred to as fallen angels.

The Alien's stare is piercing, its almond-shaped eyes are
penetrating.

                    ALIEN (V.O.)
            One of the gravest crimes in the
            "Old Empire" was violating income
            tax regulations. Taxes were a tool
            for slavery and punishment. Even
            minor errors made an IS-BE
            "untouchable" and led to
            imprisonment on Earth.

FLASHBACK:

EXT. ANCIENT MESOPOTAMIA - DAY

INSERT CARD: 6,750 BCE

Vast, arid landscapes stretch out under a blazing sun. In
the distance, towering ziggurats rise, surrounded by bustling
cities. Workers in loincloths chisel away at massive stones
in quarries, sparks flying with each strike.

EXT. ANCIENT EGYPT - DAY

The sun casts long shadows over the Giza Plateau. Laborers
haul enormous stone blocks, constructing the iconic pyramids
under the watchful eyes of overseers. A massive
communication station hums in the background, hidden within
the grandeur of the pyramids.

EXT. ANCIENT BABYLON - DAY

Imposing structures of Babylon loom over the Tigris and
Euphrates rivers. Workers carve intricate designs into the
stone walls. Spaceports discreetly blend into the
architectural marvels, with crafts landing and taking off,
hidden from the untrained eye.

EXT. ANCIENT CHINA - DAY

In the early morning mist, workers toil on colossal stone
projects, creating the foundations of pyramidal structures.

Communication towers disguised as monumental statues dot the landscape, while the Great Wall begins to take shape in the distance.

EXT. ANCIENT MESOAMERICA - DAY

Amid lush jungles, the stepped pyramids of Mesoamerica rise towards the sky. Indigenous workers move through dense foliage, transporting quarried stone. A hidden spaceport, camouflaged by the thick canopy, serves as a hub for unseen activity.

EXT. MESOPOTAMIAN SPACEPORT - DAY

At the heart of Mesopotamia, a bustling spaceport operates in secrecy. Beings from the "Old Empire" supervise as ships dock and depart. Communication stations relay messages across the empire, ensuring the smooth operation of these false civilizations.

EXT. VARIOUS SERVICE FACILITIES - DAY

Across different regions, service facilities buzz with activity. Technicians work on advanced machinery, hidden within temples and monuments. The hum of technology contrasts with the ancient settings, seamlessly integrating into the environment.

EXT. OVERVIEW OF EARTH - DAY

A view from above shows the network of pyramid civilizations spread across the globe. Each region, a cog in the grand design of the "Old Empire," operates in unison, maintaining the façade of these ancient yet advanced societies.

INT. ANCIENT EGYPTIAN TEMPLE - DAY

The grand temple is filled with intricately carved columns and statues. Sunlight filters through high windows, casting long shadows on the floor. Priests in elaborate robes perform rituals before an imposing statue of Ptah. Incense smoke curls in the air, filling the room with a mystical atmosphere.

HIGH PRIEST (AKHMOS) a stern man with a regal bearing, is dressed in an ornate robe.

                    HIGH PRIEST AKHMOS
                    (to the crowd)
                Behold, Ptah, the divine ruler, the
                Developer, who brings forth the
                spirit from the flesh.

PTAH an imposing figure in ceremonial garb, with a commanding
presence looks on.

                    PTAH
                    (with authority)
                Prepare the body for the opening of
                the mouth ceremony.

The priests carefully approach a decorated sarcophagus. They
lift the lid to reveal a mummified corpse inside.

NOVICE PRIEST (NEFER), a young eager priest, steps forward
with a ceremonial tool.

                    HIGH PRIEST AKHMOS
                    (to Nefer)
                Proceed, Nefer. Let the spirit be
                released.

Nefer, eager, is wide-eyed and nervous.

                    NEFER
                    (nervously)
                Yes, Great Leader of Craftsmen.

Nefer performs the "opening of the mouth" ceremony, reciting
ancient chants. The air crackles with energy as the ritual
reaches its climax. A faint glow surrounds the corpse, and a
ghostly figure begins to rise from it.

FUNERAL ATTENDEES Mourners in traditional attire, gathered to
witness the ceremony, gasping in awe and fear.

                    PTAH
                    (with a knowing smile)
                The spirit is freed. But its
                journey does not end here.

Unseen by the attendees, a hidden device within the temple
activates. The ghostly figure is drawn towards it,
disappearing in a flash of light. The crowd, unaware of the
true nature of the ceremony, murmurs in reverence.

                    HIGH PRIEST AKHMOS
                    (raising his arms)
                The soul has been released to the
                afterlife, to be reborn anew.

The priests close the sarcophagus and begin to lead the funeral attendees out of the temple. As the crowd disperses, Ptah and Akhmos exchange a knowing glance.

> PTAH
> (quietly, to Akhmos)
> Another soul captured, another cycle begins.

> HIGH PRIEST AKHMOS
> (nodding)
> And so, the spirit of Ptah continues to guide them, unseen and eternal.

EXT. TEMPLE COURTYARD - DAY

The attendees leave the temple, discussing the ceremony in hushed tones. Nefer, visibly shaken but proud, follows Akhmos out into the courtyard.

> NEFER
> (to Akhmos)
> Great Leader, is it true that Ptah himself oversees every reincarnation?

> HIGH PRIEST AKHMOS
> (smiling)
> Yes, Nefer. Ptah ensures the cycle remains unbroken. Our duty is to serve and uphold this sacred trust.

The grandeur of the temple and the surrounding landscape stands out prominently. The legacy of Ptah continues, hidden in plain sight, as the rituals of old keep the spirits bound to their earthly prison.

END FLASHBACK.

INT. ROSWELL ARMY AIR FORCE BASE - OFFICE

The room is dimly lit, filled with the quiet hum of machinery and the soft clacking of the stenotype machine. Army Sergeant Matilda O'Donnell MacElroy sits at a desk, reading from her notes.

The stenographer, focused and silent, transcribes her words with precision.

                    MATILDA
               (speaking clearly)
          The so-called "Divine" rulers who
          followed Ptah on Earth were called
          "Ntr," meaning "Guardians or
          Watchers" by the Egyptians. Their
          symbol was the Serpent, or Dragon,
          representing a secret priesthood of
          the "Old Empire" known as the
          "Brothers of the Serpent."

The stenographer's fingers fly over the keys, capturing every word.

                    MATILDA (CONT'D)
          The "Old Empire" engineers used
          cutting tools of highly
          concentrated light waves to carve
          and excavate stone blocks quickly.
          They also used force fields and
          spacecraft to lift and transport
          blocks of stone weighing hundreds
          or thousands of tons each.

Matilda glances at her notes, then continues.

                    MATILDA (CONT'D)
          The placement of some of these
          structures on the ground will be
          found to have geodetic or
          astronomical significance relative
          to various stars in this galactic
          region. The buildings are crude
          and impractical compared to
          building standards on most planets.
          As an engineer of The Domain, Airl
          attests that makeshift structures
          like these would never pass
          inspection on a planet in The
          Domain.

Matilda pauses, ensuring the stenographer keeps up, then resumes.

                    MATILDA (CONT'D)
          Stone blocks such as those used in
          pyramid civilizations can still be
          seen, partially excavated, in the
          stone quarries in the Middle East
          and elsewhere. Most of the
          structures were hastily built
          "props," much like the false
          façades of a Western town on the
          set of a motion picture.
                              (MORE)

                    MATILDA (CONT'D)
          They appear to be real and to have
          some use or value; however, they
          have no value. They have no useful
          purpose.

The stenographer continues to type, the clacks echoing softly in the room.

                    MATILDA (CONT'D)
          The pyramids and all other stone
          monuments erected by the "Old
          Empire" could be called "mystery
          monuments." Why would anyone waste
          so many resources to construct so
          many useless buildings? To create
          a mysterious illusion.

Matilda takes a deep breath, preparing to conclude her notes.

                    MATILDA (CONT'D)
          The fact of the matter is each one
          of the "divine rulers" were IS-BEs
          who served as operatives of the
          "Old Empire." They were certainly
          not "divine," although they were IS-
          BEs.

She closes her notes and looks up, signaling to the stenographer that she has finished. The stenographer nods, finalizing the transcript.

                    MATILDA (CONT'D)
              (softly)
          Thank you.

Matilda stands, gathers her papers, and prepares to be debriefed by Colonel William H. Blanchard. The stenographer collects the completed transcript, ready to hand it over.

INT. MILITARY BRIEFING ROOM - MOMENTS LATER

Colonel William H. Blanchard sits at a large wooden table, a stern expression on his face as he reviews the freshly typed transcripts.

The room is stark and functional, with military maps and charts lining the walls.

Army Sergeant Matilda O'Donnell MacElroy stands at attention, her demeanor professional and composed.

Captain Sheridan Cavitt leans against the wall; his curiosity is evident as he listens intently.

                    WILLIAM H. BLANCHARD
                 (looking up from the
                  transcripts)
            Sergeant MacElroy, these statements
            from Airl... they're
            extraordinary. It's hard to fathom
            the implications.

                    MATILDA
            Yes, sir. The information she
            provided is unlike anything we've
            encountered before.

Colonel Blanchard taps the papers thoughtfully, then looks
directly at Matilda.

                    WILLIAM H. BLANCHARD
            The claims about the "Old Empire"
            and the purpose of these pyramid
            civilizations... If true, it
            changes our understanding of
            history entirely. What's your take
            on the validity of Airl's
            statements?

                    MATILDA
            Sir, based on my interactions with
            Airl, she appeared sincere and
            consistent. The details she
            provided were beyond my
            comprehension yet delivered with a
            clarity that suggests truth.

Captain Cavitt steps forward, interjecting with a question.

                    SHERIDAN D. CAVITT
            Colonel, if I may... Sergeant
            MacElroy, did Airl give any
            indication of why she was so
            forthcoming with this information?
            What's her endgame?

                    MATILDA
            She mentioned that sharing this
            knowledge was part of her mission.
            Airl seemed to believe that
            understanding our true history is
            crucial for us to break free from
            the control of the "Old Empire."

Blanchard leans back in his chair, considering the weight of
the information.

                    WILLIAM H. BLANCHARD
                       (half to himself)
                    A mission to enlighten us... but
                    why now? And to what end?

He turns to Captain Cavitt, seeking his input.

                    WILLIAM H. BLANCHARD (CONT'D)
                    Captain, given your background in
                    intelligence, what's your
                    assessment? Could this be some
                    elaborate deception?

                    SHERIDAN D. CAVITT
                    It's possible, sir. But if it is a
                    deception, it's a highly
                    sophisticated one. The level of
                    detail in these transcripts...
                    it's not something easily
                    fabricated.

Blanchard nods, deep in thought, then addresses Matilda again.

                    WILLIAM H. BLANCHARD
                    Sergeant, continue to document
                    everything Airl communicates. We
                    need to gather as much information
                    as possible before making any
                    decisions.

                    MATILDA
                    Yes, sir. I'll ensure every detail
                    is recorded accurately.

The room falls into a contemplative silence, the gravity of the situation weighing heavily on the occupants. Blanchard finally breaks the silence, issuing orders.

                    WILLIAM H. BLANCHARD
                    Very well. Captain Cavitt,
                    maintain a close watch on this
                    situation. I want regular updates.
                    And Sergeant MacElroy, keep up the
                    good work. Dismissed.

Matilda salutes and exits the room, followed by Cavitt. Blanchard remains seated, poring over the transcripts, his mind racing with the potential implications of Airl's revelations.

FLASHBACK:

EXT. HIMALAYAN MOUNTAINS - DAY

INSERT CARD: 6248 BCE

The pristine peaks of the Himalayas tower against a clear blue sky. Nestled within the rugged terrain, a newly established installation of The Domain Expeditionary Force bustles with activity. Officers and crew members move efficiently, setting up equipment and fortifying their base.

> ALIEN (V.O.)
> (narration, calm and reflective)
> In 6248 BCE, active warfare began between The Domain Space Command and the surviving remnants of the "Old Empire" space fleet.

EXT. DOMAIN INSTALLATION - CONTINUOUS

The view over the installation reveals sophisticated technology integrated seamlessly into the natural surroundings. The atmosphere is one of confidence and purpose.

> ALIEN (V.O.)
> The Domain established an installation in the Himalayan mountains, unaware that Earth was maintained as a prison planet by the "Old Empire."

EXT. HIMALAYAN MOUNTAINS - NIGHT

Suddenly, the tranquility of the night is shattered by the ominous approach of enemy ships. The sky fills with the glow of spacecraft descending upon the installation, weapons primed for attack.

> ALIEN (V.O.)
> The installation was not fortified, and we were unprepared for the attack that followed.

EXT. DOMAIN INSTALLATION - NIGHT

Explosions rip through the base. Domain officers and crew members scramble to defend themselves, but the onslaught is overwhelming. The installation is rapidly consumed by fire and destruction.

                    ALIEN (V.O.)
          The "Old Empire" space forces
          attacked with relentless ferocity.

EXT. MARS - NIGHT

Captured Domain officers and crew members are led through the
barren, desolate landscapes of Mars. They are shackled and
guarded by "Old Empire" soldiers.

                    ALIEN (V.O.)
          The IS-BEs of The Domain Battalion
          were captured and taken to Mars.

INT. MARS PRISON FACILITY - NIGHT

In a dimly lit, cold facility, the captured IS-BEs are
subjected to brutal amnesia procedures. Strange machines hum
and glow, erasing memories and identities.

                    ALIEN (V.O.)
          There, they were given amnesia and
          stripped of their identities.

EXT. EARTH - VARIOUS LOCATIONS - DAY

The former Domain officers and crew, now amnesiac and
inhabiting human bodies, live ordinary lives on Earth. They
move through ancient cities, work in fields, and engage in
mundane activities, unaware of their true origins.

                    ALIEN (V.O.)
          They were sent back to Earth to
          inhabit human biological bodies,
          oblivious to their past.

EXT. HIMALAYAN MOUNTAINS - SUNSET

The serene Himalayas, now quiet and still, a stark contrast
to the earlier chaos.

                    ALIEN (V.O.)
          They are still here, hidden among
          the human population, lost to their
          true selves.

END FLASHBACK.

INT. ROSWELL ARMY AIR FORCE BASE - INTERVIEW ROOM

Airl, the diminutive alien, sits comfortably in a large recliner chair, her eyes fixed intently on Army Sergeant Matilda O'Donnell MacElroy. Sergeant MacElroy sits across from her, a notepad and pen ready on the table. The air is tense yet calm, as they engage in their unique form of communication.

> MATILDA (V.O.)
> 5,965 BCE... Investigations into the disappearance of Domain forces in this solar system...

Matilda's pen moves fluidly across the notepad, seemingly guided by an unseen force. Her eyes remain locked with the Alien's, unblinking. The words form almost magically on the paper.

> ALIEN (V.O.)
> ...led to the discovery of "Old Empire" bases on Mars and elsewhere.

The room is silent except for the soft scratching of the pen. Matilda continues to jot down notes, her face focused and attentive.

> MATILDA (V.O.)
> The Domain took over the planet Venus as a defensive position against the space forces of the "Old Empire."

IMAGES of Venus flash in Matilda's mind, conveyed telepathically by the Alien. She sees the dense, hot, sulfuric acid clouds and the few resilient life forms that manage to survive there.

> ALIEN (V.O.)
> The Domain Expeditionary Force also monitors life forms on Venus. We established secret installations or space stations in the Earth's solar system.

Matilda's hand never wavers, the notes forming almost as if on their own accord. Her eyes, still locked with the Alien, reflect the weight of the information being transmitted.

> MATILDA (V.O.)
> This solar system has a planet that is broken up -- the asteroid belt.

VISIONS of the asteroid belt appear in Matilda's mind: a vast expanse of rocky debris, serving as a low-gravity platform for spacecraft.

                ALIEN (V.O.)
      It provides a very useful low-gravity platform for takeoff and landing of spacecraft. It is used as a "galactic jump" between the Milky Way and adjoining galaxies.

The telepathic IMAGES shift, showing the strategic importance of the asteroid belt, dotted with Domain space stations and bustling with activity.

                ALIEN (V.O.)
      This broken-up planet makes an ideal space station. As a result of our war against the "Old Empire", this area of the solar system is now a valuable possession of The Domain.

Matilda finishes the last sentence, her pen coming to a stop. She breaks eye contact with the Alien for the first time, looking down at her notes. The room feels heavier with the weight of the revelations shared.

                MATILDA
           (to herself, softly)
      Unbelievable...

She looks back at the Alien, who remains calm and composed in the recliner. The understanding between them is profound, as Matilda realizes the significance of the information she's just received.

                ALIEN (V.O.)
      Between 3,450 and 3,100 BCE, The Domain Forces disrupted the intervention of the "Old Empire" operatives, or "divine gods," in Earth's affairs.

Matilda's pen moves swiftly, writing down the Alien's words with precision.

                MATILDA (V.O.)
      The "Old Empire" operatives were forced to replace themselves with human rulers.

IMAGES of ancient Egypt flash in Matilda's mind, showing the transition from "divine gods" to human rulers.

She sees the majestic splendor of ancient Egyptian civilization taking shape.

> ALIEN (V.O.)
> The First Dynasty of human Pharaohs who united Upper and Lower Egypt began with the rule of a Pharaoh named "MEN". He established the capital city called Men-Nefer, "The Beauty of Men."

Matilda ENVISIONS Men-Nefer, a thriving ancient city, its architecture and culture rich and vibrant, bustling with activity and innovation.

> MATILDA (V.O.)
> (writing)
> This began the first succession of ten human Pharaohs.

IMAGES of the first human Pharaohs ruling over Egypt appear, their reigns marked by both progress and turmoil.

> ALIEN (V.O.)
> This period brought about 350 years of chaos within the administrative ranks of the "Old Empire."

The IMAGES shift to show the confusion and disorder within the "Old Empire" as they struggled to maintain control over Earth. The once-stable hierarchy is thrown into disarray, with factions vying for power and influence.

Matilda's pen stops, and she takes a moment to absorb the gravity of the information. She looks back at the Alien, her expression a mix of awe and understanding.

> MATILDA (V.O.)
> These disruptions must have had a significant impact on Earth's development...

The Alien's eyes remain calm and focused, its telepathic message clear and steady.

> ALIEN (V.O.)
> Indeed. The transition to human rulers marked a pivotal shift in Earth's history, influenced heavily by the interventions and disruptions caused by The Domain Forces.

Matilda nods, the weight of history pressing upon her as she continues to document the revelations shared by the Alien.

Bathed in a soft, sterile light. Airl, the Alien sits in her recliner chair, serene and composed, her eyes meeting Sergeant Matilda O'Donnell MacElroy's.

Matilda's pen glides over her notepad as she transcribes the Alien's telepathic messages, their connection unbroken.

> ALIEN (V.O.)
> In 3,200 BCE, Earth was under attack between The Domain and the "Old Empire" forces.

EXT. ANCIENT EGYPTIAN LANDSCAPE - DAY

INSERT CARD: 3,200 BCE

The vibrant, bustling streets of ancient Egypt are alive with activity. Priests and common folk alike move through the grand, sand-stone cityscapes. The towering pyramids cast long shadows across the desert sands.

The voice of the Alien seeps in.

> ALIEN (V.O.)
> This does not make any sense to archaeologists or historians on Earth, as the Egyptian period is a space opera era.

INT. EGYPTIAN TEMPLE - DAY

Priests in elaborate garb chant and perform rituals. Hidden within the temple walls, advanced technology hums quietly, undetected by the untrained eye.

Again, the voice of the Alien resonates.

> ALIEN (V.O.)
> Earth historians have amnesia and assume this was only a religious period.

EXT. ANCIENT EGYPTIAN BATTLEFIELD - DAY

The sky above is filled with spacecraft from The Domain and the "Old Empire," locked in a fierce aerial battle.

Energy beams and explosions light up the sky, while below, the people of Egypt go about their daily lives, unaware of the war raging above.

The voice of the Alien comes through.

> ALIEN (V.O.)
> Technology and civilizations installed on Earth during this period were "prepackaged". They did not "evolve" on Earth.

INT. ANCIENT EGYPTIAN SCHOOL - DAY

Children are taught sophisticated mathematics, language, and writing. The teacher instructs using tools and methods far advanced for the time.

The mystifying voice of the Alien emanates.

> ALIEN (V.O.)
> There is no evidence of an evolutionary transition that resulted in these sophisticated systems. These cultures appeared as complete integrated packages.

EXT. PYRAMID SITE - DAY

Workers construct the pyramids with precision. Overseers use advanced surveying equipment disguised as rudimentary tools.

The voice of the Alien chimes in.

> ALIEN (V.O.)
> The physical evidence suggests that all traces of The Domain or "Old Empire" intervention have been carefully "cleaned up."

INT. ANCIENT EGYPTIAN LIBRARY - NIGHT

Scholars study ancient texts. Hidden among the scrolls are advanced blueprints and documents, remnants of extraterrestrial knowledge, but the scholars see only what they are meant to see.

Echoing sentiments is the voice of the Alien.

>   ALIEN (V.O.)
>   The "Old Empire" force does not
>   want IS-BEs on Earth to suspect
>   their capture and brainwashing.

EXT. ANCIENT EGYPTIAN TEMPLE - DAY

Priests chant "Amen" in unison, performing a ritual under the watchful eyes of disguised "Old Empire" operatives.

The voice of the Alien rings out.

>   ALIEN (V.O.)
>   Earth historians assume Egyptian
>   priests were not supposed to have
>   "ray guns" or other advanced
>   technology.

INT. ROSWELL ARMY AIR FORCE BASE - INTERVIEW ROOM - DAY

The room is still, with an air of anticipation. The Alien sits in her recliner chair, eyes locked with Sergeant Matilda O'Donnell MacElroy's. Matilda's pen hovers over her notepad, capturing the Alien's telepathic messages without breaking eye contact.

>   ALIEN (V.O.)
>   In 3,172 BCE, the astronomical grid
>   was laid out, connecting key mining
>   sites and astronomical buildings of
>   'the gods' in the Andes Mountains,
>   such as Tiahuanaco, Cuzco, Quito,
>   Ollantaytambo, Machu Picchu, and
>   Pachacamac.

Matilda's pen swiftly transcribes the information, her mind envisioning the vast grid across the Andean landscape.

>   MATILDA (V.O.)
>   (writing)
>   The grid-connected mining sites and
>   astronomical buildings.

>   ALIEN (V.O.)
>   Metals, including tin for making
>   bronze, were the property of "the
>   gods". There was a great variety
>   of entrepreneurial mining on Earth
>   due to the war between the "Old
>   Empire" force and The Domain.

IMAGES of ancient miners appear in Matilda's mind, showing them extracting metals and other resources from the earth.

> MATILDA (V.O.)
> (writing)
> These miners carved a few sculptures of themselves, depicted wearing mining helmets.

Matilda envisions the Ponce stela sculpture in the sunken courtyard of the Kalasasaya temple, a stone worker using an electronic, light-wave emitting stone cutter and carving tools held in a holster.

> ALIEN (V.O.)
> The "Old Empire" has maintained mining operations on planets throughout the galaxy for a very long time. The mineral resources of Earth are now the property of The Domain.

Matilda's pen stops for a moment as she processes the significance of this information. She looks back at the Alien, understanding the gravity of the historical context being shared.

> MATILDA (V.O.)
> The transition of control over Earth's resources... it must have been a significant shift...

The Alien's eyes remain calm and focused, her telepathic message clear and steady.

> ALIEN (V.O.)
> Indeed. The control of these resources was a crucial element in the ongoing conflict between The Domain and the "Old Empire".

Matilda nods, the weight of history pressing upon her as she continues to document the revelations shared by the Alien.

The room is filled with a quiet intensity. Airl, the Alien, seated calmly in the recliner, locks eyes with Sergeant Matilda O'Donnell MacElroy.

Matilda's pen moves almost instinctively, capturing the telepathic communication from Airl.

ALIEN (V.O.)
In 2,450 BCE, the Great Pyramid and the complex of pyramids near Cairo were completed. An inscription by the "Old Empire" administrators can be found in the Pyramid texts. It states that the pyramid was built under the direction of Thoth, Son of Ptah.

Matilda's mind VISUALIZES the massive structure of the Great Pyramid, understanding the historical and astronomical significance embedded within its design.

ALIEN (V.O.)
A King was never buried in the chamber, as the pyramids were not intended for burial. The Great Pyramid was precisely located at the center of all land masses of Earth, a placement requiring an aerial perspective.

IMAGES of the Earth from space flash in Matilda's mind, showcasing the precise location of the Great Pyramid.

Matilda's pen flows across the notepad.

MATILDA (V.O.)
The precision of the location and design...

ALIEN (V.O.)
Shafts within the pyramid were constructed to align with the configuration of stars in the constellation of Orion, Canis Major, specifically Sirius, and the Big Dipper, marking the home planet of the "Old Empire."

Matilda ENVISIONS the shafts inside the pyramid, perfectly aligned with the distant stars and constellations.

ALIEN (V.O.)
Also, Alnitak, Alpha Draconis, and Beta Ursae Minoris. These stars are key systems in the "Old Empire" from which IS-BEs were brought to Earth as unwanted merchandise.

The IMAGES shift in Matilda's mind, showing the pyramids and the alignment with the stars, creating a "mirror image" of the solar system and certain constellations within the "Old Empire".

Matilda's gaze is intense she is locked on the Alien's eyes.

              MATILDA (V.O.)
     The pyramids... they were more
     than just structures. They were...
     a map?

The Alien's expression remains calm, and its telepathic message is clear.

              ALIEN (V.O.)
     Yes, a map and a symbol. A
     representation of the "Old Empire"
     and a constant reminder to the IS-
     BEs on Earth of their origins and
     their captivity.

Matilda's pen stops as she absorbs the weight of this revelation, the implications settling in her mind.

INT. ROSWELL ARMY AIR FORCE BASE - BARRACKS - NIGHT

The barracks are dimly lit, casting long shadows across the room. Sergeant Matilda O'Donnell MacElroy sits alone on her bunk, her face a mask of exhaustion and deep thought. The day's telepathic interview with Airl the Alien weighs heavily on her mind.

A KNOCK at the door breaks the silence. A MILITARY POLICE OFFICER enters, carrying a tray of food. He sets the tray on the small table next to Matilda's bunk without a word, then exits, closing the door softly behind him.

Matilda glances at the tray, her eyes heavy with fatigue. She picks up a fork and takes a few bites of the food, her movements slow and mechanical. The food does little to revive her, and she soon pushes the tray away, barely touched.

With a sigh, she stretches out on the bunk, her body sinking into the thin mattress. She stares up at the ceiling, her mind racing with the day's revelations. Her eyes flutter closed, struggling to shut out the barrage of thoughts. The room is silent except for the soft hum of the air conditioning.

Matilda turns on her side, curling up slightly, seeking comfort in the familiar position.

She takes a deep breath, trying to calm her mind and find sleep. The dim light of the barracks casts a soft glow over her, a lone figure caught between the mundane and the extraordinary.

Slowly, her breathing evens out as exhaustion finally pulls her into a restless sleep, the weight of the day's discoveries lingering in the shadows around her.

EXT. ROSWELL ARMY AIR FORCE BASE - HALLWAY - DAY

The hallway is bright and sterile, lit by overhead fluorescent lights. The sound of boots echoes through the corridor as Sergeant Matilda O'Donnell MacElroy walks briskly, flanked by two MILITARY POLICE OFFICERS. The MPs' expressions are stoic, their eyes focused ahead.

As they reach the interview room door, the officers come to a stop. One of them steps forward, opening the door with a firm push. Matilda, taking a deep breath, steps through the doorway, her face set with determination.

The door closes behind her with a soft click, and the two military police officers take up their positions on either side of the entrance. They stand at attention, vigilant and ready, their presence a silent reminder of the gravity of the situation within.

The hallway remains quiet, the only sound the faint hum of the building's air system. Inside, the door to the interview room stands as a barrier between the ordinary world and the extraordinary events unfolding beyond it.

INT. ROSWELL ARMY AIR FORCE BASE - INTERVIEW ROOM - DAY

Sergeant Matilda O'Donnell MacElroy sits across from Airl, the Alien, maintaining steady eye contact. The room is quiet, the only sound is the soft hum of the air conditioning. The atmosphere is charged with the unspoken exchange between the two.

> ALIEN (V.O.)
> (telepathically)
> 2,181 BCE -- An IS-BE known as MIN emerged in Egypt, becoming the God of Fertility. Min, also known as Pan in Greek mythology, was an IS-BE who escaped the "Old Empire" amnesia system. This IS-BE influenced the religious and cultural fabric of the region, symbolizing fertility and nature.

Matilda jots down notes, her hand moving quickly across the notepad, while her eyes remain fixed on Airl, the Alien.

> ALIEN (V.O.)
> 2,160 - 2040 BCE -- The ongoing conflict between The Domain and the "Old Empire" forces weakened the control of the "divine rulers." These rulers, who had long imposed their will on the people of Egypt, were defeated and left Earth, returning to their origins in the "heavens." Human beings then ascended to power, taking the place of these so-called divine entities. The first human pharaoh shifted the capital of Egypt from Memphis to Heracleopolis, marking a new era in Egyptian history.

Matilda's face shows a mixture of fascination and disbelief as she continues to transcribe the Alien's words.

> ALIEN (V.O.)
> 1,500 BCE -- According to the high priests of Egypt, Psenophis of Heliopolis and Sonchis of Sais, this was the time of Atlantis' destruction. These accounts were later relayed to the Greek sage Solon. However, the Atlanteans referenced were not from the legendary continent of Atlantis, which existed over 70,000 years ago. They were, in fact, refugees from the Minoan civilization on Crete, fleeing the cataclysmic eruption and ensuing tidal waves of Mt. Thera. The surviving Minoans, referred to as "Kepchu" by the Egyptians, sought assistance from Egypt, the only other advanced civilization in the Mediterranean at that time.

The room seems to hold its breath as Matilda processes this flood of revelations, her pen pausing momentarily. The history of Earth, as revealed by Airl, the Alien, is far more complex and intertwined with cosmic events than she could have ever imagined.

Matilda's eyes widen slightly, absorbing the depth of the information.

The room remains silent, filled with the weight of these ancient secrets, now laid bare by the Aliens' account.

The one-way glass window observes Sergeant Matilda O'Donnell MacElroy and Airl, the Alien, in silence. The overhead camera, its red tally light glowing, stands as the lone sentry, capturing every moment.

INT. ROSWELL ARMY AIR FORCE BASE - NCO CLUB - NIGHT

The room is dimly lit, with only a few overhead lights casting shadows on the pool table and bar area. The space is mostly empty except for five men gathered around a pool table and the bar. The atmosphere is casual but charged with an underlying tension.

Colonel William H. Blanchard, in his army uniform, lines up a shot. Captain Sheridan Cavitt leans against the bar, nursing a drink. The scientist examines the cue stick thoughtfully, while the government agent sips his whiskey. The military official watches the game with a furrowed brow.

              WILLIAM H. BLANCHARD
        (serious, yet casual)
    So, gentlemen, about this
     interview with our
     "guest". The information
    in this transcript...
        (pauses to take a shot)
    ...it's not something we
    can take lightly.

              SHERIDAN D. CAVITT
        (raising an eyebrow)
You mean the part where we have
thousands of years of alien
interference and a potential
interstellar war? Yeah, kind of
hard to ignore.

              SCIENTIST
        (tapping the cue stick)
If what Airl says is true, then
Earth's history and future are far
more complicated than we ever
imagined. We're talking about
ancient battles, hidden bases, and
a very sophisticated prison system.

              GOVERNMENT AGENT
        (taking a sip)
It's a harbinger, alright.
                (MORE)

                    GOVERNMENT AGENT (CONT'D)
          If the "Old Empire" and The Domain
          have been fighting over this
          planet, who knows what kind of
          fallout we might be dealing with?

                    WILLIAM H. BLANCHARD
               (nodding, focused on the
                game)
          Exactly. And we need to figure out
          how to handle this. Public
          knowledge isn't an option. Panic
          would be the least of our worries.

                    MILITARY OFFICIAL
               (concerned)
          What about the technological
          implications? If they've been here
          for millennia, there must be tech
          we can recover or utilize. But we
          need to do it quietly.

                    SHERIDAN D. CAVITT
               (smirking)
          Quietly. That's the key. Last
          thing we need is some trigger-happy
          fool bringing attention to our
          operations.

                    SCIENTIST
               (musing)
          Airl's claims about ancient
          civilizations, the pyramid texts,
          and these so-called 'Old Empire'
          installations... if we can verify
          any of it, it could change
          everything we know about our
          past—and our future.

                    GOVERNMENT AGENT
               (finishing his drink)
          So, what's our move, Colonel? How
          do we proceed with this without
          setting off alarms?

                    WILLIAM H. BLANCHARD
               (pause, then confidently)
          We keep this contained. Limited to
          our group. We gather more intel
          from Airl, validate what we can,
          and prepare for any contingencies.
          If this is a prelude to something
          bigger, we need to be ready.

The group nods in agreement, understanding the gravity of their task. The game of pool continues, but the weight of their conversation lingers heavily in the air. The future seems uncertain, and their roles are more crucial than ever.

EXT. EGYPTIAN DESERT - 1351 BCE - DAY

Pharaoh Akhenaten stands on a sand dune, gazing out over the vast desert as the sun rises behind him. He turns and walks purposefully towards a grand construction site.

EXT. AMARNA CONSTRUCTION SITE - DAY

Thousands of workers labor under the hot sun, building the new capital city of Amarna. Massive stone blocks are hauled into place. Akhenaten supervises the construction, his presence commanding and determined.

EXT. TEMPLE OF AMUN - THEBES - DAY

The grand temple stands silent and empty. Statues of Amun look on as the last of the priests gather their belongings, casting wary glances at the vacant halls.

EXT. SPACE - 1337 BCE - DAY

In the vastness of space, two fleets of spaceships engage in a fierce battle. Beams of light and explosions illuminate the dark void. The ships of The Domain, sleek and advanced, clash with the remnants of the "Old Empire" fleet, rugged and resilient.

EXT. TROJAN PLAINS - 1,193 BCE - DAY

The city of Troy burns in the background. Warriors clash with swords and shields, their battle cries echoing through the plains. Greek soldiers breach the city walls as the Trojans fight desperately to defend their home.

EXT. SPACE - 1,193 BCE - NIGHT

Above the Earth, space stations orbit silently. Explosions and debris scatter as ships from The Domain engage the "Old Empire" forces. The struggle for control of the stations is intense and brutal.

INT. TROY - NIGHT

Troy lies in ruins, smoldering and desolate. Survivors weep and tend to the wounded. The victors loot and set fire to the remains, marking the end of a great city.

EXT. GREEK COUNTRYSIDE - 850 BCE - DAY

Homer, the blind poet, sits under an olive tree, reciting his epic tales. Around him, villagers listen in awe, their imaginations captured by the vivid stories of gods and heroes.

EXT. TEMPLE - GREECE - DAY

Scholars and scribes meticulously translate the Vedic Hymns into Greek. Scrolls and manuscripts are scattered across stone tables. This monumental task brings about a quiet revolution in thought and culture.

EXT. GREEK CITY - DAY

A bustling city square shows a blend of Greek and Eastern influences. Marketplaces are alive with activity, and the foundations of democratic society begin to take shape amidst the backdrop of newfound cultural wisdom.

EXT. EGYPTIAN TEMPLE - 638 BCE - DAY

Solon, a wise Greek philosopher, stands with two Egyptian high priests, Psenophis and Sonchis. They converse in hushed tones, and the priests point toward ancient scrolls and hieroglyphs depicting the lost civilization of Atlantis. Solon listens intently, absorbing the ancient knowledge.

INT. MILITARY BRIEFING ROOM - DAY

Colonel William H. Blanchard and Captain Sheridan Cavitt sit at a long conference table. The room is dimly lit, with the glow from the screen illuminating their faces. The video recording of the interview between Matilda and Airl the Alien plays on a monitor in front of them.

ON SCREEN: Airl, the diminutive alien, sits in a large recliner chair across from Sergeant Matilda O'Donnell MacElroy. Matilda jots down notes on a notepad through automatic writing, without breaking eye contact with Airl.

The video ends, and the room falls silent. Colonel Blanchard leans back in his chair, rubbing his chin thoughtfully. Captain Cavitt's eyes are fixed on the now-blank screen.

> WILLIAM H. BLANCHARD
> (to himself)
> This is... beyond anything we've encountered.

> SHERIDAN D. CAVITT
> (turning to Blanchard)
> You think she's telling the truth, sir? About the "Old Empire" and The Domain?

> WILLIAM H. BLANCHARD
> (gravely)
> Whether it's true or not, we can't ignore the implications. If there's even a shred of truth to what that alien says, it changes everything we know about our history and our place in the universe.

> SHERIDAN D. CAVITT
> (skeptical)
> It's a lot to take in. Intergalactic wars, amnesia, IS-BEs... it sounds like something out of a science fiction novel.

> WILLIAM H. BLANCHARD
> (nodding)
> Agreed. But we can't dismiss it outright. We need to verify as much as we can. Get our top scientists and historians on this. We need to cross-reference every bit of information.

Captain Cavitt looks thoughtful, then resolute.

> SHERIDAN D. CAVITT
> I'll get started on it right away, sir. But what about Sergeant MacElroy?

> WILLIAM H. BLANCHARD
> (exhaling deeply)
> She's crucial to this. Her ability to communicate with Airl is our only link to this information.
> (MORE)

                    WILLIAM H. BLANCHARD (CONT'D)
          We need to ensure her safety and
          keep this under wraps. No leaks,
          no speculation.

Captain Cavitt nods, understanding the gravity of the
situation.

                    CAPTAIN SHERIDAN CAVITT
          Understood, sir. I'll make sure of
          it.

The two officers sit in silence for a moment, the weight of
their discovery settling in. The screen flickers and the
recording of the interview starts to replay, filling the room
with the eerie, otherworldly presence of Airl.

INT. WHITE HOUSE - OVAL OFFICE - DAY

PRESIDENT HARRY S. TRUMAN, a white male in his early 60s,
sits behind the Resolute Desk, looking over some papers. The
room is decorated with flags and memorabilia, signifying the
importance of the space.

An AIDE opens the door, ushering in Lieutenant General Roger
M. Ramey, who walks in briskly, carrying a thick folder
marked "Above Top Secret."

                    AIDE
          Lieutenant General Ramey, sir.

                    PRESIDENT TRUMAN
          Thank you, you may leave us.

The Aide nods and exits, closing the door softly behind him.
Ramey approaches the desk and salutes. Truman returns the
salute and gestures to a chair.

                    PRESIDENT TRUMAN (CONT'D)
          Take a seat, General.

Ramey sits, placing the folder on the desk, and opening it.

                    ROGER M. RAMEY
          Mr. President, I appreciate you
          seeing me on such short notice.
          The situation at Roswell has
          escalated. We have confirmed
          contact with an extraterrestrial
          being, codename Airl.

Truman's expression remains stern but curious.

PRESIDENT TRUMAN
Go on.

Ramey pulls out a report and hands it to Truman, who begins to skim through it.

ROGER M. RAMEY
Airl has been cooperative. We've gathered substantial intelligence. However, the implications of her statements and the presence of her spacecraft are profound. We're dealing with advanced technology and potentially a new era of human-alien relations.

Truman pauses, looking up from the report.

PRESIDENT TRUMAN
And your recommendation, General?

Ramey's gaze is steady, firm.

ROGER M. RAMEY
We need to keep this contained, for now, sir. Colonel Blanchard at Roswell is managing the situation with utmost discretion. I have just received an update from him, confirming Airl's continued cooperation and the progress of our interrogations.

Truman nods thoughtfully, setting the report down.

PRESIDENT TRUMAN
Alright, General. You have my authorization to proceed as you see fit. Keep me updated on any significant developments.

Ramey stands, saluting once more.

ROGER M. RAMEY
Yes, Mr. President. Thank you.

Truman returns the salute, and Ramey exits the room, his demeanor remaining resolute and focused.

INT. ROSWELL ARMY AIR FORCE BASE - COLONEL BLANCHARD'S OFFICE - DAY

Colonel William H. Blanchard sits at his desk, a phone receiver pressed to his ear.

                  COLONEL BLANCHARD
      Understood, General Ramey. We'll
      maintain our current course and
      ensure all protocols are followed.

Blanchard hangs up the phone, looking pensive but determined.

INT. ROSWELL ARMY AIR FORCE BASE - INTERVIEW ROOM - DAY

Sergeant Matilda O'Donnell MacElroy sits across from Airl, the Alien, in the interview room. Their eyes lock in intense, telepathic communication. Matilda jots down notes on her notepad through automatic writing, never breaking eye contact with Airl.

Airl's voice echoes in Matilda's mind, conveying the following information.

                  ALIEN (V.O.)
      630 BCE -- Zoroaster established
      religious practices in Persia
      centered around Ahura Mazda. This
      was another of the monotheistic
      gods introduced by The Domain to
      replace the numerous "Old Empire"
      gods.

IMAGES of ancient Persia flash in Matilda's mind: Zoroaster teaching his followers, the sacred fire, and the symbol of Ahura Mazda.

                  ALIEN (V.O.)
      604 BCE -- Laozi, a wise
      philosopher, wrote "The Way."
      Laozi overcame the "Old Empire"
      amnesia and hypnosis machinery,
      escaping Earth. He understood the
      nature of an IS-BE deeply.
      According to legend, in his final
      lifetime, he lived in a small
      Chinese village, contemplating his
      essence and past lives. Through
      this introspection, he regained
      memory, ability, and immortality.

The IMAGE of a serene village in ancient China appears, Laozi sitting in quiet contemplation. He engages in deep thought, reflecting on his past lives and the essence of his spirit.

                    ALIEN (V.O.)
Before leaving his village, Laozi shared his wisdom, recorded as "The Way": "He who looks will not see it; He who listens will not hear it; He who gropes will not grasp it. The formless nonentity, the motionless source of motion. The infinite essence of the spirit is the source of life. Spirit is self. Walls form and support a room, yet the space between them is most important. A pot is formed of clay, yet the space formed therein is most useful. Action is caused by the force of nothing on something, just as the nothing of spirit is the source of all form. One suffers great afflictions because one has a body. Without a body what afflictions could one suffer? When one cares more for the body than for his own spirit, one becomes the body and loses the way of the spirit. The self, the spirit, creates an illusion. The delusion of Man is that reality is not an illusion. One who creates illusions and makes them more real than reality follows the path of the spirit and finds the way of heaven."

VISIONS of Laozi's teachings come to life: the village gatekeeper pleading with him, Laozi writing his wisdom, and villagers listening in awe.

Matilda's hand moves quickly across the notepad, capturing Airl's message. Her face reflects the profound impact of the information she is receiving.

                    ALIEN (V.O.)
Laozi's journey and teachings emphasize the importance of spirit over physical form, understanding one's true self, and seeing beyond the illusions of reality.

The serene IMAGE of Laozi departing to the forest, leaving behind his mortal body to reconnect with his immortal spirit.

Sergeant Matilda O'Donnell MacElroy sits across from Airl, the Alien, in their usual positions. The room is filled with a tense silence as their eyes lock, initiating their telepathic dialogue. Matilda's hand moves automatically, jotting down notes without breaking eye contact.

> ALIEN (V.O.)
> 593 BCE -- The Genesis story describes "angels" or "sons of god" mating with women of Earth. These were likely renegades from the "Old Empire" or space pirates from outside the galaxy. They may have come to steal resources or smuggle drugs. The Domain has seen many visitors to Earth, but few stay. Who would live on a prison planet by choice?

IMAGES of ancient texts flash in Matilda's mind, showing "angels" descending to Earth, mingling with humans.

> ALIEN (V.O.)
> The same book mentions Ezekiel witnessing a spacecraft near the Chebar River. His description, though archaic, is accurate for an "Old Empire" saucer. It's similar to "vimanas" seen in the Himalayas.

VISIONS of Ezekiel's encounter appear: a glowing spacecraft descending, surrounded by astonished onlookers.

> ALIEN (V.O.)
> "Yahweh" supposedly designed human bodies to last 120 years. Most biological bodies on "Sun Type 12, Class 7" planets last about 150 years. We suspect prison administrators altered human biology to die sooner, ensuring IS-BEs recycle through the amnesia mechanism more frequently.

Airl's thoughts project IMAGES of human bodies deteriorating faster, recycling through the amnesia process repeatedly.

> ALIEN (V.O.)
> Much of the "Old Testament" was written during Jewish captivity in Babylon, heavily controlled by "Old Empire" priests. It introduces false concepts of time and creation.
> (MORE)

                    ALIEN (V.O.) (CONT'D)
          The serpent, symbol of the "Old
          Empire", appears at the start,
          causing spiritual destruction of
          humans, metaphorically Adam and
          Eve.

IMAGES of ancient Babylon, with priests manipulating sacred texts, inserting false narratives appear in Matilda's mind.

                    ALIEN (V.O.)
          The Old Testament, influenced by
          "Old Empire" Forces, details IS-BEs
          being induced into biological
          bodies on Earth. It describes
          brainwashing activities: false
          memories, lies, superstitions,
          commands to forget, and traps to
          keep IS-BEs on Earth. It destroys
          the awareness that humans are
          Immortal Spiritual Beings.

Airl, the Alien, thoughts project IMAGES of ancient rituals, false memories implanted and IS-BEs trapped in an endless cycle of rebirth.

Matilda's pen continues to glide across the notepad, capturing every detail. The room remains silent, the weight of the revelations heavy in the air.

INT. DELPHI TEMPLE - DAY

INSERT CARD: 580 BCE

The ancient temple is seen nestled high in the Greek mountains. Olive trees sway gently in the breeze as the temple stands silent, its stone columns weathered by time. Inside, a robed Oracle sits before the glowing Omphalos Stone, her eyes closed in a deep trance.

                    ALIEN (V.O.)
                (soft and echoing)
          The Oracle at Delphi was but one in
          a network of communication
          centers... Each designated by the
          priests of the 'Old Empire' to
          serve a local 'god'... A false
          deity imposed upon the Earth.

A network of temples is seen from high above, forming a precise grid across the Mediterranean, stretching from Thebes to the Baltic Sea.

> ALIEN (V.O.)
> (hauntingly)
> Their temples aligned at exact intervals, connected by electronic beacons... Once powerful, now reduced to mere stones... Omphalos Stones... The remains of a grid visible only from the heavens.

The Omphalos Stone in the temple of Delphi, its glow intensifying. The Oracle's eyes flicker open, reflecting fear as if sensing something unseen.

> ALIEN (V.O.)
> (resonant)
> The symbol of their priesthood... the serpent... Python, the earth-dragon of Delphi, a guardian buried by Apollo... Another 'god' replacing the old, but the power remains...

Suddenly, the stone's glow begins to fade, its power systematically drained. The Oracle gasps, breaking free from her trance, looking around in confusion as the priests around her react with alarm.

EXT. GREEK SKYLINE - HIGH ABOVE - DAY

The Earth, the grid of temples visible once more. One by one, the points of light marking the temples dim and extinguish, leaving a dark, powerless grid.

> ALIEN (V.O.)
> (finality in her tone)
> The Domain detected this network, disabling it... One of the fatal blows to the 'Old Empire'... Their grip on this world weakened.

EXT. DELPHI TEMPLE - DAY

The Omphalos Stone now lies cold and inert. The Oracle, free from her trance, stares at the lifeless stone, realization dawning. The priests stand silent, their once-mighty power lost.

A vast expanse unfolds, with the temple fading into the rugged landscape, a remnant of a fallen empire.

                    ALIEN (V.O.)
              (whispered)
         And so, the serpent falls, buried
         beneath the stone... powerless...
         defeated...

INT. ROSWELL ARMY AIR FORCE BASE - INTERVIEW ROOM - DAY

Sergeant Matilda O'Donnell MacElroy sits across from Airl, the Alien, their eyes locked in silent communication. Matilda's hand moves automatically, jotting down notes as the telepathic exchange continues. The room is quiet, the only sound being the soft hum of the overhead lights.

                    ALIEN (V.O.)
              (calm and measured)
         In 559 BCE, the Commanding Officer
         of The Domain Battalion, lost for
         millennia, was finally detected...
         located by a search party from The
         Domain. Incarnated as Cyrus II of
         Persia, he and the Battalion who
         followed him organized a system...
         a system that allowed them to build
         the largest empire Earth had seen.

Matilda's pen glides over the notepad, recording every detail as Airl continues to relay the information, her gaze unwavering.

                    MATILDA (V.O.)
              (curious, contemplative)
         An empire... built by those who
         were lost and then found. Did they
         know? Did they feel the pull of
         something greater within them? Or
         was it just another life, lived in
         the shadow of forgotten truths?

                    ALIEN (V.O.)
              (resonant)
         The Domain Search Party scoured the
         Earth for thousands of years...
         They were 900 officers, split into
         three teams... 300 searching land,
         300 searching the oceans, 300
         searching the space around Earth...
         Humans noted their activities but
         did not understand... as always,
         the truth was hidden from them.

The room remains still, but Matilda's expression shows the intensity of the information she is receiving. Her eyes flicker as she processes the telepathic transmission.

>   MATILDA (V.O.)
>   (awed, reflective)
>   To search so relentlessly... for
>   so long... the dedication it must
>   have taken. But for those on
>   Earth, it was just another mystery,
>   another 'divine' occurrence they
>   couldn't comprehend. How much have
>   we missed, simply because we didn't
>   understand?

Airl the Alien's presence seems to intensify, her small form radiating an unseen energy that Matilda feels acutely, though she remains composed.

>   ALIEN (V.O.)
>   (explaining patiently)
>   To track the missing Battalion, The
>   Domain developed electronic
>   detection devices... capable of
>   sensing the unique electronic
>   signature of each IS-BE. On land,
>   in space, and even underwater...
>   these devices could detect life...
>   detect an IS-BE.

Matilda's pen continues its steady movement, her mind racing as she tries to piece together the enormity of what Airl the Alien is revealing.

>   MATILDA (V.O.)
>   (inquisitive, determined)
>   Electronic signatures, detection
>   devices... all to find what was
>   lost. But what if they weren't
>   found? What if some remain, hidden
>   among us, unaware of who they truly
>   are? How many more secrets are
>   buried in the fabric of our
>   reality?

Airl the Alien's voice carries a weight of ancient knowledge, each word resonating with a history that Matilda is only beginning to grasp.

>   ALIEN (V.O.)
>   (softly, with a hint of
>   reverence)
>   (MORE)

                    ALIEN (V.O.) (CONT'D)
          One such device, a 'tree of life,'
          as it appeared to the ancient
          humans... An interwoven lattice of
          electronic field generators and
          receivers... detecting IS-BEs
          whether within a body... or free
          of one. To the ancients, it
          resembled a tree... but its
          purpose was far more profound.

Matilda's face, her features reflecting a mixture of
understanding and awe as she writes furiously, capturing
every word. The scene is silent except for the scratch of
her pen and the hum of the lights, the weight of the
revelation settling in the room.

                    MATILDA (V.O.)
              (relentless, with a tinge
               of sadness)
          A tree of life... what they saw as
          a symbol of creation, of
          existence... was actually a tool,
          a device. How much of our history
          is shaped by things we don't
          understand? And how much of it is
          lost because we never questioned
          what we thought we knew?

                    ALIEN (V.O.)
              (with a tone of finality)
          And so, the search continued,
          through space, land, and sea...
          until the lost were found, and the
          path to their return was
          revealed...

Matilda's pen pauses as she takes in the magnitude of what
has been shared. The atmosphere thick with the secrets of
ancient and cosmic history, and the silent bond of
understanding that has formed between her and Airl the Alien.

FLASHBACK:

INT. ANCIENT SUMERIA - NIGHT

A SUMERIAN TEMPLE nestled in the arid landscape. Stone
carvings and reliefs cover the walls, glowing faintly in the
moonlight. The ancient artwork depicts WINGED BEINGS holding
strange, PINECONE-SHAPED INSTRUMENTS over human figures.

A carving shows an EAGLE-HEADED, WINGED BEING holding a
STYLIZED BASKET in one hand, with the PINECONE INSTRUMENT in
the other, hovering it over a human figure as if scanning it.

                    ALIEN (V.O.)
          These instruments were portable
          detection devices carried by
          members of The Domain Search Party.
          The power units, depicted as
          baskets, were essential for the
          operation of the scanners.

EXT. PERSIAN DESERT - DAY

Towering STONE RELIEFS breaks the vast expanse of the Persian
desert etched into the side of a cliff. The carvings depict
WINGED GODS with FARAVAHAR—winged spacecraft, hovering above
the ground.

                    ALIEN (V.O.)
          Humans called us "winged gods."
          Our aerial units, led by Ahura
          Mazda, searched from above,
          scanning the land for lost
          Battalion members.

EXT. SUMERIAN RIVERBANK - DUSK

Stone carvings along the riverbank show AQUATIC BEINGS with
silver suits, seemingly stepping out of the water. These
beings are depicted as having FISH-LIKE APPEARANCES, their
suits shimmering in the fading sunlight.

                    ALIEN (V.O.)
          Members of our Aquatic Unit were
          known as "Oannes" by the locals.
          They scanned the oceans, seeking
          our comrades who had taken refuge
          in the bodies of dolphins or
          whales.

Ancient carvings are seen as the light fades, leaving only
the enigmatic images visible in the dark.

                    ALIEN (V.O.)
          The truth of our presence was
          immortalized in stone, though
          misinterpreted by those who
          witnessed it.

END FLASHBACK.

INT. ROSWELL ARMY AIR FORCE BASE - INTERVIEW ROOM - DAY

Sergeant Matilda O'Donnell MacElroy sits across from Airl, the diminutive alien. The room is still, the air thick with the weight of their telepathic connection. Matilda's eyes are locked with the Alien, her notepad resting on the table untouched.

          ALIEN (V.O.)
  On land, our Search Party members
  were called "Anunnaki" by the
  Sumerians, and "Nephilim" in your
  Bible. The true purpose of our
  mission and our activities was
  never revealed to your species.

          MATILDA (V.O.)
  So, all those stories... The
  myths, the legends—they were all
  just distorted reflections of what
  really happened.

The Alien's large, dark eyes seem to shimmer with understanding. The room feels charged, as if the very walls hold their breath, waiting for more.

          ALIEN (V.O.)
  Yes. The truth was hidden from
  you, cloaked in your myths and
  religions. In the absence of
  complete and accurate data, humans
  created explanations,
  theories—fictions that made sense
  of what little they perceived.

          MATILDA (V.O.)
  So, we misinterpreted everything?
  Our history, our gods, all just...
  fragments of a misunderstood
  reality?

FLASHBACK:

EXT. ANCIENT SUMERIA - DAY

The ANUNNAKI—tall, imposing figures—walk among the ancient Sumerians. They are adorned with advanced technology, their actions precise and purposeful. The Sumerians look on in awe and fear, their primitive minds struggling to comprehend what they see.

>   ALIEN (V.O.)
>   In the absence of understanding,
>   your ancestors filled in the gaps
>   with stories—legends born from
>   fear, awe, and ignorance. They saw
>   our technology and called it magic.
>   They saw us and called us gods.
>
>   MATILDA (V.O.)
>   And we've been living those
>   misunderstandings ever since...

END FLASHBACK.

INT. ROSWELL ARMY AIR FORCE BASE - INTERVIEW ROOM - DAY

Matilda shifts slightly, her mind processing the weight of the revelations. She feels a mix of shock and clarity—pieces of the puzzle of human history slowly falling into place, yet so many questions remain unanswered.

>   ALIEN (V.O.)
>   Mythology and history, though based
>   on fragments of truth, have been
>   woven into tapestries of
>   misunderstanding. Your world's
>   past is a story half-remembered,
>   half-invented.
>
>   MATILDA (V.O.)
>   Then what is the real story, Airl?
>   Who are we really?

The room grows even quieter if that's possible. The Alien's presence feels heavier, its telepathic connection deepening.

>   ALIEN (V.O.)
>   That Sergeant is a truth still
>   buried deep within your own
>   consciousness. A truth that must
>   be uncovered, piece by piece.

Matilda's thoughts swirl with the enormity of the revelations, yet there's a strange calmness that settles over her—a sense of understanding as if a veil has been lifted ever so slightly.

>   ALIEN (V.O.)
>   I want to know, Airl. I need to
>   know...

The connection between them seems to pulse with an unspoken agreement—a promise of truths yet to be revealed.

                    ALIEN (V.O.)
          The space unit of The Domain
          Expeditionary Force is depicted in
          human records as flying in a
          "Winged Disc." This symbol is an
          allusion to the spiritual power of
          IS-BEs, as well as to the
          spacecraft used by The Domain
          Search Party.

The IMAGE of the "Winged Disc" flickers in Matilda's mind—a powerful symbol of transcendence and freedom. She feels the weight of the Alien's words pressing upon her consciousness, stirring her curiosity and awe.

                    MATILDA (V.O.)
          Winged Disc... The symbol makes
          sense now, but how could ancient
          humans have known? How much of our
          history is a misinterpretation of
          something far more profound?

Airl the Alien thoughts shift, drawing Matilda deeper into the history of the lost Battalion.

                    ALIEN (V.O.)
          The Commander of the lost
          Battalion, as Cyrus II, was
          regarded as a messiah by both the
          Jews and the Muslims. His reign,
          though brief, brought forth a
          philosophy that shaped Western
          Civilization. His
          achievements—territorial conquests,
          organizational reforms, and
          monumental projects—were
          unparalleled.

Matilda ENVISIONS Cyrus II, leading with authority, the unmistakable presence of a leader who once commanded forces beyond Earth, now reduced to a mortal life, yet still radiating an aura of greatness. The memory of his rule lingers, influencing generations long after his time.

                    MATILDA (V.O.)
          Cyrus II... More than just a man,
          more than just a king... A leader
          born from the stars, trying to
          piece together a shattered
          identity. How many others like him
          walk among us, forgotten gods of
          forgotten empires?

The Alien's thoughts convey the continued struggle to recover the lost Battalion.

> ALIEN (V.O.)
> Although we have located many of the IS-BEs in the lost Battalion, The Domain has yet to restore their memories and return them to active duty. We cannot transport IS-BEs inhabiting biological bodies to our space stations; there is no oxygen, no life support for biological entities aboard our ships.

IMAGES flash before Matilda's mind—IS-BEs, once powerful and free, now trapped in frail human forms, their memories locked away, unreachable. The tragedy of their situation overwhelms her.

> MATILDA (V.O.)
> They're still out there, lost in the vastness of this world, in these fragile bodies. They were once part of something so much greater... Can they ever be whole again?

> ALIEN (V.O.)
> Our hope lies in rekindling their awareness, memory, and identity. One day, they will be capable of rejoining us, of reclaiming their place among the stars.

Matilda feels a deep longing in Airl the Alien's thoughts, a yearning to reunite with the lost members of The Domain. It resonates within her, the desire to see these ancient beings restored to their former glory.

> MATILDA (V.O.)
> I hope... I hope they find their way back. For their sake, and for ours...

The connection between them strengthens momentarily, a silent exchange of empathy and understanding. The room feels heavy with the weight of history, of untold stories that have shaped the very fabric of the world.

Matilda's hand moves across the notepad, scribbling down notes without breaking eye contact with Airl the Alien, the automatic writing an echo of the telepathic exchange between them.

FLASHBACK:

EXT. TEOTIHUACÁN - DAY

The majestic ruins of Teotihuacán, the ancient pyramid complex bathed in the warm light of the setting sun. The Pyramid of the Sun stands tall and imposing, its silhouette stark against the sky. The Avenue of the Dead stretches out before it, lined with smaller temples and platforms.

> ALIEN (V.O.)
> 200 BCE—the last remnant of the "Old Empire" pyramid civilization stands at Teotihuacán. The Aztec name means "place of the gods" or "where men were transformed into gods."

Intricate carvings on the stone walls—serpents coiled and ready to strike, their eyes cold and menacing. The serpents are everywhere, woven into the architecture, omnipresent guardians of the ancient site.

> ALIEN (V.O.)
> Like the astronomical configuration of the Giza pyramids in Egypt, the entire complex is a precise scale model of the solar system. It accurately reflects the orbital distances of the inner planets, the asteroid belt, Jupiter, Saturn, Uranus, Neptune, and Pluto.

Looking up to the sky, focusing on the distant planets, each one perfectly aligned with the structures below. The precision is eerie, otherworldly.

> ALIEN (V.O.)
> Since the planet Uranus had only been "discovered" with modern Earth telescopes in 1787, and Pluto not until 1930, it is apparent that the builders had information from "other sources."

Looking down to the ground, following the path of the Avenue of the Dead. The imagery of serpents becomes even more prominent, their presence almost overwhelming as they seem to slither along the ancient stones, watching, waiting.

                    ALIEN (V.O.)
          A common element of the Pyramid
          Civilizations around the Earth is
          the constant use of the image of
          the snake, dragon, or serpent.
          This is because the beings who
          planted these civilizations here
          wanted to create an illusion that
          the "gods" are reptilian.

A large stone carving of a serpent, its scales intricately
detailed, its fangs bared in a menacing grin. The sky
darkens slightly, the atmosphere growing heavier.

                    ALIEN (V.O.)
          This is also a part of an illusion
          designed to perpetuate amnesia.
          The beings who placed false
          civilizations on Earth are IS-BEs,
          just like you. Many of the
          biological bodies inhabited by IS-
          BEs in the "Old Empire" are very
          similar in appearance to the bodies
          on Earth.

A view of the ancient site reveals more serpent imagery, more
signs of the once-mighty civilization. The view from above
captures the vastness of the complex, showing how it mirrors
the solar system.

                    ALIEN (V.O.)
          The "gods" are not reptiles,
          although they often behave like
          snakes.

The ancient pyramids are now under a twilight sky, their
secrets locked within the stone, guarded by serpents that
were never truly gods.

END FLASHBACK.

INT. ROSWELL ARMY AIR FORCE BASE - INTERVIEW ROOM - DAY

The room is quiet, dimly lit. The tension in the air is
palpable as Sergeant Matilda O'Donnell MacElroy sits across
from Airl, the Alien, her eyes locked onto Airl's. The
connection between them is powerful, their communication
flowing seamlessly through telepathy.

                    ALIEN (V.O.)
          Between 1,034 and 1,124 AD, the
          entire Arab world fell under the
          control of one man—Hasan ibn-al-
          Sabbah, the Old Man of the
          Mountain. His reign of terror
          spread across India, Asia Minor,
          and most of the Mediterranean
          Basin.

As Airl's voice echoes in Matilda's mind, vivid IMAGERY of a
lush garden appears, filled with beautiful, dark-eyed houris.
The air is thick with the scent of incense and the sweet
fragrance of honey. Young men, dressed in simple garments,
are seen being led into the garden, their eyes glazed with
confusion.

                    ALIEN (V.O.)
          The Old Man of the Mountain used a
          simple yet devastatingly effective
          mind control mechanism. Young men
          were kidnapped, drugged with
          hashish, and brought to this
          paradise. They were promised
          eternal bliss if they sacrificed
          themselves as assassins.

The young men are seen being taken from the garden; their
minds filled with visions of paradise. They are sent out
into the world, their eyes now filled with a single
purpose—to kill in the name of their "heaven".

                    ALIEN (V.O.)
          Meanwhile, the Old Man sent
          messengers to demand tribute—camel-
          loads of gold, spices, and other
          riches. If payment was not
          received, the assassin would be
          dispatched to kill the offending
          ruler, who had no defense against
          this unknown assailant.

A wealthy ruler is SEEN sitting in his opulent palace,
looking over a demand for payment. His face pales as he
realizes the power and reach of the Old Man of the Mountain.

                    ALIEN (V.O.)
          This is a crude yet effective
          example of how brainwashing and
          mind control can be wielded
          skillfully and forcefully.
                    (MORE)

                        ALIEN (V.O.) (CONT'D)
                    It is a microcosm of the amnesia
                    mind control operation used against
                    the entire IS-BE population of
                    Earth by the "Old Empire".

The IMAGE of the ruler fades, replaced by the stark reality of the INTERVIEW ROOM. Matilda feels a deep chill as she processes the gravity of the Alien's words, the parallels between the past and the present.

                        MATILDA (V.O.)
                    How easily minds can be bent,
                    twisted, molded into tools of
                    control... just as the Old Empire
                    has done to us all.

Her thoughts linger on the chilling realization that the amnesia and control tactics used by the Old Empire are far more pervasive and insidious than she ever imagined. The room seems to grow colder as the weight of this truth settles on her.

                        ALIEN (V.O.)
                    The entire planet has been
                    manipulated, enslaved by a system
                    that is both ancient and
                    relentless. The "Old Empire" knew
                    how to twist the mind, to create
                    illusions so convincing that even
                    the strongest IS-BE would forget
                    their true nature.

The telepathic connection between Matilda and Airl the Alien deepens, as Airl continues to share the dark history of mind control and manipulation. Matilda's resolve to uncover the truth strengthens, even as the enormity of the task before her becomes clearer.

Matilda has a determined expression, knowing that the knowledge she's gaining is crucial in the fight against the forces that have kept humanity in chains for so long.

FLASHBACK:

EXT. JERUSALEM - 1119 AD - DAY

The city bustles with activity like the KNIGHTS TEMPLAR, clad in white tunics with red crosses, march in formation. They are greeted by CROWDS OF PEOPLE, their faces a mix of reverence and curiosity. The Knights enter a grand FORTRESS, symbolizing their newly established order.

EXT. EUROPEAN BANKING HOUSES - 1135 AD - DAY

The Templars, now dressed in more formal, aristocratic attire, oversee transactions in a bustling banking house. MERCHANTS and NOBLES exchange large sacks of coins, contracts are signed, and ledgers are meticulously recorded. A HIGH-RANKING TEMPLAR nods approvingly as the operation expands across multiple locations, symbolizing their transformation into an international financial power.

EXT. SPACE - SOLAR SYSTEM - 1230 AD

The DOMAIN EXPEDITIONARY FORCE engages in a fierce battle with the remnants of the "Old Empire" space fleet. MASSIVE STARSHIPS exchange volleys of energy blasts. The battle is chaotic but decisive. EXPLOSIONS rip through the enemy fleet as the Domain forces systematically destroy each vessel, their remnants drifting lifelessly through space.

EXT. PARIS - 1307 AD - NIGHT

The TEMPLARS are dragged from their homes and fortresses by the KING'S SOLDIERS. They are shackled and beaten, their wealth seized as the soldiers loot TREASURE ROOMS filled with gold, silver, and sacred relics. KING PHILIP IV watches from a palace balcony, his expression cold and determined.

EXT. THE STAKE - 1307 AD - DAY

Under the shadow of a cathedral, TEMPLARS are tied to stakes as CROWDS gather to watch. The pyres are lit, and the flames rise high, consuming the Templars. Their faces show pain, but also defiance as they burn, a stark contrast to the SMUG EXPRESSIONS of the KING and CLERGY watching from a distance.

EXT. SWISS MOUNTAINS - 1307 AD - NIGHT

The surviving Templars flee into the mountains of SWITZERLAND. They regroup in a secluded MOUNTAIN FORTRESS. Inside, they establish a SECRET MEETING. DOCUMENTS are exchanged, gold coins clink into chests, and they plan the next steps. A MAP of Europe lies on the table, with the locations of new banks marked across the continent.

EXT. MODERN BANKING HUB - UNDETERMINED TIME - NIGHT

An INTERNATIONAL BANKING HEADQUARTERS is shown in the present, symbolizing the continuation of the Templars' influence.

Inside, HIGH-LEVEL BANKERS make decisions that influence global economies. MONEY FLOWS through digital systems, subtly financing global conflicts. The unseen hand of the "Old Empire" remains at work, manipulating nations through their control of wealth.

EXT. WAR ZONE - UNDETERMINED TIME - DAY

Images of SOLDIERS in modern combat, tanks rolling through cities, and CIVILIANS fleeing destruction flash on the screen. The cycle of war, chaos, and control continues, all part of the silent agenda to prevent IS-BEs from uniting and escaping their unseen prison.

END FLASHBACK.

INT. ROSWELL ARMY AIR FORCE BASE - OFFICE - DAY

Sergeant Matilda O'Donnell MacElroy sits at a desk, her eyes slightly glazed as she recounts the details of her interview with Airl the Alien. A stenographer sits across from her, typing diligently on a stenotype machine. The room is quiet, save for the soft clacking of the stenotype keys.

> MATILDA
> (softly, almost to
> herself)
> It's hard to say what's more disorienting... the information itself or the realization that it might all be true.

The stenographer glances up briefly, her brow furrowing slightly as she processes the strange and unsettling details being dictated.

> STENOGRAPHER
> (tentatively, with a hint
> of concern)
> Are you... sure about all this, Sergeant? It's... quite something.

> MATILDA
> (with a small, wry smile)
> Believe me, I'm as shocked as you are. But my job isn't to question it. Just to report it.

The stenographer nods, her expression still skeptical but understanding. She resumes typing, her fingers now moving more quickly as Matilda continues.

                    MATILDA (CONT'D)
                (a little more confidently
                  now)
            The perspective on Earth's history
            from The Domain... it's
            unsettling, but there's a ring of
            truth to it. Maybe that's what's
            throwing me off.

The stenographer pauses again, looking at Matilda with raised
eyebrows, then shakes her head slightly and continues typing.

                    STENOGRAPHER
            Guess it's above our pay grade to
            figure that out.

                    MATILDA
                (nodding)
            Exactly.

Matilda hands her a list of books and materials, which the
stenographer adds to the files.

                    MATILDA (CONT'D)
            Make sure these get to Airl. She
            spends all night going through
            them.

The stenographer nods and gathers her notes, giving Matilda
one last look before leaving the office. Matilda sits in
silence for a moment, her hands resting on the desk as she
stares into the distance.

INT. MILITARY BRIEFING ROOM - DAY

Colonel William H. Blanchard sits at the head of a long
table, his face stern and focused as he reviews a transcript
of the stenographic dictation. The room is dimly lit, the
only sound being the rustle of paper as Blanchard turns the
pages. Matilda stands at attention near the doorway,
watching as Blanchard works.

                    BLANCHARD
                (without looking up, his
                  tone measured)
            Sergeant, you've been through quite
            the ordeal. These... reports are
            unlike anything we've ever seen.

                    MATILDA
                (steady but with a hint of
                  nerves)
                    (MORE)

MATILDA (CONT'D)
Yes, sir. It's... it's a lot to process.

Blanchard looks up from the transcript, his gaze piercing as he studies Matilda for a moment.

BLANCHARD
(with a slight frown)
How confident are you in this information, Sergeant?

MATILDA
(meeting his gaze directly)
As confident as I can be, sir. Airl... she doesn't seem to have any reason to lie.

Blanchard considers this, flipping to the next page. His brow furrows as he reads through the detailed accounts. He pauses, his fingers tapping lightly on the table.

BLANCHARD
(more to himself)
These implications...

He stands up and walks over to a nearby window, staring out into the distance.

BLANCHARD (CONT'D)
(still facing the window)
We're dealing with something far beyond our understanding, Sergeant. Something that could change... everything.

MATILDA
(quietly)
I know, sir.

Blanchard turns to face her, his expression hardening with resolve.

BLANCHARD
Keep doing your job, Sergeant. We need every piece of information we can get.

MATILDA
(sharp nod)
Yes, sir.

Blanchard nods back and watches her leave. He returns to the table, picking up the transcript once more, his face set with grim determination.

INT. ROSWELL ARMY AIR FORCE BASE - INTERVIEW ROOM - DAY

INSERT CARD: OFFICIAL TRANSCRIPT OF THE U.S. ARMY AIR FORCE ROSWELL ARMY AIR FIELD, 509TH BOMB GROUP SUBJECT: ALIEN INTERVIEW, 28. 7. 1947, 1ST SESSION

The room is eerily quiet as Matilda maintains eye contact with Airl, her notepad resting lightly on her lap, her pen poised but motionless. The telepathic connection between them hums with energy, the air thick with anticipation.

>> ALIEN (V.O.)
> The origins of this universe and life on Earth, as discussed in the textbooks I have read, are very inaccurate.

Matilda feels a flicker of unease. She shifts slightly in her chair but keeps her focus on Airl the Alien, knowing the importance of what is about to be shared.

>> MATILDA (V.O.)
> Inaccurate? How?

>> ALIEN (V.O.)
> The text of books I have been given on subjects related to the function of life forms contains information that is based on false memories, inaccurate observation, missing data, unproven theories, and superstition.

Matilda's hand tightens on the pen. Confusion and doubt are etched on her face.

>> MATILDA (V.O.)
> I've spent years studying, trusting the knowledge passed down through generations. Could it all be flawed?

>> ALIEN (V.O.)
> Just a few hundred years ago, your physicians practiced bloodletting as a means to release supposed ill humor from the body in an attempt to relieve or heal a wide variety of physical and mental afflictions.

									MATILDA (V.O.)
							(a touch defensive)
						But we've moved past that.
						Medicine has advanced.

									ALIEN (V.O.)
							(gently)
						Although this has been corrected
						somewhat, many barbarisms are still
						being practiced in the name of
						medical science.

Matilda's mind reels. She thinks of the procedures, the treatments still used today. How much of it, she wonders, is still rooted in misunderstanding?

									ALIEN (V.O.)
						Many primary errors that Earth
						scientists make are the result of
						ignorance of the nature and
						relative importance of IS-BEs as
						the source of energy and
						intelligence that animate every
						life form.

Matilda leans forward slightly, her curiosity piqued.

									MATILDA (V.O.)
						IS-BEs... You've mentioned them
						before. They're... what exactly?

									ALIEN (V.O.)
						The Immortal Spiritual Beings, the
						true essence that animates all
						life. Without understanding IS-
						BEs, your scientists miss the core
						of what life truly is.

Matilda's pen moves slightly, jotting down the words almost automatically. Her thoughts, however, are focused entirely on Airl's revelations.

									ALIEN (V.O.)
						The Domain Communications Office
						has authorized me to provide you
						with some information. This may
						help you to discover more effective
						solutions to the unique problems
						you face on Earth.

									MATILDA (V.O.)
						You mean... there's more I need to
						know?

                    ALIEN (V.O.)
          The correct information about the
          origins of biological entities has
          been erased from your mind, as well
          as from the minds of your mentors.
          In order to help you regain your
          own memory, I will share with you
          some factual material concerning
          the origin of biological entities.

Matilda swallows, her throat suddenly dry. The enormity of
what Airl the Alien is saying hits her like a tidal wave.
She steadies herself, ready to absorb whatever comes next.

                    MATILDA (V.O.)
                (determined)
          I'm ready. Tell me everything.

Airl's presence in her mind grows stronger, more focused, as
the alien begins to share knowledge that has been hidden from
humanity for millennia.

                    ALIEN (V.O.)
                (thoughts resonating with
                 calm clarity)
          You will find "evolution" mentioned
          in the ancient Vedic Hymns.

Matilda listens intently, absorbing each word as Airl
continues to share her knowledge telepathically.

                    ALIEN (V.O.)
          The Vedic texts are like folk tales
          or common wisdom and superstitions
          gathered throughout the systems of
          The Domain. These were compiled
          into verses, like a book of rhymes.
          For every statement of truth, the
          verses contain as many half-truths,
          reversals of truth, and fanciful
          imaginings, blended without
          qualification or distinction.

Matilda raises an eyebrow slightly, reflecting on the
complexities Airl describes.

                    ALIEN (V.O.)
                (with a hint of
                 frustration)
          The theory of evolution assumes
          that the motivational source of
          energy that animates every life
          form does not exist.
                         (MORE)

ALIEN (V.O.) (CONT'D)
It assumes that an inanimate object or a chemical concoction can suddenly become "alive" or animate accidentally or spontaneously. Or perhaps an electrical discharge into a pool of chemical ooze will magically spawn a self-animated entity.

Matilda nods subtly as if beginning to grasp the concept.

ALIEN (V.O.)
There is no evidence whatsoever that this is true, simply because it is not true. Dr. Frankenstein did not really resurrect the dead into a marauding monster, except in the imagination of the IS-BE who wrote a fictitious story one dark and stormy night.

Matilda's thoughts echo a silent agreement as she reflects on the influence of such fictional stories on human understanding.

ALIEN (V.O.)
(with a tone of revelation)
No Western scientist ever stopped to consider who, what, where, when, or how this animation happens. Complete ignorance, denial, or unawareness of the spirit as the source of life force required to animate inanimate objects or cellular tissue is the sole cause of failures in Western medicine.

Matilda, processing the weight of Airl's words, feels a deep sense of understanding washes over her.

MATILDA (V.O.)
(thoughtful)
"The spirit as the source of life force..." It changes everything we think we know.

The room falls into a contemplative silence, with Matilda still locked in telepathic communication with Airl the Alien, her mind opening to new possibilities.

ALIEN (V.O.)
This is the knowledge that has been erased from your understanding.
(MORE)

                  ALIEN (V.O.) (CONT'D)
        Without it, humanity fumbles in the
        dark, trying to piece together a
        puzzle with missing pieces.

Matilda takes a deep breath, her mind reeling yet determined to comprehend the depth of this revelation.

                  MATILDA (V.O.)
          (resolute)
        I must remember this. Somehow, I
        need to make them see—make them
        understand.

Airl's thoughts convey a sense of calm certainty.

                  ALIEN (V.O.)
        I will share more with you,
        Matilda. We will uncover the truth
        together.

Matilda, feeling a newfound resolve, prepares herself for what comes next, ready to learn more from Airl.

                  MATILDA (V.O.)
          (resolute)
        I'm ready, Airl. Let's continue.

Airl's presence seems to fill the room with an unspoken promise of deeper revelations yet to come.

INT. ROSWELL ARMY AIR FORCE BASE - BARRACKS - NIGHT

Matilda lies in her bunk, her eyes open but unfocused, staring into the darkness of the barracks.

The room is silent, except for the faint hum of the base's operations filtering through the walls. She shifts slightly, trying to find a comfortable position, but sleep eludes her. Her mind races, replaying the day's events, the telepathic interview, and the overwhelming information Airl shared.

                  ALIEN (V.O.)
          (echoing in Matilda's
           mind)
        Evolution does not occur
        accidentally. It requires a great
        deal of technology, carefully
        manipulated under the supervision
        of IS-BEs.

Matilda closes her eyes tightly, as if trying to shut out the voice, but it only grows stronger, more insistent.

213.

> ALIEN (V.O.)
> (echoing)
> The idea that human bodies evolved naturally from ape-like forms is incorrect.

Matilda's brow furrows in concentration. Her hands clutch the blanket, pulling it up closer to her chin as if seeking protection from the onslaught of thoughts invading her mind.

> ALIEN (V.O.)
> (echoing)
> The notion that modern humanoid bodies evolved on this planet is a hypnotic lie, designed to prevent your recollection of the true origins of Mankind.

Matilda's breathing quickens, her chest rising and falling in time with the rhythm of Airl's words, as if the voice is taking over her very breath.

> ALIEN (V.O.)
> (echoing)
> Humanoid bodies have existed in various forms throughout the universe for trillions of years.

A deep sense of unease washes over Matilda. Her eyes snap open, wide and alert. She pushes herself up, leaning against the wall, her mind racing with questions and doubts.

The weight of the knowledge presses down on her, making her feel small, insignificant, yet somehow connected to a vast and ancient truth.

Matilda sits there, staring into the void of the darkened room, as the voice of Airl fades into the background of her thoughts, leaving behind an indelible mark on her consciousness.

INT. ROSWELL ARMY AIR FORCE BASE - CONTROL ROOM - DAY

Colonel William H. Blanchard and Captain Sheridan Cavitt stand side by side, observing the interview room through the one-way glass window. Their eyes are fixed on Airl the Alien and Matilda.

> WILLIAM H. BLANCHARD
> (leaning closer to the glass)
> Airl knows we're watching, doesn't she?

                    SHERIDAN D. CAVITT
               (nods)
          No doubt about it. Airl's
          awareness is... unsettling. You'd
          think this glass would give us some
          sense of control.

                    WILLIAM H. BLANCHARD
          It's just a formality now. We're
          fooling ourselves if we think we're
          not part of this conversation.

Cavitt glances at Blanchard, concern evident.

                    SHERIDAN D. CAVITT
          Do you think it's wise to let this
          continue? What if she's
          manipulating us through Matilda?

                    WILLIAM H. BLANCHARD
               (pauses, thoughtful)
          We have to take that risk. We need
          to know what she knows. Every word
          she conveys could be vital.

They both turn their attention back to Airl and Matilda, the weight of uncertainty hanging heavily between them.

                    SHERIDAN D. CAVITT
          I just hope Matilda can handle
          this. The information... it's
          beyond anything we've ever dealt
          with.

                    WILLIAM H. BLANCHARD
               (softly)
          She's tougher than she looks. But
          even the toughest have their
          breaking point. We'll have to keep
          a close watch on her, too.

Blanchard's eyes narrow slightly, betraying a hint of doubt as he continues to study the interaction between the alien and the sergeant.

                    SHERIDAN D. CAVITT
          Whatever happens, we can't let this
          get out. The world's not ready for
          what's on the other side of that
          glass.

Blanchard nods, resolute.

                    WILLIAM H. BLANCHARD
          Agreed. This stays between us and
          Airl... for now.

They continue to observe the silence of the room filled with
the tension of the unknown.

INT. ROSWELL ARMY AIR FORCE BASE - MESS HALL - DAY

The mess hall is mostly empty, with two MILITARY POLICE
OFFICERS standing guard near the entrance. At a table in the
middle, three men sit together, picking at their meals.

The Military official, a hardened veteran, glares at his food
before looking up at the others.

                    MILITARY OFFICIAL
          This is getting old. We've been
          part of this operation from day
          one. Now we're being sidelined
          like we don't matter.

The government agent, wearing a drab suit with a perpetual
frown, nods, leaning forward.

                    GOVERNMENT AGENT
          Blanchard acts like he's the only
          one who can handle this. We barely
          get any time with the alien, and
          when we do, it's like he's watching
          our every move.

The scientist, wearing a lab coat and glasses, taps his fork
against the table, clearly agitated.

                    SCIENTIST
              (annoyed)
          I've been asking for direct access
          to Airl for weeks. I need more
          than just brief glimpses to
          understand what's really going on.
          Blanchard just keeps saying it's
          "classified."

                    MILITARY OFFICIAL
          He's overstepping. We're supposed
          to be a team, but he's treating us
          like outsiders. We need full
          access to Airl to do our jobs.
          This is bigger than just one man's
          jurisdiction.

                    GOVERNMENT AGENT
          Exactly. The way he's handling
          this, it's like he's got something
          to hide. What's so dangerous that
          he can't trust us with it?

                    SCIENTIST
               (sighs)
          I don't think he realizes the
          potential here. Airl has knowledge
          that could change everything we
          know about science, about history.
          We're wasting time with all these
          restrictions.

                    MILITARY OFFICIAL
          If we push too hard, we risk
          getting cut out completely. But if
          we don't push, we're just wasting
          time. We need to make Blanchard
          understand—we're in this together.
          He can't keep treating us like
          we're the enemy.

                    GOVERNMENT AGENT
               (leaning back)
          Maybe it's time we had a little
          talk with the Colonel. Make him
          see reason. This is our operation
          too. We can't let him lock us out.

                    SCIENTIST
               (quietly)
          We don't have much choice. It's
          either we push for more access, or
          we sit here twiddling our thumbs
          while the biggest discovery in
          human history slips through our
          fingers.

The three men exchange determined looks, each silently
agreeing that things need to change. The guards remain at
their posts, unaware of the plans forming just a few feet
away.

INT. ROSWELL ARMY AIR FORCE BASE - INTERVIEW ROOM - DAY

Sergeant Matilda O'Donnell MacElroy sits across from Airl,
the Alien, in the dimly lit interview room. Matilda's eyes
are focused, her notepad resting on her lap. Airl's large,
dark eyes seem to stare beyond the walls as if lost in a
distant memory. The room feels heavy with the weight of
their silent communication.

                    ALIEN (V.O.)
               (ethereal and calm)
          Thousands of years ago, when our
          forces established a base in the
          Himalayan Mountains, some of my
          comrades sought to interact with
          the local inhabitants. They found
          the humans to be curious and eager
          to learn. Perhaps it was boredom
          or a desire to share, but the
          verses of the Vedic Hymns were
          taught to them.

FLASHBACK:

EXT. HIMALAYAN MOUNTAINS - NIGHT

The snow-capped peaks of the Himalayas rise under a starry
sky. A small group of humans gathers around a glowing fire,
their faces illuminated by the flickering light. Domain
officers, distinct in their otherworldly presence, stand
among them, gesturing gently with their hands. The humans
listen intently, eyes wide, as if absorbing the mysteries of
the universe.

                    ALIEN (V.O.)
               (sublime tone)
          It was not a directive from The
          Domain. These teachings were a
          departure from protocol, a
          momentary lapse, as they felt the
          urge to share knowledge with the
          primitive beings of Earth. I
          understand now that it seemed like
          an innocent diversion at the time.
          A way to pass down wisdom to
          creatures who looked to the stars
          with wonder.

END FLASHBACK.

INT. ROSWELL ARMY AIR FORCE BASE - INTERVIEW ROOM - DAY

Airl continues to sit, unmoving, yet an aura of presence
fills the room. Matilda captivated, jots down notes as if
the words are flowing straight from Airl's mind to her pen.

                    ALIEN (V.O.)
               (a hint of regret)
          The Vedic Hymns carried fragments
          of truth, mixed with human
          interpretations and imaginations.
                         (MORE)

                    ALIEN (V.O.) (CONT'D)
          Though they were mere echoes of the
          vast knowledge held by The Domain,
          these hymns have shaped the
          spiritual foundations of many
          civilizations on Earth.

MONTAGE:

EXT. HIMALAYAS - DAY

A sequence of scenes showing humans from different ages and places, chanting the Vedic Hymns. A sage in an ancient forest, a young student by a river, a congregation in a vast temple. Their voices blend into a single, continuous chant, resonating with a knowledge that transcends time.

END MONTAGE.

INT. ROSWELL ARMY AIR FORCE BASE - INTERVIEW ROOM - DAY

Matilda's face shows a mix of awe and comprehension as she absorbs Airl's revelation. The room is quiet, save for the subtle hum of the base outside.

                    ALIEN (V.O.)
               (softly)
          But such actions, though well-
          intentioned, have unforeseen
          consequences. The truths we shared
          have been diluted, misinterpreted,
          and turned into tools of control.
          This is the burden of knowledge,
          Matilda: to see the light but
          understand the shadows it casts.

Matilda nods slightly, her understanding deepening. She knows that what she learns here could change everything, not just for her, but for all of humanity.

Airl remains seated, her gaze steady and unblinking, as she conveys her thoughts to Matilda. Matilda's hand moves almost automatically, writing down everything she receives, her eyes never leaving Airl's.

                    ALIEN (V.O.)
               (serene and thoughtful)
          The Vedic Hymns were not intended
          to be anything more than stories, a
          simple diversion for those who
          shared them.
                              (MORE)

> ALIEN (V.O.) (CONT'D)
> Yet, over the millennia, these verses were passed down verbally through the generations, from the foothills of the Himalayas and eventually spreading throughout India.

MONTAGE:

I/E. INDIA - DAY AND NIGHT

Scenes of different teachers and disciples through the ages: a bearded sage sits under a tree, a young boy listens intently, a woman in simple clothing teaches a group of children. Their mouths move in silent recitation, the rhythm of the verses binding them together across time and space.

> ALIEN (V.O.)
> (hint of irony)
> In The Domain, no one credits the Vedic Hymns as factual material. They are regarded with the same gravity as your 'Grimm's Fairy Tales' might be. But on Earth, where all IS-BEs have had their memories erased, it's no surprise that these tales and fantasies could be mistaken for truth.

END MONTAGE.

INT. ROSWELL ARMY AIR FORCE BASE - INTERVIEW ROOM - DAY

Matilda writes furiously, her pen moving across the paper, recording every detail. Her face is a mix of fascination and concern as she absorbs Airl's revelations. Airl's presence remains calm, almost dispassionate, as she continues to share her knowledge.

Airl the Alien voice is heard, she cautiously expounds.

> ALIEN (V.O.)
> The humans who learned the Vedic verses began to tell others that these stories came from 'the gods.' Over time, the metaphorical language and allegorical nature of the verses were lost. What was once a poetic expression of ideas was soon adopted as literal truth.

MONTAGE:

I/E. INDIA - DAY AND NIGHT

Various scenes of priests and scribes inscribing the verses onto palm leaves, teaching groups of followers, and the verses being recited in grand temples. Statues of gods and goddesses are worshipped, rituals are performed, and devotees bow in reverence.

Airl's voice expresses a touch of sadness.

                    ALIEN (V.O.)
     The original philosophical essence
     of the Vedic teachings was ignored.
     Instead, the literal interpretation
     of the verses became the basis for
     nearly every religious practice on
     Earth, particularly in what you
     know as Hinduism.

END MONTAGE.

INT. ROSWELL ARMY AIR FORCE BASE - INTERVIEW ROOM - DAY

Matilda stops writing for a moment, looking up at Airl with wide eyes. She takes a deep breath, feeling the weight of the information pressing on her. Airl's eyes remain steady, filled with an ancient wisdom that seems beyond human comprehension.

                    ALIEN (V.O.)
     The minds of Earth's inhabitants
     have been shaped by these verses,
     their thoughts and beliefs molded
     by words meant to entertain rather
     than to educate. The truth has
     been lost, buried under the weight
     of devotion and dogma.

Matilda nods slightly, acknowledging the profound implications of Airl's words. She feels a mixture of awe and unease, realizing that what she is learning could change everything she thought she knew about human history and belief.

                    ALIEN (V.O.)
     As an officer and pilot of The
     Domain, I rely on facts, not
     philosophy, to accomplish my
     missions.
                      (MORE)

                    ALIEN (V.O.) (CONT'D)
          Our discussion of history is based
          on actual events, long before IS-
          BEs arrived on Earth, or the 'Old
          Empire' came to power. I can share
          some of this history from personal
          experience.

Matilda's pen suddenly and rapidly jots notes on the notepad,
her eyes locked with Aril's.

                    MATILDA (V.O.)
          It's a complex form of deception,
          and all for what?

FLASHBACK:

EXT. ARCANE GALAXY - SPACE - NIGHT

A vibrant galaxy, far from the Milky Way, twinkles with
millions of star systems. Uninhabited planets orbit their
suns, lifeless and barren, waiting for creation.

                    ALIEN (V.O.)
               (steady, reflective)
          Many billions of years ago, I was a
          member of a vast biological
          laboratory in a distant galaxy. It
          was called the Arcadia Regeneration
          Company. Our mission was to create
          life—new forms to populate
          uninhabited planets.

EXT. ARCANE PLANET - DAY

A sprawling, advanced laboratory complex sits on the surface
of a lush planet. Beings of various shapes and sizes work
meticulously, their hands and instruments moving with
precision and purpose.

                    ALIEN (V.O.)
               (calm, focused)
          I was a biological engineer,
          working alongside a large team of
          technicians. It was our business
          to manufacture and supply life
          forms to planets waiting to be
          inhabited.

INT. ARCANE LABORATORY - MAIN WORKSHOP - DAY

Airl, in a sleek, streamlined form, oversees technicians manipulating genetic sequences. They mold and alter genetic patterns, creating unique and varied species. Tubes and vats filled with glowing liquids pulse with life, awaiting deployment.

> ALIEN (V.O.)
> There were millions of star systems with millions of planets ready for life. Our work was to ensure each planet received species suited to its environment. The basic genetic material was common to all life forms, so most of our work involved subtle manipulations—alterations to fit the needs of each world.

EXT. NEWLY POPULATED PLANET - DAY

Lush greenery and alien creatures thrive on the surface of a once-barren planet. Beings of diverse shapes and sizes roam the landscape, perfectly adapted to their surroundings.

> ALIEN (V.O.)
> (softly)
> There were many biological laboratories like ours, each specializing in different kinds of life forms, depending on the 'class' of the planet. Over time, we developed a vast catalog of species across the galaxies.

INT. ARCANE LABORATORY - ARCHIVE ROOM - DAY

Shelves upon shelves of data crystals and holographic records line the walls. Each one catalogs a species, a planet, and a creation.

> ALIEN (V.O.)
> (solemn)
> Our work was to ensure the continuation of life, to populate the stars with diverse and thriving ecosystems. A legacy of creation spread throughout the universe.

EXT. ARCANE GALAXY - SPACE - NIGHT

The galaxy spins on, teeming with life, thanks to the efforts of the Arcadia Regeneration Company and countless others like them.

> ALIEN (V.O.)
> (whispering)
> That was my life, long before Earth, long before the 'Old Empire'... a time when creation itself was my mission.

END FLASHBACK.

INT. ROSWELL ARMY AIR FORCE BASE - CONFERENCE ROOM - DAY

Tension fills the air. The government agent, scientist, and military official sit across the table from Colonel William H. Blanchard. Their faces are a mix of frustration and impatience. The walls seem to close in as their grievances take center stage.

> GOVERNMENT AGENT
> (leaning forward)
> Colonel, we're all professionals here. But this restricted access is hindering our ability to assess the situation properly. We need more interaction with the entity.

> SCIENTIST
> (nodding in agreement)
> We're talking about an unprecedented opportunity for research. Every moment without direct access is a lost opportunity for discovery. I can't conduct any meaningful study with these limitations.

> MILITARY OFFICIAL
> (slightly agitated)
> And from a security standpoint, Colonel, my team needs to be more involved. The situation is too volatile to keep us on the sidelines. We should be in that room, monitoring every interaction.

Colonel Blanchard listens calmly, his face unreadable. He waits for them to finish before speaking.

                    WILLIAM H. BLANCHARD
                (steady and firm)
            I understand your concerns. But
            let's not forget what we're dealing
            with here. This isn't a science
            project or a political maneuver.

                    GOVERNMENT AGENT
                (interrupting)
            With all due respect, Colonel, this
            is more than just about security.
            The implications of this situation
            go far beyond Roswell.

                    SCIENTIST
                (urgently)
            We need data, Colonel. Real data.
            And for that, we need more access.

Blanchard's eyes narrow slightly. He leans forward, his
voice dropping a notch.

                    WILLIAM H. BLANCHARD
                (intense)
            I get it. You all have your roles
            to play. But my responsibility is
            the overall security and
            containment of this... situation.

                    MILITARY OFFICIAL
                (pressing)
            Colonel, we—

                    WILLIAM H. BLANCHARD
                (cutting him off)
            No. This isn't up for debate.
            It's contingent on a need-to-know
            basis. And right now, you don't
            need to know more than what you're
            being given.

The room falls silent. The government agent, scientist, and
military official exchange frustrated glances, knowing
there's no arguing with the Colonel's final word.

                    WILLIAM H. BLANCHARD (CONT'D)
                (standing up)
            This meeting is over.

Colonel Blanchard exits the room, leaving the three men to
simmer in their discontent.

INT. ROSWELL ARMY AIR FORCE BASE - OFFICE - NIGHT

The room is dimly lit, shadows cast by the single desk lamp flicker across Colonel Blanchard's stern face. The weight of the day hangs heavy on his shoulders. He reaches for a Top-Secret memo marked with the insignia of Lieutenant General Roger M. Ramey. The envelope is crisp, sealed with authority. As he opens it and begins to read, the voice of General Ramey echoes in his mind, deep and resolute.

> ROGER M. RAMEY (V.O.)
> It is of the utmost importance that "I," General Ramey be apprised immediately of the situation with the Alien.

Blanchard's brow furrows as he continues reading, the seriousness of the situation deepening with each word.

> ROGER M. RAMEY (V.O.)
> President Truman is aware of the situation and is forming a top-secret committee to oversee the whole operation.

Blanchard's grip tightens on the paper. He leans back in his chair, the weight of the memo sinking in. His eyes scan the room, settling momentarily on the picture of his family on the desk. The stakes have just been raised, and the burden of what lies ahead presses down on him.

He folds the memo carefully and places it back on his desk, staring at it as if it might somehow provide the answers he needs. The silence in the room is deafening, broken only by the faint ticking of the clock on the wall.

Blanchard exhales slowly, gathering his thoughts, knowing that every decision he makes from here on out could change the course of history.

INT. ROSWELL ARMY AIR FORCE BASE - INTERVIEW ROOM - DAY

Matilda listens intently, her expression a mixture of fascination and concentration. Airl's telepathic voice fills her mind, calm yet laden with the weight of vast experience.

> ALIEN (V.O.)
> The "Arcadia Regeneration Company" specialized in mammals for forested areas and birds for tropical regions.
> (MORE)

                    ALIEN (V.O.) (CONT'D)
               Our marketing staff negotiated
               contracts with various planetary
               governments and independent buyers
               from all over the universe.

Matilda takes a deep breath, her mind trying to grasp the
magnitude of what Airl is describing.

                    ALIEN (V.O.)
               Technicians created animals that
               were compatible with variations in
               climate, atmospheric and
               terrestrial density, and chemical
               content. We were also paid to
               integrate our specimens with
               biological organisms already living
               on a planet, engineered by other
               companies.

Matilda scribbles notes, though her mind is fully engaged in
telepathic communication. She hesitates for a moment, then
mentally asks the question that has been forming in her mind.

                    MATILDA (V.O.)
               You mentioned working with other
               companies. How did you communicate
               with them across such vast
               distances?

                    ALIEN (V.O.)
               We communicated through industry
               trade shows, publications, and a
               variety of information supplied
               through an association that
               coordinated related projects. This
               was not much different from how
               your corporations interact with one
               another on Earth.

Matilda nods to herself, her pen moving quickly across the
paper.

                    ALIEN (V.O.)
               Our research required extensive
               interstellar travel to conduct
               planetary surveys. That is when I
               learned my skills as a pilot.

Matilda pauses, intrigued by the mention of Airl's piloting
skills.

                    MATILDA (V.O.)
               So, you were not only a biological
               engineer but also a pilot?

                    ALIEN (V.O.)
          Yes. The data gathered from our
          surveys was accumulated in massive
          computer databases, then evaluated
          by biological engineers like
          myself. We needed to understand the
          unique conditions of each planet to
          ensure that the life forms we
          created would thrive.

Matilda absorbs this, her thoughts racing to keep up with the
flow of information.

                    MATILDA (V.O.)
          It sounds so... advanced. Beyond
          anything we could imagine.

                    ALIEN (V.O.)
          To you, it may seem that way. But
          to us, it was simply our work—our
          purpose.

Matilda feels a deep sense of awe, realizing that she is
hearing about an era and an industry that predates everything
she knows.

The room falls into a heavy silence, broken only by the faint
hum of equipment, as Matilda continues to process the
extraordinary knowledge being shared with her.

Matilda sits in silence, her eyes wide as Airl's telepathic
voice echoes in her mind.

                    ALIEN (V.O.)
          A computer is an electronic device
          that serves as an artificial brain,
          capable of storing information,
          making computations, solving
          problems, and performing mechanical
          functions.

MONTAGE:

EXT. PLANETARY ADMINISTRATION CENTER - GALACTIC SYSTEM - DAY

Massive, shimmering towers stretch into the sky, glowing with
energy. A vast computer hub hums within, its circuits
endlessly processing data and overseeing planetary functions.

                    ALIEN (V.O.)
          In most of the galactic systems of
          the universe, huge computers are
          commonly used to run the routine
          administration, mechanical
          services, and maintenance
          activities of an entire planet or
          planetary system.

INT. BIOLOGICAL LABORATORY - ARCOSIS PLANET - NIGHT

Technicians in sleek uniforms input data into a colossal
computer system. Holographic displays show detailed
planetary surveys, while 3D models of life forms rotate in
the air.

                    ALIEN (V.O.)
          Based on the survey data gathered,
          designs and artistic renderings
          were made for new creatures.

EXT. INTERSTELLAR AUCTION HOUSE - STARPORT - DAY

A bustling interstellar auction house filled with alien
buyers. Holographic screens display life forms for sale:
majestic birds, fearsome predators, and elegant mammals.

                    ALIEN (V.O.)
          Some designs were sold to the
          highest bidder.

INT. PRIVATE LABORATORY - CUSTOM BIO-ENGINEERING FACILITY -
NIGHT

Scientists craft a unique creature from scratch, responding
to the exact specifications of an alien client. The client's
image hovers on a communication screen, approving the design.

                    ALIEN (V.O.)
          Other life forms were created to
          meet the customized requests of our
          clients.

EXT. TROPICAL PLANET - DAY

Newly created birds soar through vibrant forests, their
exotic colors blending perfectly with the surroundings. A
peaceful mammal grazes nearby, its design a perfect fit for
the lush environment.

                    ALIEN (V.O.)
          These creations were designed to
          integrate seamlessly into their
          environments, ensuring balance and
          harmony across the galaxies.

END MONTAGE.

INT. ROSWELL ARMY AIR FORCE BASE - INTERVIEW ROOM - DAY

Matilda leans forward, absorbing the incredible scope of the
galactic bio-engineering industry. Airl's presence fills the
room, both distant and deeply connected.

                    ALIEN (V.O.)
          To us, it was a vast network of
          creation and design—a complex
          system that spanned galaxies,
          driven by the need to populate
          worlds with life.

EXT. ROSWELL ARMY AIR FORCE BASE - BARRACKS - NIGHT

Two stern-faced MILITARY POLICE stand guard outside the
barracks door. Their post is silent, save for the distant
hum of night insects and the occasional shuffle of boots on
gravel. The sky above them is a vast canvas of stars,
stretching endlessly across the darkened landscape.

INT. ROSWELL ARMY AIR FORCE BASE - BARRACKS - NIGHT

Matilda is alone, sitting on the edge of her bunk. Her hands
rest on her lap, fingers absentmindedly twisting together as
her mind races. The sterile room feels even colder tonight,
the hum of the fluorescent lights overhead almost oppressive.

She rises slowly, drawn to the window as if by an invisible
force. The night outside is crystal clear, and the stars
glimmer like distant beacons. Matilda presses her palm
against the cool glass, her breath fogging up a small circle
as she gazes out, captivated by the vastness of the universe.

Her mind is consumed by the revelations Airl shared with
her—the unimaginable expanse of life beyond Earth, the
intricate web of creation and manipulation across galaxies,
and the idea that everything she once believed may be just a
fragment of the truth.

A sense of wonder mixes with a creeping unease. The world
she thought she knew seemed smaller, less significant now.

She closes her eyes for a moment, trying to quiet her racing thoughts, but Airl's words echo in her mind.

> ALIEN (V.O.)
> The stars you see are only a fraction of the whole—each one a gateway, a link in the endless chain of life that spans the universe. And yet, the truths hidden behind them are far more complex than you could ever imagine.

Matilda opens her eyes, feeling both overwhelmed and enlightened. She knows that her life, her understanding of the world, has been irrevocably changed. The vast night sky stares back at her, indifferent yet full of secrets.

She takes a deep breath, standing still at the window, as the weight of what she has learned begins to settle within her. Somewhere, beyond those stars, lies the truth—a truth she is only beginning to grasp.

EXT. FORT WORTH ARMY AIRFIELD - DAY

The bright blue sky is pierced by the roaring engine of a P-38 "Lightning" fighter plane. Its sleek silhouette glides through the air with precision, the landing gear extended as it prepares for descent.

The plane touches down on the runway with a smooth bounce, its tires screeching against the asphalt before it slows to a steady roll.

INT. FORT WORTH ARMY AIRFIELD - OFFICE OF ROGER M. RAMEY - DAY

The office is a blend of military efficiency and personal pride. A large map of the United States hangs on one wall, with various strategic markers pinned on it. The room smells faintly of leather and polished wood.

Seated behind a formidable desk is Lieutenant General Roger M. Ramey, wearing his meticulously decorated Air Force uniform. He is focused intently on a document stamped with "EYES ONLY," his eyes scanning each line with a critical gaze.

A sharp knock on the door breaks the silence. General Ramey barely glances up from the document.

> ROGER M. RAMEY
> (without looking up)
> Enter.

An ARMY OFFICER steps inside, his posture stiff with protocol.

> ARMY OFFICER
> Sir, Colonel William H. Blanchard has arrived.

> ROGER M. RAMEY
> (nodding)
> Show him in.

The officer exits, and moments later, Colonel William H. Blanchard enters the room. Blanchard's expression is serious, and his uniform is neatly pressed. He moves with the confidence of someone used to bearing heavy responsibilities. He takes a seat across from Ramey.

General Ramey closing the document and setting it aside.

> ROGER M. RAMEY (CONT'D)
> Colonel Blanchard, I trust your journey was uneventful.

> WILLIAM H. BLANCHARD
> (with a slight nod)
> Yes, sir. Straightforward flight.

General Ramey leans forward slightly, his tone growing more intense.

> ROGER M. RAMEY
> Good. Now, what's the latest on our... visitor?

Blanchard straightens, his voice measured but low.

> WILLIAM H. BLANCHARD
> Sir, the situation remains delicate. The entity—Airl—continues to cooperate, but her communications are complex. The information she's providing is... beyond anything we've encountered before. It's above top secret, sir. Even our most secure channels feel inadequate.

General Ramey's eyes narrow slightly, absorbing the gravity of the situation.

>   ROGER M. RAMEY
>   And her intentions? Do we have any
>   indication of a threat?
>
>   WILLIAM H. BLANCHARD
>   None so far. She seems more
>   interested in sharing knowledge
>   than causing harm. But the scope
>   of what she knows... it could
>   change everything, sir. We're
>   still assessing the full extent.

Ramey taps his fingers on the desk, considering Blanchard's words carefully.

>   ROGER M. RAMEY
>   We need to ensure that this
>   knowledge stays contained.
>   President Truman is aware, and he's
>   forming a top-secret committee to
>   oversee the operation. But until
>   then, all information stays between
>   us and the necessary personnel. No
>   leaks, no exceptions.
>
>   WILLIAM H. BLANCHARD
>   (gravely)
>   Understood, sir. We're taking
>   every precaution.

Ramey nods, satisfied for the moment.

>   ROGER M. RAMEY
>   Good. Keep me informed, Colonel.
>   This is far from over.
>
>   WILLIAM H. BLANCHARD
>   (standing up)
>   Yes, sir.

Blanchard turns to leave, but there's a heaviness in the air as both men understand the magnitude of what they're dealing with. As Blanchard exits, Ramey watches him go, his mind already racing with the implications of the situation.

The door closes softly behind Blanchard, leaving Ramey alone in the office once more. He looks down at the "EYES ONLY" document, his expression unreadable as the weight of the secrets he holds settles over him like a shroud.

FLASHBACK:

EXT. ALIEN PLANET - DAY

A lush, tropical landscape filled with strange, vibrant plant life. Exotic creatures roam the terrain, each one uniquely adapted to the environment.

> ALIEN (V.O.)
> After a new life form was introduced, we closely monitored their interaction with the planetary environment and the other indigenous life forms. It was essential to ensure harmony.

EXT. ALIEN PLANET - RIVERBANK - DAY

A newly introduced species of mammal drinks from a river. Nearby, a native creature watches cautiously.

> ALIEN (V.O.)
> Conflicts between incompatible organisms often arose. When they did, we entered negotiations with other companies.

INT. BIOLOGICAL LABORATORY - DAY

A vast, futuristic lab filled with engineers and technicians. Airl, in her human-like form, stands before a large holographic map of the planet, discussing the issues with a group of alien technicians.

> ALIEN (V.O.)
> These talks usually led to compromises. Modifications to our creations, or theirs, were necessary.

EXT. ALIEN PLANET - FOREST - DAY

A new, modified creature interacts peacefully with a native species. The ecosystem thrives.

> ALIEN (V.O.)
> This delicate process of negotiation and alteration is part of what you might call "Eugenics." But for us, it was an art form—one that required balance and care.

END FLASHBACK.

INT. ROSWELL ARMY AIR FORCE BASE - INTERVIEW ROOM - DAY

The dimly lit room feels heavy with tension. The invasive eye of a camera mounted in the corner quietly hums, its unblinking lens focused on the small table where Airl, the extraterrestrial being, sits opposite Matilda. Behind them, the one-way glass window looms, an ever-present reminder that they are under constant surveillance.

Matilda's eyes lock onto Airl's. Their gaze is intense, unwavering. No words are spoken aloud, yet the air feels thick with conversation as if an invisible current of thought passes between them.

> ALIEN (V.O.)
> In some cases, we made alterations to the planetary environment itself, though such measures were rare. Planet building, you see, is far more complex than making adjustments to a single life form.

Matilda listens intently, her brow furrowed slightly as she absorbs the information. Airl's presence is calm but powerful, her thoughts flowing effortlessly into Matilda's mind.

> ALIEN (V.O)
> Coincidentally, a friend and fellow engineer from the Arcadia Regeneration Company once shared with me a story. This was long after I had left the company. They had contracted a project to deliver life forms to Earth. This was done to replenish the planet after a war in this region of the galaxy had devastated nearly all life forms here.

Matilda's eyes widen slightly, her mind racing to comprehend the vastness of the information.

> MATILDA (V.O.)
> Seventy million years ago?

> ALIEN (V.O.)
> Yes. Around that time. The project involved introducing new species to Earth, filling the void left by the destruction. The remnants of that event still echo in your planet's history.

Matilda's grip tightens on the edge of the table as the weight of the revelation settles in. The hum of the camera continues in the background, a constant reminder that every moment of this conversation is being monitored, dissected, and analyzed.

Matilda remains seated across from Airl, her expression a mix of awe and deep contemplation. The quiet hum of the camera persists in the background, but Matilda's focus is entirely on the telepathic voice in her mind.

> ALIEN (V.O,)
> The skill required to modify this planet into an ecologically interactive environment capable of supporting billions of diverse species was immense. Specialized consultants from nearly every biotechnology company in the galaxy were involved.

Matilda's thoughts swirl as she envisions the magnitude of such a project, her fingers tapping the table in nervous rhythm.

> ALIEN (V.O.)
> What you see now on Earth—the vast array of life forms—is the result of that collaboration. Your scientists mistakenly attribute this diversity to a "theory of evolution." In truth, all life forms on this planet, and on any other, were created by companies like ours.

Matilda's eyes narrow in thought, trying to reconcile this information with everything she has known.

> MATILDA (V.O.)
> But how could such a grand design be mistaken for natural evolution? The sheer complexity...

> ALIEN (V.O.)
> How else can you explain the millions of completely divergent and unrelated species on land and in the oceans of this planet? The truth is the spiritual animation that defines every living creature is not a product of random chance.

Matilda leans forward slightly, her curiosity piqued.

                    MATILDA (V.O.)
               You speak of spiritual animation...
               the soul?

                    ALIEN (V.O.)
               Yes. To say it is the work of
               "god" is far too simplistic. Every
               IS-BE, every sentient being, has
               many names, many faces, across
               different times and places. Every
               IS-BE is, in essence, a god. When
               they inhabit a physical object,
               they are the source of life.

Matilda absorbs Airl's words, her mind struggling to grasp
the implications. The understanding that every living being,
every form of life, is animated by a sentient spirit—a god in
its own right—upends everything she has ever believed.

                    MATILDA (V.O.)
               So... every living thing here...
               is more than just flesh and bone?

                    ALIEN (V.O.)
               Indeed. Each IS-BE is a source of
               life. You, too, are an IS-BE,
               Matilda.

The room seems to grow even quieter as the weight of Airl's
revelation hangs in the air. Matilda's gaze drifts for a
moment, her mind contemplating the interconnectedness of all
things, the vast network of life across the universe, all
tied together by this mysterious force—IS-BEs.

She returns her focus to Airl, feeling a strange sense of
kinship with this alien being who seems to hold the secrets
of the universe in her telepathic grasp.

INT. ROSWELL ARMY AIR FORCE BASE - OFFICE - EVENING

Colonel William H. Blanchard sits behind his desk, the dim
light casting a shadow across his furrowed brow. His fingers
tap rhythmically on the pile of transcripts in front of him —
transcripts from Matilda's interviews with Airl the Alien.

Blanchard's eyes scan the page, his focus sharp, absorbing
the words that seem to jump off the paper. The ticking of a
nearby clock is the only sound in the room, though
Blanchard's thoughts are racing.

                    ALIEN (V.O.)
               There are millions of species of
               insects.
                         (MORE)

                    ALIEN (V.O.) (CONT'D)
          About 350,000 of these are species
          of beetles. There may be as many
          as 100 million species of life
          forms on Earth at any given time.
          In addition, there are many times
          more extinct species of life on
          Earth than there are living life
          forms. Some of these will be
          rediscovered in the fossil or
          geological records of Earth.

Blanchard stops, lifting his gaze, staring into the distance, but his mind is back in the interview room. Airl's words echo through his thoughts, turning everything, he knows about Earth and evolution into something foreign and unsettling.

He rubs his temples, grappling with the weight of the revelation.

                    ALIEN (V.O.)
          The current 'theory of evolution'
          of life forms on Earth does not
          consider the phenomena of
          biological diversity. Evolution by
          natural selection is science
          fiction. One species does not
          accidentally, or randomly evolve to
          become another species, as the
          Earth textbooks indicate, without
          manipulation of genetic material by
          an IS-BE.

Blanchard exhales slowly. The truth in front of him shakes the foundation of all known science. His military training, so steeped in discipline and rigid understanding, struggles to reconcile with these new concepts. His hand unconsciously grips the edge of the desk as Airl's voice continues in his head.

                    ALIEN (V.O.)
          A simple example of IS-BE
          intervention is the selective
          breeding of a species on Earth.
          Within the past few hundred years,
          several hundred dog breeds,
          hundreds of varieties of pigeons,
          and dozens of Koi fish have
          'evolved' in just a few years,
          beginning with only one original
          breed.

Blanchard flips through more pages, reading faster now, as though the words themselves might unravel the mysteries of the universe before him. His heart races, but outwardly, his face remains stoic.

> ALIEN (V.O.)
> Without active intervention by IS-BEs, biological organisms rarely change.

Blanchard closes the transcript, resting his hands on top of it. He leans back in his chair, staring at the ceiling for a moment, lost in thought. What does this mean for humanity? For everything they've been taught. He swallows hard, feeling the weight of responsibility. The revelation is too immense to comprehend fully, yet he knows he must.

The clock continues its steady ticking as Blanchard prepares himself for the inevitable confrontation between the known and the unknown.

> WILLIAM H. BLANCHARD
> (muttering)
> What in God's name are we dealing with?

The room feels smaller now, as though the boundaries of the world he once knew have been shattered, leaving only the vast unknown ahead.

INT. ROSWELL ARMY AIR FORCE BASE - INTERVIEW ROOM - DAY

The hum of the overhead lights buzzes softly as Matilda sits across from Airl the Alien, her notepad untouched, her mind solely focused on the telepathic exchange. The sterile room feels eerily silent, save for the constant reminder of the one-way glass and camera looming in the background.

> ALIEN (V.O.)
> The development of an animal like the 'duck-billed platypus' required a lot of very clever engineering. Imagine the complexity — combining the body of a beaver with the bill of a duck, and then making it a mammal that lays eggs. That was no accident, I assure you.

Matilda's eyes flicker, intrigued by the notion. The alien's thoughts flow into hers like a calm stream, each revelation adding weight to the extraordinary story.

MATILDA (V.O.)
           (telepathic)
A special order?

                    ALIEN (V.O.)
          Undoubtedly. Some wealthy client
          must have placed a request — a
          'special order' for amusement or as
          a gift. The sheer design of it! I
          am sure a laboratory of one of the
          biotechnical companies spent years
          perfecting the platypus, making it
          a self-replicating life form.

Matilda's brow furrows slightly as the thought of creatures being crafted for amusement settles in her mind. It challenges everything she knows about nature.

                    MATILDA (V.O.)
          And yet, on Earth, this is seen as
          the result of natural evolution.
          Coincidental, random
          interactions...

                    ALIEN (V.O.)
          Absurdity. The notion that any
          life form could arise from random
          chemical reactions moldering up
          from primordial ooze—"

There's a slight pause in the exchange. Airl's thoughts sharpen, almost like an exasperated sigh filling the air.

                    ALIEN (V.O.)
          —it defies reason. Life is not
          random. Every detail of the life
          forms you see on Earth is
          engineered, either by beings like
          us or through IS-BE intervention.

Matilda leans forward, her focus intensifying. The words feel larger than the room itself.

                    MATILDA (V.O.)
          So... even the bacteria we
          consider ancient and foundational?

                    ALIEN (V.O.)
          Factually, yes. Take
          Proteobacteria, for example. Its
          origins are not of Earth.
                         (MORE)

                    ALIEN (V.O.) (CONT'D)
          These organisms are modifications
          of a Phylum designed for specific
          planetary environments—ones with
          anaerobic atmospheres. Planets
          that The Domain classifies as 'Star
          Type 3, Class C' planets.

Matilda mentally visualizes the classification, her mind
struggling to wrap itself around such a vast cosmic concept.

                    MATILDA (V.O.)
          Where would these planets be?

Airl's thoughts send an image flooding into Matilda's mind: a
constellation of stars, bright blue and fiercely burning.

                    ALIEN (V.O.)
          Planets near intensely hot blue
          stars, such as those in the
          constellation Orion's Belt in this
          galaxy. What Earth scientists call
          'natural selection' has nothing to
          do with the creation of these
          organisms. They were designed for
          very specific environments, not by
          chance, but by intent.

Matilda absorbs the information, a quiet awe spreading across
her expression. The complexities of creation, so often
attributed to time and nature, now seem impossibly small in
comparison to the cosmic scale she's being exposed to.

                    MATILDA (V.O.)
          The scale... is beyond anything
          we've ever imagined.

                    ALIEN (V.O.)
          And it is only the beginning.

Matilda sits unmoving, her mind enveloped by Airl's
telepathic voice. The sterile room seems to fade away,
leaving only the intensity of their connection. Airl
continues, her thoughts clear and unwavering.

                    ALIEN (V.O.)
          Creating life forms is very
          complex, highly technical work for
          IS-BEs who specialize in this
          field. The intricacies are beyond
          anything your Earth scientists
          currently understand.

Matilda's breath catches. She can sense the vastness of the knowledge being imparted, an ocean of information where her comprehension barely scratches the surface.

> MATILDA (V.O.)
> But Earth biologists study life with such precision. Why can't they see this?

> ALIEN (V.O.)
> Because they are blinded. Genetic anomalies, which should raise obvious questions, are baffling to them. This is not a failure of their intelligence, but a result of memory erasure. Earth scientists—like all humans here—have had their memories of the past erased by the Old Empire.

The mention of the "Old Empire" sends a shiver down Matilda's spine. The words carry a weight of control, manipulation, a force beyond the reach of human understanding.

> MATILDA (V.O.)
> False memories... So, they can't see the truth? Even when it's in front of them?

> ALIEN (V.O.)
> Precisely. The false memory implantations make them incapable of observing the most obvious of anomalies. They have been programmed to see only what is permitted by the Old Empire. Evolution, as they see it, is an illusion crafted for their limited perspective.

Matilda's mind races. The very foundation of human understanding, of life itself, suddenly feels fragile—artificial.

> MATILDA (V.O.)
> If they could remember... if they knew the truth... would they see things differently?

> ALIEN (V.O.)
> Undoubtedly. They would see that the creation of life forms is not random.
> (MORE)

> ALIEN (V.O.) (CONT'D)
> It is not a matter of chance, but of design, perfected over billions of years. The greatest technical challenge of biological organisms was the invention of self-regeneration.

Matilda's eyes widen as she pictures the concept.

> MATILDA (V.O.)
> Self-regeneration... you mean reproduction?"

> ALIEN (V.O.)
> Yes. Sexual reproduction. It was invented as the solution to a major problem: the constant need to manufacture replacement creatures. Early life forms, you see, were often destroyed or consumed by other organisms. This required planetary governments to continually buy replacement animals, which became... inconvenient and costly.

Airl's thoughts are infused with a sense of practicality, as though these monumental feats of creation were simply a matter of efficiency.

> MATILDA (V.O.)
> So... sexual reproduction was designed to make life self-sustaining?

> ALIEN (V.O.)
> Exactly. Rather than constantly manufacturing new creatures, the ability to reproduce solved the issue. Life forms could now sustain themselves without constant intervention, a far more economical solution.

Matilda's mind reels. What humanity had always believed to be natural, primal, instinctive was, in fact, a grand design—a system built for convenience, an engineered solution.

> MATILDA (V.O.)
> It seems so... calculated.

                    ALIEN (V.O.)
          Because it was. Every life form,
          every process, was carefully
          crafted. The work of life creation
          is a science—one that only IS-BEs
          with immense skill and knowledge
          can truly master. It is far beyond
          the comprehension of those with
          erased memories.

Matilda lets the words sink in. Airl's revelations have
shattered the delicate framework of everything she knew.
Life, as it exists on Earth, was a cosmic equation,
engineered and perfected over time, by beings far beyond
human reach. She stares into Airl's eyes, the alien's
presence both calming and overwhelming, as the magnitude of
it all settles deeply into her thoughts.

FLASHBACK:

EXT. UNKNOWN PLANET - FUTURISTIC CONFERENCE HALL - DAY

INSERT CARD: TRILLIONS OF YEARS AGO

Perched atop a mountain, glistening beneath multiple suns.
The hall is filled with representatives from countless
biotechnology companies—creatures of various shapes, sizes,
and technologies, some floating in the air, others
slithering, walking, or hovering in sleek, egg-shaped craft.

Airl the Alien's docile voice like the flow of water seeps
in.

                    ALIEN (V.O.)
          The Council of Yuhmi-Krum... where
          the fate of countless life forms
          across the galaxies was sealed.

As the representatives bicker, their voices blend into a
chaotic cacophony. The tension is thick, and there is
palpable greed in the air.

Airl's voice is calm and controlled.

                    ALIEN (V.O.)
          Arguments over the production of
          new species had reached a breaking
          point. Too many vested interests,
          too much power at stake. The
          biotechnology industry had become a
          battlefield.

244.

INT. COUNCIL CHAMBER - DAY

One of the leading representatives, a towering figure with insect-like features and elongated limbs, taps his finger-like appendages on the surface of the holographic table.

Airl's voice emanates like that of a passive observer.

> ALIEN (V.O.)
> It was this company, the largest in the insect and flowering plant business, that proposed a solution—a solution that would alter life forever.

A holographic projection of a complex ecosystem springs to life in the middle of the room. It shows plants blooming, insects pollinating, animals hunting, and others being hunted. The display rotates, demonstrating the interdependency of life forms.

The company's representative looks on, a smug smile creeps across his insectoid face.

Again, Airl's voice subtly drifts in.

> ALIEN (V.O.)
> Their proposal was simple. Creatures must consume other life forms as a source of energy. They called it the 'food chain.' A way to limit overpopulation, to introduce balance.

Council members exchange dark, knowing glances. Behind the scenes, silent deals are made. One COUNCIL MEMBER—small, humanoid with a crystalline body—whispers to a shadowy figure in the back of the room.

Airl's voice bears witness to the shady activities of the council.

> ALIEN (V.O.)
> Compromises were reached. Bribes were made. And those who could not be persuaded...

QUICK FLASH: A member of the council collapses, gasping, their crystalline body fracturing into a thousand pieces.

> ALIEN (V.O.)
> Were eliminated.

INT. COUNCIL CHAMBER - DAY

In the BACKGROUND, a final agreement is reached. The Council members nod to each other in mutual, cold understanding. The towering insectoid representative activates a device, and the decision is logged in a vast galactic database.

> ALIEN (V.O.)
> And thus, the food chain was born—a system of life forms dependent on one another for survival, all for the benefit of the companies profiting from the endless cycle.

EXT. PLANET - DAY

MONTAGE:

As the decision ripples across galaxies, creatures are genetically engineered to fulfill the food chain's cruel logic.

A PACK OF PREDATORS is released into the wilderness, devouring herbivores.

INSECTS crawl across flowering plants, their movement synchronized like a machine.

PARASITES burrow into helpless hosts, feasting on their bodies.

Airl's voice seems almost analytical.

> ALIEN (V.O.)
> The idea became a universal standard. Creatures consuming one another, plants relying on insects, parasites thriving. The cycle of death and regeneration was profitable... efficient.

END MONTAGE.

FLASHBACK:

INT. COUNCIL CHAMBER - DAY

The insectoid representative leans back in satisfaction, watching as the Council disperses. The deed is done.

Airl the Alien's voice is steady and forthcoming.

ALIEN (V.O.)
          It was a system of survival by
          design. Not by nature. Not by
          chance.

END FLASHBACK.

INT. ROSWELL ARMY AIR FORCE BASE - INTERVIEW ROOM - DAY

Matilda sits frozen, her eyes wide as Airl's voice fades from
her mind.

                    ALIEN (V.O.)
          The Earth is but one small
          experiment in a vast catalog of
          life forms. Nothing here happened
          by accident.

Matilda, still gazing at Airl, absorbs the weight of this
revelation. The silence between them deepens as the truth
lingers in the air, heavy and undeniable.

The room is still, save for the faint hum of the lights
overhead and the occasional sound of the Military Police
shifting outside the door.

Matilda's eyes are fixed on Airl, her mind a whirl of
unanswered questions and astonishing revelations. Her brows
furrow in concentration as the telepathic connection between
Matilda and Airl deepens.

Airl's voice echoes within Matilda's consciousness, calm and
steady.

                    ALIEN (V.O.)
          The company I mentioned earlier...
          their name, roughly translated into
          your language, would be 'Bugs &
          Blossoms.' They specialized in
          designing creatures with unique
          symbiotic relationships, but their
          ambitions grew darker.

FLASHBACK:

INT. UNKNOWN PLANET - BOARDROOM OF BUGS & BLOSSOMS - DAY

In a sleek, futuristic boardroom. EXECUTIVES of BUGS & BLOSSOMS—alien figures dressed in opulent robes of shimmering fabric—sit around a glowing table, their faces illuminated by projections of parasitic organisms, carnivores, and strange, otherworldly plants. One EXECUTIVE—an insectoid figure with translucent wings—stands up, addressing the room.

> EXECUTIVE (V.O.)
> (telepathically, in a
> different alien language)
> The market for parasitic creatures is dwindling. But if we can establish a new, fundamental law of biology—that all life forms must consume other life forms for energy—then we create an endless need for our products.

Airl's voice calmly sounds off.

> ALIEN (V.O.)
> They wanted to justify the manufacturing of parasitic creatures, but there was little demand for organisms that simply decomposed organic matter. So, they invented the food chain.

END FLASHBACK.

MONTAGE:

INT. ANIMATION HALLS AND LOBBYING - CORPORATE CAMPAIGN - DAY

PUBLIC RELATIONS FIRMS produce sleek HOLOGRAPHIC PROMOTIONS and animated advertisements glorifying the "circle of life" where creatures feed on one another in a "natural" cycle.

LOBBYISTS from Bugs & Blossoms walk through the HALLS OF GALACTIC GOVERNMENTS, shaking hands with officials, offering lavish gifts, and whispering promises.

In a massive GOVERNMENT CHAMBER, LAWS are drafted, documents bearing alien symbols are signed into existence.

Airl the Alien's voice is poised, balanced.

> ALIEN (V.O.)
> They hired public relations firms, political lobbyists—whatever it took to glorify this new idea.
> (MORE)

248.

> ALIEN (V.O.) (CONT'D)
> They pushed forward the narrative that all life forms needed 'food' for energy, a complete fabrication. Before that, life forms consumed only sunlight, minerals, or vegetation. Never one another.

END MONTAGE.

INT. ROSWELL ARMY AIR FORCE BASE - INTERVIEW ROOM - DAY

Matilda's lips part in shock, though she remains silent, processing the weight of Airl's words. She tries to form a question in her mind, but Airl's thoughts continue, smooth and uninterrupted.

> ALIEN (V.O.)
> Once this false theory was accepted, Bugs & Blossoms went into the carnivore business. They began designing predators—creatures whose sole purpose was to hunt and consume others. It was a grotesque business model, but it thrived.

FLASHBACK:

INT. FACTORIES OF BUGS & BLOSSOMS - DAY

The vast alien LABORATORIES and GENETIC FACTORIES, where engineers labor over holographic blueprints of carnivorous animals. GIANT TANKS bubble with embryonic life forms—clawed beasts, sharp-toothed predators, and parasitic organisms—all being created, tested, and refined.

Airl the Alien's ethereal voice chimes in.

> ALIEN (V.O.)
> With carnivores, the ecosystem began to unravel. Soon, entire populations of herbivores were wiped out. The demand for replacement creatures became insurmountable. It was a biological arms race, and the planets could not keep up.

INT. GOVERNMENT HEARING - PLANETARY LEADERS - DAY

PLANETARY GOVERNORS, frustrated, debating in front of the COUNCIL.

                    GOVERNOR (V.O.)
                (telepathically, in alien
                 language)
            We cannot keep replenishing these
            creatures. The destruction is too
            great, and the cost is too high!

Airl the Alien is heard quite succinctly.

                    ALIEN (V.O.)
            Planetary governments grew tired of
            constantly replenishing the animals
            that were being eaten. They
            demanded a solution.

INT. EXECUTIVE MEETING AT BUGS & BLOSSOMS - DAY

The INSECTOID EXECUTIVE again, speaking before a group of
shareholders. He gestures toward a massive hologram of
creatures engaging in sexual reproduction.

The descriptive ethereal voice of Airl the Alien is heard.

                    ALIEN (V.O.)
            And so, Bugs & Blossoms offered
            another solution: sexual
            reproduction. It was a novel
            concept in biological engineering.
            Until then, creatures were
            manufactured individually, not self-
            replicating. But now, these life
            forms could replenish themselves.

END FLASHBACK.

INT. ROSWELL ARMY AIR FORCE BASE - INTERVIEW ROOM - DAY

Matilda's eyes widen as the pieces fall into place. She
inhales slowly, her mind buzzing with the shocking
implications. The telepathic session continues.

                    MATILDA (V.O.)
            So... the entire system of life on
            Earth—the food chain,
            reproduction—all of it was
            engineered?

                    ALIEN (V.O.)
            Yes. Life was never meant to
            devour itself. That is a product
            of greed, exploitation.
                    (MORE)

ALIEN (V.O.) (CONT'D)
And now, on your planet, it is seen as 'natural'—a lie that has been passed down for eons.

Matilda sits back, her heart pounding, as she struggles to reconcile everything she has just learned.

ALIEN (V.O.)
(calmly)
It is not your fault, Matilda. The deception has been flawless. Even now, your scientists cling to theories that blind them to the truth.

The room falls into a deep, unnerving silence as Matilda processes Airl's revelations.

The low hum of the lights fills the room as Matilda and Airl continue their silent, yet intense, exchange. Matilda's eyes remain locked on Airl the Alien, her notepad untouched on the table as their telepathic conversation persists.

ALIEN(V.O.)
(a sense of contemplation and regret)
As expected, the patent licenses for the biological engineering process required to implant stimulus-response mating, cellular division, and preprogrammed growth patterns for self-regenerating animals were owned by 'Bugs & Blossoms'. They controlled the intellectual property, making it impossible for other biotechnology companies to function without purchasing the licenses.

Matilda blinks, absorbing the weight of the statement, though her thoughts still swirl in disbelief.

ALIEN (V.O.)
(continuing, with growing intensity)
Through the next few million years, laws were passed that forced these companies to incorporate the programs. Every life form, no matter how simple or complex, had to conform to the standard model of reproduction. The expense was astronomical.
(MORE)

                    ALIEN (V.O.) (CONT'D)
          It crippled smaller companies and
          slowly eroded the creativity and
          ingenuity that once fueled the
          biological industry.

A brief pause, as Matilda's mind races to catch up.

                    ALIEN (V.O.)
              (a tinge of bitterness)
          This awkward, impractical
          concept—food and sex as essential
          drives for survival—became the
          cornerstone of biology across the
          galaxies. It was a doomed
          experiment from the start. Over
          time, as species consumed one
          another and the reproductive
          mechanisms became faulty or
          misused, the entire biotechnology
          industry collapsed. 'Bugs &
          Blossoms,' like the others, was
          driven into ruin.

Matilda's brow furrows, feeling the weight of an entire
industry's demise.

                    ALIEN (V.O.)
              (slightly melancholic)
          When species became extinct, there
          was no way to replace them. The
          technology of creating life had
          been lost forever. What was once
          an extraordinary, vibrant
          marketplace of creativity and
          biological diversity dwindled to
          nothing.

A stillness falls between them. The enormity of the
knowledge presses down on Matilda, filling her mind with
images of vanished species, forgotten technology, and a
universe once teeming with endless possibilities now
restrained by laws, greed, and corruption.

                    ALIEN (V.O.)
              (a soft conclusion)
          None of this technology was ever
          known on Earth, and probably never
          will be.

Matilda lets out a slow breath, the implications
overwhelming. The complexity and loss of the universe
outside Earth now feels more tangible, more tragic.

INT. ROSWELL ARMY AIR FORCE BASE - CONFERENCE ROOM - DAY

The harsh fluorescent lights illuminate the sterile, gray room. Seated around the table are three men: The government agent, wearing a sharp suit, the scientist, in a lab coat, and the military official, dressed in a crisp uniform, medals displayed prominently. They sit rigidly, their eyes trained on Colonel William H. Blanchard, who is seated opposite them, flipping through a thick file labeled "EYES ONLY".

Colonel Blanchard's face is impassive, but his eyes are intent as he reads aloud from the transcript.

                COLONEL BLANCHARD
            (reading with precision)
    'Bugs & Blossoms' controlled the
    patent licenses for biological
    engineering, including the
    implantation of cellular division
    and reproduction programs in all
    species. The monopoly crushed
    other companies, leading to the
    eventual collapse of the entire
    biotechnology industry.

A stunned silence fills the room. The government agent shifts in his seat, incredulous.

                GOVERNMENT AGENT
            (breaking the silence,
             barely containing his
             disbelief)
    So, you're telling me an entire
    industry that shaped the life forms
    across the galaxy collapsed because
    of a single company?

                COLONEL BLANCHARD
            (without looking up)
    That's correct.

The scientist, leaning forward, his hands clasped tightly, shakes his head in disbelief.

                SCIENTIST
    Do you understand what this means?
    We're talking about the
    manipulation of life itself,
    trillions of years of biological
    history wiped out, forgotten...
    and we've never even known about
    it.

The military official, always the skeptic, rubs his chin thoughtfully.

                     MILITARY OFFICIAL
        This... 'Bugs & Blossoms'—could
        they have had any influence here?
        Could that same technology have
        been planted on Earth somehow?

                     COLONEL BLANCHARD
              (looking up from the
                transcript)
        There's no indication that this
        technology was ever introduced to
        Earth. According to Airl, it was
        lost long before humanity ever came
        into existence.

The government agent leans forward, his face now serious, almost desperate.

                     GOVERNMENT AGENT
        We need access to this information,
        Colonel. I'm not sure you
        understand the magnitude of what
        we're dealing with. A full copy of
        the transcript—

                     COLONEL BLANCHARD
              (cutting him off, firmly)
        It's classified. 'For eyes only.'

The agent bristles, anger creeping into his voice.

                     GOVERNMENT AGENT
        We're all on the same team here,
        Colonel. Keeping us in the dark
        doesn't help anyone.

Blanchard's eyes narrow as he slowly closes the file.

                     COLONEL BLANCHARD
        And as far as this information
        goes, you're in the dark for a
        reason. Need-to-know only, and
        right now, you don't need to know.

A tense silence falls over the room. The military official glances between Blanchard and the others, sensing the tension rising.

                     SCIENTIST
              (in a calm, measured tone)
                (MORE)

                    SCIENTIST (CONT'D)
          Colonel, the science alone is
          invaluable. The applications—if we
          could understand this technology,
          it could change everything. You
          can't seriously expect us to just
          sit back and—

                    COLONEL BLANCHARD
               (leaning forward, his
                voice low but commanding)
          You will sit back and follow
          protocol, Doctor. This isn't some
          scientific playground. It's above
          your clearance, all of you. That's
          the end of it.

The government agent clenches his jaw, fists tightening, but he says nothing. The scientist looks down, clearly frustrated. The military official remains quiet, observing, but the tension in the room is palpable.

Blanchard stands, pushing the closed file aside.

                    COLONEL BLANCHARD (CONT'D)
          This meeting is over.

The three men exchange glances, reluctant but unable to argue further. One by one, they stand and file out of the room, leaving Blanchard alone, the "EYES ONLY" file still resting on the table in front of him.

INT. ROSWELL ARMY AIR FORCE BASE - CONTROL ROOM - DAY

The low hum of the AEG Magnetophon reel-to-reel tape recorder fills the room, accompanied by the rhythmic clicks and whirrs of military personnel operating the console. On the TV monitor, the image of Airl the Alien and Matilda locked in an intense, silent gaze flickers in black and white. The magnetic tape spins steadily, recording every moment of the mysterious telepathic exchange.

Military personnel man the console, their hands swiftly turning knobs, adjusting dials, pushing buttons, and flicking switches. They move with precision, as though handling something too delicate to misstep.

The door swings open, and Colonel William H. Blanchard strides in with purpose, followed by Lieutenant General Roger M. Ramey and President Harry S. Truman. Their presence instantly alters the room's atmosphere—tense, weighty.

Blanchard gestures toward the one-way glass window, revealing the surreal sight of Matilda seated across from the diminutive figure of Airl. Both appear to be locked in a mental, unspoken exchange, their gazes fixed on one another with a stillness that makes the air feel thick.

President Truman stands quietly at the window, his face carefully composed, betraying little. But beneath that reserved exterior, the weight of the moment presses heavily on him. He watches the monitor, then shifts his gaze to the live view through the window, struggling to reconcile what he sees with his understanding of the world.

Behind him, General Ramey stands just as motionless, but his eyes dart between Truman and the monitor. The bewilderment bubbling beneath his stern expression is palpable, though he tries to mask it with an air of military discipline.

The President's hands rest behind his back, gripping tightly. Though he says nothing, it's clear that his mind is racing, grappling with the incomprehensible nature of the scene before him. His thin veneer of control barely contains the profound disbelief, or perhaps fear, churning within.

A small shift from Blanchard, who remains focused on the live feed of the interview, pulls them from their thoughts.

              COLONEL BLANCHARD
          (softly, to Ramey)
    They've been at it for hours. No
    breaks. No words spoken aloud.

Ramey doesn't respond, his eyes narrowing slightly as he watches Matilda's calm, almost serene demeanor.

              PRESIDENT TRUMAN
          (voice low, controlled)
    Is she... receiving something?
    From it?"

Blanchard and Ramey exchange a glance. It's clear neither of them fully understands the mechanics of what is happening in that room.

              COLONEL BLANCHARD
          (barely above a whisper)
    Yes, sir. Telepathy.

President Truman inhales deeply, his brow furrowing. His attention shifts back to the one-way glass. Whatever was said, or unsaid, weighs heavily on all of them.

The reel-to-reel recorder continues spinning, a silent sentinel documenting the unfathomable exchange taking place beyond the glass.

Without a word, Truman moves closer to the window, staring intently at Airl. Something profound is unfolding before his eyes, something that defies every protocol, every norm he's ever known.

In the dim glow of the control room, they stand as silent witnesses to a moment in history that will never be spoken of outside these walls.

INT. ROSWELL ARMY AIR FORCE BASE - INTERVIEW ROOM - DAY

Matilda and Airl sit across from each other, locked in their telepathic exchange. Matilda's face remains calm, but her mind races with the information she is receiving. Airl's telepathic voice fills Matilda's thoughts, steady and precise.

> ALIEN (V.O.)
> There are still computer files on some planets far from here that record the procedures for biological engineering. Possibly the laboratories and computers still exist somewhere. However, there is no one around doing anything with them.

Matilda furrows her brow slightly, absorbing the enormity of the statement. She jots down a few notes, but her mind remains deeply connected to Airl's message.

> ALIEN (V.O.)
> This is why it is so important for The Domain to protect the dwindling number of creatures left on Earth.

Airl's thoughts linger for a moment before she continues, sending another wave of revelations to Matilda.

> ALIEN (V.O.)
> The core concept behind 'sexual reproduction' technology was the invention of a chemical/electronic interaction called "cyclical stimulus-response generators". This programmed genetic mechanism causes a seemingly spontaneous, recurring impulse to reproduce.

Matilda's pen hesitates on the page for a moment before she writes down "cyclical stimulus-response generators."

                    ALIEN (V.O.)
The same technique was later adapted and applied to biological flesh bodies, including Homo Sapiens.

Matilda's hand trembles slightly as she scribbles "Homo Sapiens" on the pad, feeling the weight of the information.

                    ALIEN (V.O.)
Another important mechanism used in the reproductive process, especially with Homo Sapiens-type bodies, is the implantation of a "chemical-electrical trigger" mechanism in the body.

A small frown forms on Matilda's lips as she processes the mention of the "trigger" mechanism.

                    ALIEN (V.O.)
The "trigger" which attracts IS-BEs to inhabit a human body, or any kind of "flesh body," is the use of an artificially imprinted electronic wave that uses "aesthetic pain" to attract the IS-BE.

Matilda feels a cold shiver as the weight of the words sink in. She pauses, pen frozen over the paper. Her mind swirls with questions, but she knows her role is to listen, to document. The room remains eerily silent, except for the sound of her pen scratching faintly against the pad.

In her mind, the pieces of the puzzle are coming together, but she can sense there's much more to uncover.

The room remains still as Airl continues transmitting telepathically to Matilda. Matilda, locked in her focused gaze, listens intently, her mind processing the depth of the information.

                    ALIEN (V.O.)
Every trap in the universe, including those used to capture IS-BEs who remain free, is "baited" with an aesthetic electronic wave.
                       (MORE)

                    ALIEN (V.O.) (CONT'D)
          The sensations caused by the
          aesthetic wavelength are more
          attractive to an IS-BE than any
          other sensation.

Matilda's brow furrows slightly, reflecting on the concept.
She hesitates for a moment before responding telepathically.

                    MATILDA (V.O.)
          So... beauty and pain? They're
          combined, and that's what traps us
          here? That's why we stay?

Her thoughts echo softly, curious and tentative, but they
reach Airl directly.

                    ALIEN (V.O.)
          Exactly. When the electronic waves
          of pain and beauty are combined
          together, this causes the IS-BE to
          get "stuck" in the body.

Matilda absorbs this, a subtle tension crossing her features
as she continues jotting down notes.

                    ALIEN (V.O.)
          The "reproductive trigger" used for
          lesser life forms—cattle, other
          mammals—is simpler. It's triggered
          by chemicals emitted from scent
          glands, combined with reproductive
          chemical-electrical impulses
          stimulated by testosterone or
          estrogen.

Matilda writes rapidly, capturing every word as her mind
races to comprehend the scientific precision behind Airl's
words.

                    ALIEN (V.O.)
          These impulses are also interactive
          with nutrition levels. When
          deprived of food, life forms
          reproduce more in an attempt to
          perpetuate survival through future
          regenerations.

                    MATILDA (V.O.)
          Survival through starvation...
          even when there's nothing left to
          sustain them.

Airl's voice comes back, calm yet powerful.

ALIEN (V.O.)
Exactly. These fundamental principles have been applied throughout all species of life. The addiction to the "sexual aesthetic-pain" electronic wave is the reason that the ruling class of The Domain does not inhabit flesh bodies.

Matilda sits back slightly, letting the weight of that realization settle in.

MATILDA (V.O.)
So... they don't get trapped. They're... immune to it?

ALIEN (V.O.)
Correct. This is also why officers of The Domain Forces only use doll bodies. This wave has proven to be the most effective trapping device ever created in the history of the universe, as far as I know.

Matilda shifts in her seat, feeling a cold chill ripple down her spine. The concept of these invisible, irresistible forces manipulating existence stirs a mixture of fear and curiosity within her.

She stares at Airl, her mind racing.

MATILDA (V.O.)
How do we even begin to escape such a powerful trap?

Airl doesn't respond immediately, and the silence deepens, leaving Matilda with more questions than answers.

The connection between them lingers, unbroken, as Matilda prepares herself for whatever revelations are still to come.

FLASHBACK:

EXT. COSMIC LANDSCAPE - UNKNOWN GALAXY

A vast and sprawling galaxy stretches out, shimmering with distant stars and planets. The scene feels serene yet teeming with underlying complexity. In the distance, planets under the rule of The Domain and the "Old Empire" are faintly visible, structured and orderly.

                    ALIEN (V.O.)
          The civilizations of The Domain and
          the "Old Empire" both depend on a
          device to "recruit" and maintain a
          workforce of IS-BEs who inhabit
          flesh bodies on planets and
          installations.

EXT. INDUSTRIAL PLANET - DAY

A massive industrial planet hums with activity. Thousands of humanoid figures, the "working class" IS-BEs, labor tirelessly in colossal factories. Some are carrying out construction work, others labor in harsh environments, endlessly repeating their tasks. They are trapped within the physical form of their bodies, oblivious to their true nature.

                    ALIEN (V.O.)
          These IS-BEs are the "working
          class" beings who do all of the
          slavish, manual, undesirable work
          on planets.

INT. FACTORY COMPLEX - DAY

Inside one of the factories, IS-BEs, their faces blank and hollow, operate machinery that forges large metal components. Sweat drips from their brows as the clanking and grinding of machinery fill the air. They are utterly subjugated, bound to their physical forms. Above them, the factory overseers—figures cloaked in shadow—watch, controlling every movement.

                    ALIEN (V.O.)
          As I mentioned, there is a very
          highly regimented and fixed
          hierarchy or "class system" for all
          IS-BEs throughout the "Old Empire"
          and The Domain.

EXT. A DOMINION CITY - DAY

A beautiful, well-ordered city floats above the chaos of the industrial planet. In contrast to the dim and drudgery below, this city glows with light, inhabited by "free" IS-BEs. Ethereal beings move effortlessly, unbound by physical bodies. They glide freely through the streets, interacting through thought, sharing knowledge and ideas. Their world is filled with creativity and power.

                    ALIEN (V.O.)
          The highest class are "free" IS-
          BEs. They are not restricted to
          the use of any type of body and may
          come and go at will...

EXT. SPACE STATION - DAY

In the depths of space, an elegant, towering space station
orbits a planet. Free IS-BEs move about in control rooms,
governing over the planetary operations. They oversee the
laborers on the planet below through holographic screens.
These free IS-BEs make decisions without physical
limitations.

                    ALIEN (V.O.)
          ...Provided that they do not
          destroy or interfere with the
          social, economic, or political
          structure.

EXT. PLANETARY SYSTEM - NIGHT

A distant, harsh world under "Old Empire" rule. Massive,
walled cities surround enslaved populations. Laborers toil
in mines and fields, working endlessly. A ship flies
overhead, a majestic craft belonging to the higher strata of
IS-BEs who remain free to roam.

                    ALIEN (V.O.)
          Below this class are many strata of
          "limited" IS-BEs who may or may not
          use a body from time to time.

EXT. CONTROL ROOM - SPACE STATION - NIGHT

The leaders of both The Domain and "Old Empire" gather in
regal control rooms, their movements fluid and unburdened by
physical limitations. They discuss the social order,
dictating the fates of countless beings below them. The IS-
BEs below carry out their will without question.

                    ALIEN (V.O.)
          Limitations are imposed on each IS-
          BE regarding the range of power,
          ability, and mobility they can
          exercise.

EXT. COSMIC VOID - NIGHT

The focus is on the vast expanse of stars and galaxies, as Airl's voice continues to echo with somber wisdom.

> ALIEN (V.O.)
> This is the structure that has endured for eons... where freedom is reserved for few, and labor is imposed on many.

The stars shimmer quietly, as if observing the distant hierarchy of civilizations from an incomprehensible distance.

END FLASHBACK.

INT. ROSWELL ARMY AIR FORCE BASE - OFFICE - DAY

The afternoon sun casts a soft light through the small windows. Matilda sits across from the stenographer, her notepad resting on her lap. The stenographer sits with fingers poised above the stenotype machine, ready to transcribe. Matilda flips through the notes, scanning the pages, her voice calm yet deliberate.

> MATILDA
> (reading from her notes)
> "Below these are the 'doll body' classes, to which Airl belongs. Nearly all space officers and crew members of spacecraft are required to travel through intergalactic space. Therefore, they are each equipped with a body manufactured from lightweight, durable materials."

The stenographer's fingers dance across the stenotype, capturing every word. Matilda pauses, taking a breath, then continues.

> MATILDA (CONT'D)
> (reading)
> "Various body types have been designed to facilitate specialized functions. Some bodies have accessories, such as interchangeable tools or apparatus for activities like maintenance, mining, chemical management, navigation..."

She pauses again, her mind drifting momentarily to the enormity of what she's recounting. Her eyes flick up to the stenographer, who waits patiently.

> MATILDA (CONT'D)
> (slightly shaking her head)
> "And... there are many gradations of this body type, which also serve as an 'insignia' of rank. Below these are the soldier class."

Matilda flips the page slowly, the weight of Airl's revelations clearly heavy on her mind. The stenographer watches her briefly, sensing the tension but saying nothing.

> MATILDA (CONT'D)
> (continuing)
> "The soldiers are equipped with a myriad of weapons and specialized armaments designed to detect, combat, and overwhelm any imaginable foe. Some soldiers are issued mechanical bodies. Most soldiers, however, are merely remote-controlled robots with no class designation."

Matilda's eyes linger on the final line, the reality of what she is reading sinking in further. She exhales softly and closes the notepad.

> MATILDA (CONT'D)
> (looking down at her hands)
> That's it for this section.

The stenographer finishes typing, the click of the keys come to a final halt as silence fills the room. They sit quietly for a moment, both aware of the magnitude of the information they are documenting.

The weight of truth presses heavily in the air.

INT. ROSWELL ARMY AIR FORCE BASE - OFFICE - EVENING

The fading sunlight outside barely filters through the closed blinds. Colonel William H. Blanchard and Captain Sheridan Cavitt sit across from each other, copies of the transcript from Airl's interview spread out on the desk between them. Both men wear expressions of astonishment as they read over the latest revelations. Cavitt, looking tense, begins to read aloud, his voice thick with disbelief.

                    CAPTAIN CAVITT
               (reading)
          "The lower classes are limited to
          'flesh bodies.' Of course, it is
          not possible for these to travel
          through space for obvious reasons.
          Flesh bodies are far too fragile to
          endure the stresses of gravity,
          temperature extremes, radiation
          exposure..."

Cavitt trails off for a moment, shaking his head before
continuing.

                    CAPTAIN CAVITT (CONT'D)
               (continuing)
          "Atmospheric chemicals... the
          vacuum of space. The logistical
          inconveniences of food, defecation,
          sleep... air pressure. And then
          this—"

He points to the page, glancing at Blanchard who remains
fixated on his own copy.

                    CAPTAIN CAVITT (CONT'D)
               (quoting aloud)
          "Most flesh bodies will suffocate
          in only a few minutes without a
          specific combination of atmospheric
          chemicals. After 2 or 3 days,
          bacteria cause severe odors to be
          emitted. Odors of any kind are not
          acceptable in a space vessel."

Cavitt lowers the transcript, running a hand through his
hair. Blanchard, silent up until now, lifts his head, his
eyes wide with shock but his tone measured as he speaks.

                    COLONEL BLANCHARD
               (nods slowly)
          "And... 'flesh bodies are utterly
          useless for military duty.' A
          single shot from an electronic
          blast gun and—"
               (he taps the page)
          "—instantly turns a flesh body into
          noxious vapor."

The weight of the statement lingers in the room. Cavitt
leans back in his chair, still processing the information.

                    CAPTAIN CAVITT
               (with a hint of sarcasm,
                shaking his head)
          Sounds like we're lucky to even be
          standing, let alone fighting a war.

Blanchard sets his transcript down and stares into the
distance, lost in thought. The office is quiet except for
the soft ticking of the clock on the wall.

                    COLONEL BLANCHARD
               (grimly, after a pause)
          This changes everything...

The room falls into silence again, both men grappling with
the vast implications of what they've just read. The eerie
reality of Airl's words hangs thick in the air, casting long
shadows over their next steps.

INT. ROSWELL ARMY AIR FORCE BASE - BARRACKS - SHOWER - NIGHT

The steady rush of water echoes off the tiled walls, drowning
out the hum of the base just outside. Water cascades down
Matilda's face, her expression weary but focused. She stands
under the stream, letting the warmth soothe her tense
muscles, her forehead pressed lightly against the shower
wall. For a brief moment, the heat of the water provides a
small sense of relief from the intensity of the day's events.

The rhythmic sound of the falling water is the only noise,
but Matilda's thoughts race beneath the surface.

QUICK FLASHBACK:

The telepathic connection with Airl surge through Matilda's
mind. Her brow furrows as she remembers the overwhelming
weight of the alien's revelations—the origins of life, the
manipulation of genetics, the nature of the universe itself.
It's almost too much to bear.

BACK TO SCENE.

Matilda stands still, the water pouring down her, lost in the
gravity of it all. But then, her shoulders straighten. The
daunting task that lies ahead for her and humanity can't be
escaped. Yet, despite the overwhelming responsibility, a
quiet resolve begins to grow within her. She knows what must
be done. Airl's revelations are only the beginning, and
Matilda is resigned to see the interviews through, no matter
the cost.

The water continues to flow, but her mind is set. As she reaches up to turn off the faucet, Matilda takes a deep breath. She steps out of the shower, determination now etched into her features. Whatever challenges come with her next interview with Airl, she is prepared to face them.

Matilda wraps herself in a towel, her reflection in the mirror showing a woman no longer weighed down by fear but fortified by purpose.

INT. ROSWELL ARMY AIR FORCE BASE - HALLWAY - DAY

Matilda walks down the long, sterile hallway, her footsteps echoing in sync with the two military police officers flanking her. The dim overhead lights cast shadows on the floor, the soft hum of fluorescent bulbs filling the silence.

Her expression is focused, though her eyes dart between the clipboard in her hands and the path ahead. She flips through her notes, but the questions seem to blur together as her mind races. She inhales deeply, trying to shake off the weight of the day's revelations and focus.

The military police officers remain silent, their presence a constant reminder of the seriousness of the task at hand. Matilda's fingers tighten around the clipboard, the words she's rehearsed in her mind almost feel inadequate now. She mentally runs through possible responses Airl might give, envisioning each scenario, but uncertainty gnaws at her.

They approach the heavy, steel door at the end of the hallway. Matilda halts, glancing at it as if it were a portal to another world—one that she's both eager and hesitant to enter. Her chest rises with another deep breath. She knows that every word exchanged in that room could shift the entire foundation of what she knows about human existence.

One of the officers steps forward and opens the door. Matilda straightens, slipping her clipboard under her arm. Without hesitation, she steps through.

The door closes behind her, the soft clank of the lock sealing her inside with the unknown.

INT. ROSWELL ARMY AIR FORCE BASE - INTERVIEW ROOM - DAY

Matilda steps into the room, clipboard in hand, her eyes locking instantly with Airl's steady gaze. The alien sits calmly in the recliner, radiating a presence that fills the sterile room with otherworldly energy.

The ever-present one-way glass looms in the background, but it feels distant now. To Matilda, only Airl matters.

She takes her seat across from Airl, her breath steady but her mind brimming with the enormity of what she's about to learn. The quiet hum of the room is broken only by the soft scratch of Matilda's pen against the notepad as she jots down her thoughts, her gaze never breaking from Airl's.

> ALIEN (V.O.)
> IS-BEs who inhabit flesh bodies have lost much of their native ability and power. Although it is theoretically possible to regain or rehabilitate these abilities, no practical means has been discovered or authorized by The Domain.

Matilda's brow furrows slightly as she processes the implications of this. She knows this is a piece of a much larger puzzle — one that spans beyond the limits of Earth's history. Her pen pauses as Airl continues the telepathic message.

> ALIEN (V.O.)
> Even though spacecraft of The Domain travel trillions of 'light years' in a single day, the time required to traverse the space between galaxies is significant, not to mention the length of time to complete just one set of mission orders, which may require thousands of years.

Matilda shifts in her seat, intrigued by the vast expanse of time that Airl the Alien speaks of. She imagines the infinite stretches of space, the missions spanning millennia, and what it means for beings like Airl who are not tethered to the fleeting lifespan of human bodies.

> ALIEN (V.O.)
> Biological flesh bodies live for only a very short time — only 60 to 150 years, at most — whereas doll bodies can be re-used and repaired almost indefinitely.

Matilda feels a subtle shift in the energy around them. The truth of the fragile human form sinks in, feeling smaller, more transient than ever before. The idea of living for mere decades, compared to the near eternity of reusable doll bodies, strikes a chord. Her pen scratches across the page once more, documenting everything with meticulous precision.

> ALIEN (V.O.)
> The first development of biological
> bodies began in this universe about
> seventy-four trillion years ago.
> It rapidly became a fad for IS-BEs
> to create and inhabit various types
> of bodies for an assortment of
> nefarious reasons: especially for
> amusement, to experience various
> physical sensations vicariously
> through the body.

Airl's revelation pulls Matilda deeper into thought. She looks at her own hands, suddenly aware of the temporary nature of the body she inhabits. She considers what it must have been like for these ancient beings, creating bodies for entertainment, for sensation, only to become trapped in them.

Matilda meets Airl's eyes again. The alien's calm, ever-knowing gaze holds her there. Her role, her understanding of existence, feels minute in comparison to the grandeur of time, of life, of the universe Airl is revealing to her.

Matilda takes a breath, her telepathic voice speaks softly, carrying the weight of her thoughts.

> MATILDA (V.O.)
> So, the bodies we live in now,
> they're just... shells? Temporary
> forms we've forgotten we ever
> chose?

Airl's silence is affirmation enough. The gravity of it settles over Matilda like a heavy fog. Matilda sits in her usual position across from Airl. Their eyes lock, and once again, the telepathic exchange begins.

> ALIEN (V.O.)
> Since that time, IS-BEs have
> continued to devolve in their
> relationship with bodies. What
> began as an innocent exploration of
> life in physical form turned into a
> trap. Initially, IS-BEs created
> and inhabited bodies for amusement,
> to feel the sensations of a
> physical existence. But over time,
> certain tricks were introduced that
> trapped IS-BEs in the very bodies
> they once enjoyed.

Matilda listens intently, her hand poised over the notepad, but she doesn't write, her focus fixed solely on Airl's words.

                    ALIEN (V.O.)
          One such trick was the creation of
          fragile bodies—delicate enough
          that, when an IS-BE used their
          natural power to create energy,
          they might accidentally harm or
          destroy the body. The IS-BE,
          remorseful for the damage caused,
          would pull back their power,
          careful not to injure the body
          further. This reduction of power
          became a habit, and over time, IS-
          BEs weakened themselves in an
          attempt to protect these fragile
          forms.

Matilda feels a surge of unease, the weight of the
realization growing.

                    MATILDA (V.O.)
          So, by trying to protect the
          bodies, they became more dependent
          on them?

                    ALIEN (V.O.)
          Exactly. The IS-BE began to feel a
          sense of responsibility for the
          bodies they inhabited. This paved
          the way for manipulation. Over
          time, these beings who once had the
          ability to exist freely began to
          get trapped in physical forms,
          unable to leave. A long history of
          treachery and deceit followed,
          leading to a growing number of IS-
          BEs becoming permanent prisoners
          within bodies.

Matilda furrows her brow, absorbing the gravity of what she's
hearing.

                    MATILDA (V.O.)
               (mind racing)
          And those who trapped them...
          profited?

                    ALIEN (V.O.)
          Indeed. Some IS-BEs, realizing the
          power they held, took advantage of
          this situation. They enslaved
          others, trapping them in bodies and
          diminishing their ability to escape
          or resist.
                         (MORE)

                    ALIEN (V.O.) (CONT'D)
          The enslavement became widespread,
          evolving into what you would
          recognize as a hierarchy—a class
          system where the power of the IS-BE
          is reflected by the type of body
          they inhabit.

The depth of the conversation hangs in the air, as Matilda feels the weight of generations of exploitation.

                    ALIEN (V.O.)
          Trillions of years of enslavement.
          Entire civilizations built upon
          this structure—both in the 'Old
          Empire' and in The Domain. Bodies
          became symbols of class, of power,
          of control.

                    MATILDA (V.O.)
          And it continues even now?

                    AIRL (V.O.)
          Yes. To this day, the remnants of
          those manipulations are still felt,
          and the hierarchy of IS-BEs trapped
          in bodies persists.

The enormity of the situation presses down on Matilda. She struggles to grasp the implications of what Airl is revealing. As the telepathic silence lingers, she sits back, overwhelmed, but determined to continue their exchange.

INT. ROSWELL ARMY AIR FORCE BASE - BRIEFING ROOM - DAY

The room is dimly lit, a single light casting a soft glow over a desk. At the center of the desk lies a stack of transcripts from the interview with Airl. Pages rustle gently as the scientist, sitting alone, flips through them with focused intent. His brow furrows, deep in thought.

The silence of the room is broken only by the faint shuffling of papers. His fingers linger on an excerpt from the transcript. He reads silently, the words reverberating in his mind.

                    SCIENTIST (V.O.)
          "The vast majority of IS-BEs
          throughout the galaxies of this
          universe inhabit some form of flesh
          body.
                              (MORE)

SCIENTIST (V.O.) (CONT'D)
The structure, appearance, operation, and habitat of these bodies vary according to the gravity, atmosphere, and climatic conditions of the planet they inhabit."

The scientist taps his pen absently against the page, lost in contemplation. He gazes up briefly, eyes scanning the room as if looking for answers in the shadows.

His eyes return to the transcript.

SCIENTIST (V.O.)
"Body types are predetermined largely by the type and size of the star around which the planet revolves, the distance from the star, and the geological, as well as atmospheric components of the planet."

He pauses, pondering the complexity of what he's reading. His mind races, trying to reconcile Airl's knowledge with the limited scope of Earth's understanding of astronomy and biology.

He whispers under his breath, barely audible, as if speaking to no one but himself.

SCIENTIST
(Softly)
Body types... predetermined by the stars themselves...

He looks at the page once more.

SCIENTIST (CONT'D)
"For example, Earth is identified, roughly, as a 'Sun Type 12, Class 7 planet'. That is a heavy gravity, nitrogen/oxygen atmosphere planet, with biological life forms, in proximity to a single, yellow, medium-size, low radiation sun or 'Type 12 star'. The proper designations are difficult to translate accurately due to the extreme limitations of astronomical nomenclature in the English language."

The scientist leans back in his chair, staring blankly at the ceiling.

The weight of the universe seems to press down on him, the vastness of its scope incomprehensible. His lips move silently as he repeats to himself:

                SCIENTIST (V.O.)
     Sun Type 12, Class 7...

He sits forward again, eyes narrowed in deep thought. The enormity of what he is learning makes him feel small like a man trying to grasp the ocean with his bare hands. The mysteries Airl has revealed leave more questions than answers, and for the first time in his life, the scientist feels truly lost in the vastness of the cosmos.

He sets the papers down carefully, staring at them as though they might leap up and offer him more insight. But they remain still, silent, enigmatic—just like the universe they describe.

                SCIENTIST
         (Murmuring)
     There's so much more than we ever
     imagined...

The room feels heavy with the burden of this newfound knowledge. Alone with his thoughts, the scientist contemplates the vastness of existence, his mind racing to grasp the truths Airl has revealed, and the profound implications they hold for Earth—and for him.

INT. ROSWELL ARMY AIR FORCE BASE - INTERVIEW ROOM - DAY

Matilda sits across from Airl, their eyes locked in telepathic communication. The tension in the room is palpable, but Matilda maintains her calm demeanor. Her notepad rests on the table, but she isn't writing—her focus is entirely on absorbing every word that passes from Airl's mind to hers.

                ALIEN (V.O.)
     The vast majority of IS-BEs
     throughout the galaxies of this
     universe inhabit some form of flesh
     body.

Matilda nods slightly, absorbing the scale of Airl's words. Her brow furrows as she tries to comprehend the unimaginable diversity of life forms across the universe.

                    ALIEN (V.O.)
                (continuing)
            The structure, appearance,
            operation, and habitat of these
            bodies vary according to the
            gravity, atmosphere, and climatic
            conditions of the planet they
            inhabit. Body types are
            predetermined largely by the type
            and size of the star around which
            the planet revolves, the distance
            from the star, the geological, as
            well as atmospheric components of
            the planet.

FLASHBACK:

Matilda's eyes widen as visions of alien worlds and countless creatures flicker in her mind, projected from Airl's thoughts.

END FLASHBACK.

                    ALIEN (V.O.)
                (continuing)
            On average, these stars and planets
            fall into gradients of
            classification which are fairly
            standard throughout the universe.
            Earth is identified, roughly, as a
            "Sun Type 12, Class 7 planet". That
            is a heavy gravity, nitrogen/oxygen
            atmosphere planet, with biological
            life forms, in proximity to a
            single, yellow, medium-size, low
            radiation sun or "Type 12 star".

Matilda begins to jot down brief notes, her handwriting shaky but quick. Her thoughts race, filled with the implications of what she's hearing.

                    ALIEN (V.O.)
                (continuing)
            The proper designations are
            difficult to translate accurately
            due to the extreme limitations of
            astronomical nomenclature in the
            English language.

Matilda pauses, pen resting on the paper, feeling the immensity of Airl's knowledge pressing against her limited understanding.

                    ALIEN (V.O.)
                (continuing)
            There are as many varieties of life
            forms as there are grains of sand
            on the beach. You can imagine how
            many different creatures and types
            of bodies have been manufactured by
            millions of companies such as "Bugs
            & Blossoms" for all of the myriad
            planetary systems during the course
            of seventy-four trillion years!

Matilda's pen is completely still. She exhales deeply, her
mind racing to fathom the sheer scale of the universe as
described by Airl. The silent intensity between them builds.

                    MATILDA (V.O.)
                (responding)
            Seventy-four trillion years...
            It's incomprehensible. And all
            those life forms, scattered across
            countless stars...

Her thoughts trail off, overwhelmed by the vastness of the
revelation. Airl's calm yet penetrating gaze doesn't waver,
sensing Matilda's astonishment.

                    ALIEN (V.O.)
                (gently)
            This is only the beginning.

Matilda takes a deep breath, preparing herself for the next
wave of unimaginable knowledge. The task at hand—this
seemingly endless interview—is becoming more daunting than
ever. Yet, she is resolute. She can't stop now.

The room feels heavier with the weight of the information.
The clock ticks softly in the background, but neither Matilda
nor Airl notice. They are locked in a moment that transcends
time, one human mind trying to process the boundless
knowledge of the universe, shared by an IS-BE who has seen it
all.

INT. ROSWELL ARMY AIR FORCE BASE- CONTROL ROOM - DAY

Colonel William H. Blanchard stands behind the glass, his
eyes focused on the interview in progress on the other side
of the one-way window. In the room, Sergeant Matilda
O'Donnell MacElroy sits across from Airl the Alien, their
eyes locked in telepathic communication. The silence in the
control room is only broken by the hum of equipment, a subtle
tension growing with each passing second.

Blanchard notices the shift in Matilda's expression — her face pale, brows furrowing. The conversation with Airl has clearly taken its toll. She blinks, and for the first time, her gaze falters. Her breathing deepens, and slowly, she breaks eye contact with the alien.

Matilda stands, shaky but resolute, pushing her chair back with an audible scrape. Blanchard stiffens as he watches her step away from the chair. Her movements are deliberate, almost heavy, as though she's walking against an invisible force. Airl remains seated, unblinking, but Blanchard can sense the weight of the telepathic exchange lingering in the air.

Matilda approaches the door, pausing for a moment with her hand on the handle. She takes one last breath, opens the door, and walks out of the interview room, her face still marked by the weight of what she has just experienced.

Blanchard's jaw tightens as he watches her leave, the pressure of the situation evident on his face. He glances at the screen that monitors the session, but his attention drifts back to the empty chair where Matilda once sat.

INT. ROSWELL ARMY AIR FORCE BASE - BARRACKS - DAY

Matilda sits on the edge of her bunk, hunched over with her elbows resting on her knees, staring blankly at the floor. Her eyes are hollow, and her hands tremble slightly as she wrings them together. The emotional toll of the interview with Airl weighs heavily on her shoulders, her confidence visibly shaken.

The door creaks open, but Matilda hardly notices. Colonel William H. Blanchard steps into the room quietly, his demeanor calm yet commanding. He takes in the sight of Matilda, clearly worn down by the overwhelming pressure of her task.

Blanchard approaches the bunk, his footsteps soft, and sits down beside her. For a moment, neither of them speaks. Matilda remains in her own world, her eyes unfocused, lost in the emotional burden that taunts her mind.

     WILLIAM H. BLANCHARD
   (softly)
 Sergeant...

Matilda blinks as if waking from a trance, but she still doesn't look at him. Her body language is tense, her breath shallow.

WILLIAM H. BLANCHARD (CONT'D)
(imploring)
Matilda, you have to see this mission through.

She doesn't respond, her gaze still fixed on the floor. Blanchard leans forward slightly, his voice taking on a firmer, yet understanding tone.

WILLIAM H. BLANCHARD (CONT'D)
Your country depends on you. What we're dealing with... it's bigger than any one of us.

Matilda clenches her jaw, her lip trembling. She can feel the weight of his words, but the fear and uncertainty grip her tightly. Blanchard sighs, softening his tone once more.

WILLIAM H. BLANCHARD (CONT'D)
You've already come this far. No one else can do what you're doing, Matilda.

He waits, hoping his words will reach her. She finally looks up, her eyes meeting his for the first time since he entered the room.

MATILDA
(barely above a whisper)
I don't know if I can...

Blanchard looks at her with a quiet intensity, his voice unwavering.

WILLIAM H. BLANCHARD
You don't have a choice, Sergeant. This is what you've been called to do.

There's a long pause. Matilda bites her lip, wrestling with her thoughts, before nodding slowly. She knows, deep down, that Blanchard is right.

WILLIAM H. BLANCHARD (CONT'D)
(standing up, placing a hand on her shoulder)
We're counting on you. Don't let us down.

He walks toward the door, leaving Matilda to her thoughts. She sits there, her confidence still fragile, but a spark of resolve flickers in her eyes. The weight of the mission may be crushing, but she knows she must endure.

INT. ROSWELL ARMY AIR FORCE BASE - CONFERENCE ROOM - DAY

The room is stark, the air tense. Seated around the table are three men: the Government Agent, the Scientist, and the Military Official. Captain Sheridan Cavitt sits close by, observing the proceedings quietly. Colonel William H. Blanchard leans forward, arms crossed, his stern gaze fixed on Matilda, who is sitting at the head of the table.

A stack of transcripts lay in front of Matilda. Her hands rest on them for a moment as she gathers her thoughts. The room falls silent, everyone waiting for her to speak.

She picks up the transcripts, her eyes scanning the words briefly before lifting her gaze to the others.

> MATILDA
> (steady, but
>   contemplative)
> Today, Airl told me about some very technical things. I took a few notes to remind myself, so I can repeat what she said as closely as possible.

The room remains still. Eyes dart across the table, but no one interrupts. Matilda pauses, gathering her thoughts, then continues.

> MATILDA (CONT'D)
> (careful, as if choosing
>   her words)
> She began with an analogy... about scientific knowledge.

She places the transcripts down carefully, her fingers resting on the pages, as the tension grows in the room. All eyes are on Matilda, who now holds their undivided attention.

INT. ROSWELL ARMY AIR FORCE BASE - INTERVIEW ROOM - DAY

INSERT CARD: TOP SECRET OFFICIAL TRANSCRIPT OF THE U.S. ARMY AIR FORCE ROSWELL ARMY AIR FIELD, 509TH BOMB GROUP SUBJECT: ALIEN INTERVIEW, 29. 7. 1947, 1ST SESSION

Matilda sits across from Airl, her gaze fixed on the alien, the intensity of the telepathic connection almost overwhelming. The weight of the conversation, and the sheer depth of information being conveyed, fills the room.

                    ALIEN (V.O.)
               (calm yet profound voice)
          Can you imagine how much progress
          could have been made on Earth if
          people like Johannes Gutenberg, Sir
          Isaac Newton, Benjamin Franklin,
          George Washington Carver, Nicola
          Tesla, Jonas Salk, and Richard
          Trevithick were living today? What
          if they never died, never forgotten
          everything they knew, and continued
          to learn and work forever?

Matilda shifts slightly in her chair, taking it all in, her
mind grappling with the implications of such a statement.

                    ALIEN (V.O.)
               (thoughtfully)
          Imagine the level of technology and
          civilization that could be attained
          if Immortal Spiritual Beings, like
          these, were allowed to continue to
          create -- in the same place, and at
          the same time -- for billions or
          trillions of years. The Domain is
          one such civilization that has
          existed for trillions of years with
          relatively uninterrupted progress.
          Knowledge has been accumulated,
          refined, and improved upon in
          nearly every field of study
          imaginable.

Matilda's thoughts race as she processes the unimaginable
concept of endless progression, free from death or memory
loss. She tries to envision Earth under such conditions.

                    MATILDA (V.O.)
               (curious yet unsettled
                tone)
          And all this time, this knowledge
          was simply... kept? Perfected?

                    ALIEN (V.O.)
          Yes. Originally, the interaction
          of IS-BE illusions or inventions
          created the very fabric of the
          physical universe -- the microcosm
          and the macrocosm. Every particle,
          every star, every subatomic
          structure -- all brought into
          existence by an IS-BE, just like
          you.

Matilda furrows her brow, her thoughts swirling. The sheer magnitude of Airl's explanation is difficult to fathom.

> MATILDA (V.O.)
> (questioning)
> So... everything was just... imagined into being?"

> ALIEN (V.O.)
> (conviction)
> Everything. From the size of a dust particle to a Magellanic cloud. Every thought manifest from nothingness. Even the tiny cells that sense and navigate within a body were conceived in this way.

Matilda feels a shiver down her spine, realizing the power of creation she has forgotten.

> ALIEN (V.O.)
> (gently but firmly)
> You, and every IS-BE on Earth, participated in the creation of this universe. Despite the flesh body you now inhabit, despite only living for 65 short years, and despite the overwhelming electric shock treatments to erase your memory... you still know who you are.

Matilda remains quiet, reflecting. She begins to recall small, distant memories—flashes of understanding and awareness from her past lives.

> ALIEN (V.O.)
> (comforting)
> And how else can one explain the child prodigy? A three-year-old playing concertos without formal training. It is not by chance; it is memory, thousands of lifetimes in front of a keyboard, on planets long forgotten.

Matilda's breath catches, stunned by the simple truth. Deep down, she begins to feel the weight of her true self, the potential she has forgotten.

> MATILDA (V.O.)
> (shaken but determined)
> So... the Old Empire's influence has been weakening?

> ALIEN (V.O.)
> (with certainty)
> Yes. In the past hundred years, humankind has developed more than in the previous two thousand. The influence of the Old Empire over the mind and affairs of Mankind has diminished, allowing for growth once more.

Matilda sits quietly, absorbing the enormity of Airl's revelation. The truth of her existence, her potential, begins to settle in.

INT. ROSWELL ARMY AIR FORCE BASE - CONFERENCE ROOM - DAY

Seated around the table are the Government Agent, the Scientist, the Military Official, Captain Sheridan Cavitt, and Colonel William H. Blanchard. At the head of the table, Matilda O'Donnell MacElroy sits quietly, her hands resting on the transcripts of her interview with Airl the Alien.

The room is still, tense with anticipation as the men await Matilda's words. After a moment, Matilda exhales softly, picking up the transcript. She scans the pages briefly before speaking.

> MATILDA
> (steady, but with an
>   undercurrent of emotion)
> "A renaissance of invention on Earth began in 1,250 AD with the destruction of the 'Old Empire' space fleet in the solar system. During the next 500 years, Earth may have the potential to regain autonomy and independence..."

The men around the table exchange uneasy glances. The Scientist leans forward, his curiosity piqued.

> SCIENTIST
> (interrupting)
> Potential for autonomy? Are we talking full independence from external control?

> MATILDA
> (nods slightly,
>   continuing)
>   (MORE)

                    MATILDA (CONT'D)
          "...but only to the degree that
          humankind can apply the
          concentrated genius of the IS-BEs
          on Earth to solve the amnesia
          problem."

The Government Agent raises an eyebrow, scribbling a note on
his pad. He seems skeptical.

                    GOVERNMENT AGENT
          IS-BEs, concentrated genius,
          solving amnesia. Sounds far-
          fetched, doesn't it?

Matilda holds his gaze for a moment, her voice unwavering as
she presses forward.

                    MATILDA
               (firmly)
          "However, on a cautionary note, the
          inventive potential of the IS-BEs
          who have been exiled to this planet
          is severely compromised by the
          criminal elements of the Earth
          population. Specifically,
          politicians, warmongers, and
          irresponsible physicists create
          unlimited weapons..."

She pauses, letting the gravity of the statement sink in.
Captain Cavitt shifts in his seat, his brow furrowed.

                    CAPTAIN CAVITT
          Unlimited weapons? You mean like
          nuclear bombs?

Matilda glances at him and nods.

                    MATILDA
          Yes, nuclear bombs, chemicals,
          diseases, and social chaos. These
          have the potential to extinguish
          all life forms on Earth, forever.

The tension in the room grows palpable as the men absorb her
words. Colonel Blanchard folds his hands, leaning forward
slightly, his face tight with concern.

                    COLONEL BLANCHARD
          How close are we to that scenario?

Matilda sighs softly before continuing, her eyes briefly
scanning the transcript again.

                    MATILDA
          "Even the relatively small
          explosions that were tested and
          used in the past two years on Earth
          have the potential to destroy all
          of life if deployed in sufficient
          quantities. Larger weapons could
          consume all of the oxygen in the
          global atmosphere in a single
          explosion."

The Military Official straightens, clearly alarmed.

                    MILITARY OFFICIAL
          Wait... all the oxygen?

Matilda nods.

                    MATILDA
          Yes, in a single explosion.

A tense silence falls over the room. The Scientist speaks
again, his voice a mixture of disbelief and curiosity.

                    SCIENTIST
          But... this can't just be about
          weapons. What's the real issue
          here?"

Matilda places the transcript on the table and meets their
eyes one by one. She picks up the transcript and continues
reading.

                    MATILDA
          "The most fundamental problems that
          must be solved to ensure that Earth
          will not be destroyed by technology
          are social and humanitarian
          problems. The greatest scientific
          minds on Earth, despite their
          genius, have never addressed these
          problems."

                    GOVERNMENT AGENT
                (leaning back, muttering)
          Figures.

Matilda continues, her voice softening with the weight of the
truth she must deliver.

                    MATILDA
          "Therefore, do not look to
          scientists to save Earth or the
          future of humanity.
                    (MORE)

MATILDA (CONT'D)
Any science that is solely based on the paradigm that existence is composed only of energy and objects moving through space... is not true science. It utterly ignores the creative spark originated by an individual IS-BE."

The Government Agent crosses his arms, glancing sideways at the Scientist, who frowns but stays silent.

MATILDA (CONT'D)
"And that is the problem. This ignorance, instilled by the 'Old Empire,' has trapped IS-BEs on this planet, robbing them of their innate ability to create space, energy, and matter. As long as the awareness of the spiritual self is ignored, humanity will remain imprisoned."

Her voice falters slightly as she delivers the final warning.

MATILDA (CONT'D)
"Until the day of its own... self-destruction and oblivion."

The room falls into an uneasy stillness, the weight of Matilda's words hanging in the air. The men exchange glances, shaken by the enormity of what they've just heard.

Without waiting for more questions, Matilda lowers the transcript, gazing at the group as they process the warning Airl has conveyed through her.

INT. WHITE HOUSE - OVAL OFFICE - DAY

President Harry S. Truman sits behind his desk, a solemn expression etched on his face. In his hands, he holds a stack of transcripts from the Roswell Army Air Force Base. His eyes scan the pages, and as he reads, the voice of Airl the Alien echoes in his mind.

ALIEN (V.O.)
"Do not rely on the dogma of physical sciences to master the fundamental forces of creation any more than you would trust the chanted incantations of an incense-burning shaman. The net result of both of these is entrapment and oblivion.
(MORE)

                    ALIEN (V.O.) (CONT'D)
          Scientists pretend to observe, but
          they only suppose that they see and
          call it fact. Like the blind man,
          a scientist cannot learn to see
          until he realizes that he is
          blind."

Truman's gaze hardens as he continues reading, his mind
absorbing the alien's philosophical critique of human
knowledge.

                    ALIEN (V.O.)
          "The "facts" of Earth science do
          not include the source of creation.
          They include only the result or
          byproducts of creation. The
          "facts" of science do not include
          any memory of the nearly infinite
          past experience of existence. The
          essence of creation and existence
          cannot be found through the lens of
          a microscope or telescope or by any
          other measurement of the physical
          universe."

Truman leans back in his chair, setting the papers down for a
moment, his fingers briefly rubbing his temples. The weight
of the words hangs heavy in the air.

                    ALIEN (V.O.)
          "How can a blind man teach others
          to see the nearly infinite
          gradients that comprise the
          spectrum of light? The notion that
          one can understand the universe
          without understanding the nature of
          an IS-BE is as absurd as conceiving
          that an artist is a speck of paint
          on his own canvas."

Truman's eyes close for a moment, as if to find a sense of
clarity amidst the overwhelming information. He takes a deep
breath and adjusts his glasses, then looks at the transcripts
once more. The revelations shake the very foundation of
everything he thought he knew.

                    ALIEN (V.O.)
          "Religion says the creator is all,
          and the creation is nothing. These
          two extremes are the bars of a
          prison cell. They prevent
          observation of all phenomena as an
          interactive whole."

Truman gently places the transcripts on his desk, the weight of Airl's words pressing down on his shoulders. He stares out the nearby window, the distant hum of Washington life muted by the enormity of the knowledge he now holds.

He takes another deep breath, his hand instinctively moving to straighten the papers as though organizing the chaos in his mind. The room is silent, but the thoughts race, leaving the President to ponder the implications of what he has just read.

After a long pause, Truman leans forward, his expression one of steely resolve. Whatever decision lies ahead, the truth in these transcripts cannot be ignored.

INT. ROSWELL ARMY AIR FORCE BASE - INTERVIEW ROOM - DAY

Matilda sits across from Airl, her notepad untouched, eyes locked with the alien. Her breathing is slow and deliberate as the telepathic connection deepens between them. Airl's thoughts flood into her mind, washing over her like a tide of complex emotions and revelations.

> ALIEN (V.O.)
> The study of creation without knowing the IS-BE, the source of creation, is futile. When you sail to the edge of a universe conceived by science, you fall off the end into an abyss of dark, dispassionate space and lifeless, unrelenting force.

Matilda shifts slightly in her chair, her fingers trembling ever so slightly. The weight of the information is bearing down on her, but she steels herself, focusing on Airl's voice resonating within her mind.

> ALIEN (V.O.)
> On Earth, you have been convinced that the oceans of the mind and spirit are filled with gruesome, ghoulish monsters that will eat you alive if you dare to venture beyond the breakwater of superstition.

QUICK FLASHBACK:

Matilda's mind flickers with images: the fears and superstitions of mankind, the societal taboos against seeking too deeply into one's soul. The image of her religious upbringing flashes before her—traditions that suddenly seem like shackles, holding her from a deeper truth.

BACK TO THE SCENE.

>   ALIEN (V.O.)
>   The vested interest of the "Old
>   Empire" prison system is to prevent
>   you from looking at your own soul.
>   They fear that you will see in your
>   own memory the slave masters who
>   keep you imprisoned. The prison is
>   made of shadows in your mind. The
>   shadows are made of lies, pain,
>   loss, and fear.

Her heart beats faster. Memories of her life on Earth rise—pains she thought were healed, losses she thought forgotten. But now, they feel like pieces of a larger puzzle she had never understood. Airl's words slice through the illusions of comfort she once held.

>   ALIEN (V.O.)
>   The true geniuses of civilization
>   are those IS-BEs who will enable
>   other IS-BEs to recover their
>   memory and regain self-realization
>   and self-determination. This issue
>   is not solved through enforcing
>   moral regulation on behavior, or
>   through the control of beings
>   through mystery, faith, drugs,
>   guns, or any other dogma of a slave
>   society.

Matilda's mind swims, her hands clenching into fists. She realizes she's been given a chance to glimpse something profound—a key to a door she never knew existed. She exhales slowly, overwhelmed by the responsibility of what she is learning.

>   ALIEN (V.O.)
>   And certainly not through the use
>   of electric shock and hypnotic
>   commands! The survival of Earth
>   and every being on it depends on
>   the ability to recover the memory
>   of skills you have accrued through
>   the trillenia; to recover the
>   essence of yourself.

Matilda feels a pang of sorrow and anger at the thought of the suffering caused by these primitive techniques of control—methods that strip away the essence of what makes someone whole. She recalls the institutional horrors, the mind-numbing procedures. Her chest tightens as Airl's words bring those thoughts to the surface.

> ALIEN (V.O.)
> Such an art, science, or technology has never been conceived in the "Old Empire". Otherwise, they would not have resorted to the "solution" that brought you to your current condition on Earth.

Matilda's eyes momentarily lower to the floor, the full scope of humanity's enslavement weighing heavily on her. The idea that the solution to their imprisonment has never even been attempted—never even considered—gnaws at her.

> ALIEN (V.O.)
> Neither has such technology ever been developed by The Domain. Until recently, the necessity of rehabilitating an IS-BE with amnesia has not been needed. Therefore, no one has ever worked on solving this problem. So far, unfortunately, The Domain has no solution to offer.

The room feels colder, the weight of those final words settling over her like a dark cloud. The helplessness in Airl's voice echoes in Matilda's mind. The truth is far worse than she could have imagined—there is no solution, not yet. No one is coming to save them.

Matilda remains still, trying to absorb the gravity of the situation, her determination wavering. She inhales sharply, refocusing, knowing she has to continue, no matter how insurmountable it all feels.

INT. SPACECRAFT IN EARTH'S ORBIT - COMMAND CENTER

The vast darkness of space stretches beyond the control room's wide observation windows. Far below, Earth hovers, a blue and green sphere swathed in clouds. Inside the spacecraft, the command center is filled with Alien officers of The Domain Expeditionary Force, who work intently at a series of sophisticated consoles.

Seated in a central command chair is a high-ranking Domain officer, radiating an aura of calm yet focused authority. His sleek, doll-like body gleams under the ambient light, devoid of any expression but quietly observant.

On an array of monitoring screens, the telemetry of Matilda's conversation with Airl streams in waves and symbols, translated into the visuals of soundwaves, brainwave patterns, and telepathic emissions.

An officer turns to the COMMANDER, nodding in quiet understanding.

> COMMANDER (V.O.)
> (via telepathy)
> She is progressing. Airl's methods seem effective. The Earthling is absorbing the information.

The TACTICAL OFFICER, operating a holographic console, initiates a scan of Earth's atmosphere and biosphere. The hologram displays data streams: air quality, water purity, the stability of ecosystems. He pauses, his gaze fixed on a segment of data.

> TACTICAL OFFICER (V.O.)
> (via telepathy)
> Commander, it is crucial we advance the planetary preservation protocols. The human population is endangering their environment.

The Commander inclines his head slightly, a sign of silent acknowledgment.

OBSERVATION PANEL - SPACE BEYOND

Outside the observation panel, another Domain spacecraft floats, silently stationed beside this one. Farther off in the distance, a faint shimmer of stars hints at other Domain ships, invisible but ever watchful.

The ANALYST officer's console glows softly as he tunes into a telepathic relay of Airl's words. A figure appears on the screen — the image of Nikola Tesla in a historical photograph, his eyes piercing, his demeanor stoic.

> ANALYST (V.O.)
> (via telepathy)
> Tesla achieved significant advancements but was limited by Earth's understanding of energy. We must identify others with similar latent potential. A delicate task, yet... necessary.

> COMMANDER (V.O.)
> (via telepathy)
> Indeed. While limited, some humans possess unusual capacity. The technology within Airl's vessel can be utilized to accelerate understanding... carefully.

He gestures toward the ship's interior, where unseen compartments are filled with complex machinery and alien artifacts, each containing secrets yet to be uncovered by human technology.

The TACTICAL OFFICER glances toward the Commander, his thoughts trailing into a silent yet powerful message.

> TACTICAL OFFICER (V.O.)
> (via telepathy)
> When the time is right, Commander, pieces of Airl's craft could be dispersed discreetly. Each holds knowledge that, if properly interpreted, could guide their scientists forward.

The Commander gazes out over Earth, his thoughts focused on the fragile future of the planet below.

> COMMANDER (V.O.)
> (via telepathy)
> Patience. Humanity's understanding must evolve slowly, lest it be squandered. The intention is to preserve Earth's systems, not to hasten its decline.

He pauses, his gaze unyielding as Earth turns silently below.

INT. ROSWELL ARMY AIR FORCE BASE - INTERVIEW ROOM - DAY

Matilda sits across from Airl, the small gray alien, their eyes meeting in the familiar, intense gaze that bridges their telepathic connection. Matilda, holding her notepad with faintly trembling hands, mentally prepares herself as Airl's voice begins to echo in her mind, resonating with information that stretches the limits of her understanding.

> ALIEN (V.O.)
> The materials of my craft are beyond the capability of Earth's current resources. Many of the metals have taken billions of years to perfect and are processed in ways unfathomable to human engineers.

Matilda listens, her brow furrowing as she tries to comprehend.

                    ALIEN (V.O.)
          The craft's navigation system
          itself is bonded to my own
          wavelength. It requires not only
          control, but a deep integration —
          one that cannot be replicated
          without an IS-BE trained
          specifically to interface with the
          neural network.

Matilda's mind races. She scribbles a note, but the
implications make her pause, pen hovering over the page.
Airl's thoughts, deep and steady, continue flowing.

                    ALIEN (V.O.)
          Some of the craft's components will
          stir recognition in certain Earth
          scientists. There are those among
          you who, in past existences,
          wielded similar knowledge in realms
          far removed from this one. They
          have the latent ability to unlock
          some of this technology, to recall
          the understanding they once held.

Matilda is taken aback, her mind spinning with thoughts of
forgotten knowledge and scientists who might carry these
dormant memories.

                    MATILDA (V.O.)
               (thoughtfully, in
                response)
          So... these minds, these brilliant
          minds of Earth... you're saying
          they might remember? They might...
          rediscover what they once knew?

                    ALIEN (V.O.)
          Indeed. Just as some on Earth
          "remembered" how to recreate the
          electric generator, refrigeration,
          or antibiotics — these flashes of
          genius are remnants of memories,
          fragments of understanding
          returning to them. Your
          civilization is built on these
          fragments. In time, through study
          of my craft, other vital knowledge
          may resurface.

Matilda's heart beats faster. The responsibility of it
weighs heavily on her, and she can feel her pulse echoing in
the silence of the room.

                    MATILDA (V.O.)
                (telepathically)
            Then this... this is not only a
            study of technology but a chance to
            reclaim pieces of ourselves that
            were lost.

Airl's eyes, steady and unblinking, seem to acknowledge the profundity of her realization.

                    ALIEN (V.O.)
                (via telepathy)
            Precisely. Earth's progress
            depends on this reclamation. The
            reawakening of dormant skills will
            not be easy, but within your
            species, the potential remains.
            You carry the memories, the
            knowledge of a thousand
            civilizations, waiting to emerge.

Matilda takes a deep, steadying breath, feeling the enormity of their conversation press into her heart. She lowers her gaze, almost reverent, as the weight of Airl's revelations settles within her.

INT. WHITE HOUSE - OVAL OFFICE - DAY

President Harry S. Truman sits behind his grand oak desk, his expression reserved, stern, and unmoved. Sunlight seeps softly through the tall, heavy curtains, casting a warm glow over the polished wood and framed photographs around him. But Truman's focus is entirely on the Top Secret transcript in his hands.

He reads slowly, his eyes scanning over the intricate words, absorbing their weight and complexity. Airl's ethereal voice, calm and clear, echoes in his mind as he reads:

                    ALIEN (V.O.)
            "The following are the specific
            systems embodied in my craft that
            contain useful components..."

A pause, as Truman's gaze lifts briefly, his brow furrowed, before he returns to the text.

                    ALIEN (V.O.)
          "1) There is an assortment of
          microscopic wiring or fibers within
          the walls of the craft that control
          such things as communications,
          information storage, computer
          function, and automatic
          navigation."

Truman's hand tightens slightly around the paper as he reads
on, the vast implications beginning to register.

                    ALIEN (V.O.)
          "2) The same wiring is used for
          light, sub-light, and ultra-light
          spectrum detection and vision."

The President's gaze shifts, distant. His mind absorbs the
alien's words, but his face remains an unreadable mask.

                    ALIEN (V.O.)
          "3) The fabrics of the interior of
          the craft are far superior to any
          on Earth at this time and have
          hundreds or thousands of
          applications."

Truman closes his eyes briefly, processing the magnitude of
the technology described.

                    ALIEN (V.O.)
          "4) You will also find mechanisms
          for creating, amplifying, and
          channeling light particles or waves
          as a form of energy."

The silence in the Oval Office grows heavier, and Truman's
jaw tightens subtly. He opens his eyes, the deep focus
sharpening in them as he reads further.

                    ALIEN (V.O.)
          "As an officer, pilot, and engineer
          of The Domain Forces, I am not at
          liberty to discuss or convey the
          detailed operation or construction
          of the craft in any way, other than
          what I have just disclosed.
          However, I am confident that there
          are many competent engineers on
          Earth who will develop useful
          technology with these resources."

Truman's fingers trace the edge of the transcript as he
reaches the final lines.

                    ALIEN (V.O.)
          "I am providing these details to
          you in the hope that the greater
          good of The Domain will be served."

Truman sets the paper down slowly, his hand resting on top of
it, as he stares into the distance with a reserved but
penetrating gaze. The weight of what he has read settles
heavily on his shoulders, yet his expression remains firm,
unmoved.

INT. ROSWELL ARMY AIR FORCE BASE - INTERVIEW ROOM - DAY

The lone camera sits mounted in the corner of the room, its
red tally light blinking steadily, an unblinking sentinel
capturing every moment. Matilda sits across from the
diminutive figure of Airl, their gazes locked in an intense
connection. The faint hum of the room is the only sound as
their telepathic exchange continues.

Matilda's eyes dart briefly to the one-way glass window. She
is acutely aware of the watchers behind it but quickly
refocuses on Airl. Her pen rests on the notepad in front of
her, motionless, as her attention is consumed entirely by the
silent dialogue unfolding in her mind.

                    ALIEN (V.O.)
          Immortal Spiritual Beings, or IS-
          BEs, are the creators of illusions.
          In their original, unfettered
          state, each IS-BE is an eternal,
          all-powerful, all-knowing entity.

Airl's calm, telepathic voice reverberates in Matilda's mind.
She takes a steadying breath, absorbing the enormity of the
alien's words.

                    ALIEN (V.O.)
          IS-BEs create space by imagining a
          location. The intervening distance
          between themselves and the imagined
          location is what you perceive as
          space. IS-BEs are not bound by the
          physical universe. They are a
          source of energy and illusion.

Matilda tilts her head slightly, her gaze narrowing as she
processes the concept.

                    ALIEN (V.O.)
          An IS-BE can choose to exist within
          an illusion of space and time, to
          create objects and events, to cause
          motion and animate forms. Any form
          animated by an IS-BE is called
          life. Yet, the creation of an
          illusion demands constant attention
          to sustain it. Without this
          attention, the illusion ceases to
          exist.

Airl's serene tone contrasts with the intensity of the ideas
she conveys. Matilda's brow furrows, the sheer depth of the
explanation stretching the limits of her understanding.

                    ALIEN (V.O.)
          One common denominator of IS-BEs is
          their desire to avoid boredom.
          Imagine having the power to
          conceive anything, perceive
          everything, and cause anything to
          happen at will. Now imagine if you
          could do nothing else. Would you
          not grow bored?

Matilda's lips part slightly as her thoughts race. The
notion is both alien and oddly relatable. She shifts
slightly in her seat, her fingers twitching over her notepad.

                    ALIEN (V.O.)
          IS-BEs diminish their abilities to
          create games to play. They
          willingly endure pain, suffering,
          and challenges to introduce
          unknowns, barriers, and
          opponents—elements that make a game
          worth playing. The physical
          universe is made up of unadmired
          illusions, crafted and sustained by
          IS-BEs seeking admiration or
          entertainment.

Matilda's gaze softens, her curiosity melding with a hint of
sadness. She glances at her untouched notepad, then back at
Airl, as though searching for a way to encapsulate the
enormity of these revelations.

                    ALIEN (V.O.)
          Your universe began as a collection
          of individual illusions, imagined
          as homes by IS-BEs.
                         (MORE)

> ALIEN (V.O.) (CONT'D)
> Over time, these illusions
> collided, merged, and coalesced,
> resulting in shared creation. The
> game was born of their desire to
> solve the problem of boredom.

Airl's telepathic presence feels warm yet vast, like a boundless horizon. Matilda straightens slightly, a flicker of resolve replacing her earlier uncertainty.

The hum of the room continues, and the flashing red tally light remains steady as the silent, profound exchange between the two persists.

DREAM SEQUENCE:

EXT. INFINITE VOID - TIMELESS

Matilda stands barefoot in an endless void of shimmering white light. There is no horizon, no sound, only stillness. Her breath echoes faintly as she glances around, her body weightless yet solid.

Suddenly, faint outlines of **galaxies** begin to materialize in the void, swirling gently. Stars burst into life with vibrant colors, forming nebulas and constellations that stretch infinitely in all directions.

> ALIEN (V.O.)
> All space, galaxies, suns, and
> **planets** were created by IS-BEs.
> They exist because we agree they
> exist.

Matilda watches as planets take shape before her, floating within reach. Each planet is unique—some vibrant and lush, others barren and rocky. She touches a nearby planet, and a rush of life forms appear, populating its surface.

EXT. VERDANT PLANET - DAY

Matilda is now standing in a **verdant alien world.** Lush forests filled with towering; bioluminescent trees hum softly. Strange creatures roam the land—graceful, deer-like beings with crystalline antlers and birds with radiant, trailing feathers.

Above her, **two suns** burn brightly in a green-tinged sky. A warm breeze rustles the leaves as sparkling streams wind through the terrain.

                    ALIEN (V.O.)
          Every IS-BE constructs their own
          universe, their own rules. Some
          are solitary, others collaborative.
          These creations form infinite
          layers of existence.

The verdant world shifts suddenly. The forest dissolves into
swirling mist.

EXT. CONVERGING UNIVERSES - UNKNOWN

Matilda stands between **colliding universes**. One is vibrant,
filled with pulsating colors and fluid motion. The other is
dark and angular, its sharp geometric shapes spinning
violently.

She watches as they merge, their edges interlocking like
puzzle pieces. A glowing lattice forms between them,
stabilizing their collision.

                    ALIEN (V.O.)
          When universes converge, IS-BEs
          join forces. They create and
          destroy, share and compete. This
          is how existence expands.

Matilda steps forward, and the lattice glows brighter.

EXT. INFINITE OCEAN - SUNSET

Matilda now stands at the edge of an **infinite ocean** under a
fiery orange sunset. The waves sparkle with golden light,
carrying fragments of memories and illusions. Each wave
reflects fleeting images of universes and beings—lovers
embracing, empires rising, stars dying.

She steps into the water, and the memories flood her mind.

                    ALIEN (V.O.)
          IS-BEs create illusions to play
          games, to avoid boredom. But the
          price of creation is maintaining
          the illusion.

As Matilda moves deeper into the water, the waves rise,
carrying her upward.

EXT. STARLIT MAZE - NIGHT

The water disappears, and Matilda finds herself in a **starlit maze**. The walls are made of shifting light, reflecting distorted versions of herself. She reaches out to touch one wall, and the reflection shatters into fragments of stars.

> ALIEN (V.O.)
> To play the game, IS-BEs forget their power. They trap themselves in a maze of their own creation, pretending there is no escape.

Matilda begins running through the maze, the walls shifting and closing in. She feels panic rise, but suddenly stops.

She closes her eyes, takes a deep breath, and whispers:

> MATILDA
> This isn't real.

The maze walls dissolve into stardust, revealing a boundless universe.

EXT. COSMIC SKY - TIMELESS

Matilda floats in a **cosmic sky** surrounded by infinite stars. She feels weightless and free, as if she is one with the universe.

> ALIEN (V.O.)
> You are the creator of your own prison, and only you hold the key.

Matilda stretches out her arms, her body glowing with a soft, golden light. A peaceful smile crosses her face as the stars pulse around her, acknowledging her presence.

THE DREAM FADES TO WHITE.

INT. ROSWELL ARMY AIR FORCE BASE - INTERVIEW ROOM - DAY

Matilda jolts awake in her chair, her breathing quick. Airl the Alien watches her silently, her eyes reflecting the infinite expanse Matilda just experienced.

Matilda steadies herself, realizing the enormity of what she has just witnessed. She meets Airl's gaze, her own eyes filled with wonder and quiet determination.

                    MATILDA (V.O.)
                (telepathically)
            I've never felt anything like that
            before... so vast, so
            interconnected. It's overwhelming.
            How... how do you carry the weight
            of knowing all this?

Airl tilts her head slightly, as if studying Matilda's
question.

                    ALIEN (V.O.)
                (telepathically)
            Knowledge is not a weight. It is
            the absence of it that burdens you.
            The illusion of separation and
            ignorance is the heaviest chain.

Matilda's brow furrows as she absorbs Airl's words. Her
hands slowly relax, her breathing steadies, but her mind
races with questions.

                    MATILDA (V.O.)
            You said we create our own cages.
            That we forget who we are. Why?
            Why would anyone willingly do this
            to themselves?

Airl's gaze sharpens, carrying an almost imperceptible edge
of urgency.

                    ALIEN (V.O.)
            On Earth, you are taught that the
            gods are responsible. That only a
            god can create universes. In doing
            so, responsibility is placed on
            another: another IS-BE, another
            "god." Never oneself.

Matilda leans back slightly, the words sinking in. Her lips
part as if to speak, but she hesitates. Airl continues, her
voice unwavering yet compassionate.

                    ALIEN (V.O.)
            This is the source of your
            entrapment. To believe that
            creation comes from outside of you,
            that your existence is owed to
            another, is to deny your own
            divinity. You are taught that you
            are powerless, that you are at the
            mercy of forces beyond you.
                        (MORE)

ALIEN (V.O.) (CONT'D)
But the truth is simple: you, individually and collectively, are gods.

Matilda flinches slightly at the weight of the statement, her fingers curling around the edge of the table.

MATILDA (V.O.)
(softly)
Gods? We... we're taught that's blasphemy.

Airl the Alien tilts her head again, her expression unreadable.

ALIEN (V.O.)
Blasphemy is a construct designed to maintain control. To keep you from looking inward. The fear of such a label ensures obedience to the illusion. But an IS-BE is not bound by illusions, except by their own agreement to be so.

Matilda's throat tightens. The enormity of the revelation feels both liberating and paralyzing. She searches Airl's eyes for reassurance.

MATILDA (V.O.)
If... if we're all gods, why don't we feel like it? Why does it feel like we're trapped, lost?

Airl leans forward slightly, her presence emanating calm.

ALIEN (V.O.)
Because you have been taught to forget. To believe in limits. To trust in lies. Responsibility for creation has been assigned to something other than yourself. You are taught to worship, to obey, to doubt your own power. Until you remember, you will remain in a self-made labyrinth.

Matilda takes a deep, shaky breath, her hands gripping the edge of the table as though bracing herself.

MATILDA (V.O.)
How do we remember? How do we take back what we've lost?

Airl's eyes soften, her voice carrying the faintest hint of compassion.

> ALIEN (V.O.)
> Begin by questioning. By rejecting the stories of gods who demand your servitude. By seeing the illusion for what it is. Responsibility is the key to freedom. You must reclaim it.

Matilda closes her eyes for a moment, centering herself. When she opens them again, her gaze is resolute.

> MATILDA (V.O.)
> I'll try. But... it feels impossible.

> ALIEN (V.O.)
> Every journey begins with a single step. Remember, the labyrinth you navigate was built by your own hands. Only you can find the way out.

Matilda's lips press into a determined line. The tension in the room shifts, the air thick with the unspoken weight of possibility. For the first time, she feels the faintest flicker of hope amidst the enormity of what she has learned.

FLASHBACK:

INT. ROSWELL ARMY AIR FORCE BASE - BRIEFING ROOM - EVENING

The dim light casts long shadows over the room, amplifying the tense atmosphere. Colonel William H. Blanchard stands at the head of the table, his hands gripping the edge with white-knuckled intensity. Captain Sheridan Cavitt leans against the wall, arms crossed, his gaze fixed on Matilda, who sits in the center of the room, clutching a transcript to her chest like a lifeline.

The table is cluttered with documents, maps, and ashtrays filled with cigarette butts, remnants of an extended and heated discussion.

Matilda's voice cuts through the thick air, her tone resolute and unwavering.

> MATILDA
> (holding up the
> transcript)
> This transcript speaks for itself.
> (MORE)

                    MATILDA (CONT'D)
          I relayed Airl's exact
          communication as faithfully as
          possible.

Colonel Blanchard's jaw tightens. He exhales sharply, pacing
the room as though trying to contain his mounting
frustration.

                    WILLIAM H. BLANCHARD
                      (almost to himself)
          The implications... the military
          implications of this—

He stops mid-thought, turning sharply toward Matilda.

                    WILLIAM H. BLANCHARD (CONT'D)
                      (voice rising)
          Do you understand what's at stake
          here? If even half of what's in
          this transcript is true—

Captain Cavitt interjects, his voice measured but dripping
with concern.

                    CAPTAIN CAVITT
          We're talking about a level of
          power and knowledge that could
          change everything. Or destroy
          everything.

Matilda's grip on the transcript tightens. She looks down at
the pages, then back at the two men, her expression a mixture
of defiance and conviction.

                    MATILDA
          I understand the weight of this
          better than anyone. But Airl
          wasn't speaking in terms of
          destruction. Her message is bigger
          than that. She's talking about
          responsibility—ours, as a species.

Blanchard's face hardens, his military instincts wrestling
with the enormity of what's been laid out before him.

                    WILLIAM H. BLANCHARD
          And what if this responsibility is
          a Trojan horse? A vulnerability we
          can't afford.

The room falls into a heavy silence. The sound of the base's
operations faintly hums in the background, a distant reminder
of the world outside.

Matilda places the transcript gently on the table, her voice now softer but unyielding.

			MATILDA
		If we let fear dictate our actions,
		we've already lost. Airl's words
		were not a threat—they were a
		warning. It's up to us to decide
		how we use this knowledge.

Blanchard and Cavitt exchange a long, weighted look. Neither speaks, but the flicker of doubt and understanding passes between them.

The transcript rests on the table, highlighting a single phrase underlined in pencil that demands attention:

"You are gods. Accept responsibility."

END FLASHBACK.

INT. ROSWELL ARMY AIR FORCE BASE - INTERVIEW ROOM - DAY

INSERT CARD: OFFICIAL TRANSCRIPT OF THE U.S. ARMY AIR FORCE ROSWELL ARMY AIR FIELD, 509TH BOMB GROUP SUBJECT: ALIEN INTERVIEW, 31. 7. 1947, 1ST SESSION

The room is still, yet electric with the unspoken tension between Matilda and Airl. The faint hum of the camera in the corner provides a subtle rhythm to the otherwise silent atmosphere. Matilda sits straight-backed, her hands resting lightly on the notepad in her lap. Across from her, Airl's unblinking gaze locks onto Matilda's, an unspoken telepathic intensity passing between them.

			ALIEN (V.O.)
		It is my personal belief that truth
		should never be sacrificed on the
		altar of political, religious, or
		economic expediency. Such actions
		lead only to the enslavement of IS-
		BEs, perpetuating their ignorance
		and suffering.

Matilda nods faintly, her fingers tightening on the pen as she jots down Airl's words without breaking eye contact.

			ALIEN (V.O.)
			(continuing)
		As an officer, pilot, and engineer
		of The Domain, it is my duty to
		protect the greater good of The
		Domain and its possessions.
			(MORE)

                    ALIEN (V.O.) (CONT'D)
          However, even I cannot defend
          against forces of which I am
          unaware.

A shadow of concern crosses Airl's face, though her composure remains steady.

                    ALIEN (V.O.)
          The isolation of Earth from the
          rest of civilization serves as a
          barrier. It prevents me from
          discussing many subjects with you
          at this time. Security protocols
          restrict me from revealing
          specifics about the plans and
          activities of The Domain.

Matilda's gaze wavers briefly.

                    MATILDA (V.O.)
              (hesitantly)
          But what you've shared so far...
          it's already so much. Can't you
          stay longer? There's still so much
          I don't understand.

Airl's expression softens, her gaze holding an unexpected kindness.

                    ALIEN (V.O.)
          I have given you as much as I feel
          ethically able to offer within the
          bounds of my duties. My intention
          was to provide you with knowledge
          that might aid the IS-BEs of Earth.
          But I must return to my assigned
          duties on the 'space station' now.

Matilda leans forward slightly, her thoughts racing.

                    MATILDA (V.O.)
              (urgently)
          You're leaving? When?

Airl's response is calm, yet resolute.

                    ALIEN (V.O.)
          As an IS-BE, I will depart from
          Earth within the next 24 hours.

Matilda's breath catches, her mind struggling to process the finality of Airl's words.

                    MATILDA (V.O.)
                (telepathically)
            What happens after you're gone?
            What happens to... all of this?

Airl tilts her head slightly, her eyes narrowing as if choosing her words carefully.

                    ALIEN (V.O.)
            That is for you, and the IS-BEs of
            Earth, to decide. What I have
            given you is a fragment of truth.
            What you do with it will determine
            the future of this world.

Matilda looks down at her notepad, the weight of responsibility settling heavily on her shoulders.

                    ALIEN (V.O.)
            Remember, knowledge alone is not
            enough. It is the will to act upon
            that knowledge which defines your
            existence.

A long silence hangs between them as Matilda gathers her thoughts. When she finally looks up, Airl's gaze is unwavering, a silent farewell passing between them.

INT. ROSWELL ARMY AIR FORCE BASE - BARRACKS - EVENING

The soft glow of a desk lamp lights the room, casting elongated shadows on the plain walls. Matilda sits on her bunk, her notepad resting on her lap. The pen in her hand hovers above the blank page as her thoughts swirl. She takes a deep breath, then begins to write. Her voice is heard in a quiet voice-over, though her lips occasionally move as she murmurs parts aloud to herself.

                    MATILDA (V.O.)
            Today, Airl told me she would leave
            within 24 hours. She explained
            that her "doll"—her body—will
            remain behind for us to study. She
            has no attachment to it. To her,
            it's just a tool, something she can
            replace. Yet, to us, it's an alien
            wonder, a treasure trove of
            technology we barely understand.

Matilda pauses, her pen still. She looks out the small window at the evening sky, where the stars begin to pierce the growing darkness. The vastness of the universe stares back at her, and she murmurs softly.

                    MATILDA
          A body as simple and disposable as
          an old pair of boots...

She shakes her head and resumes writing, her voice continuing
in voice-over.

                    MATILDA (V.O.)
          I should feel relieved. The
          military will be ecstatic to have
          her body to examine, and my role in
          all this will come to an end. But
          I'm not relieved. Not at all.
          Instead, I feel... torn. Torn
          between my duty and this
          inexplicable connection I've formed
          with her.

She sets her pen down for a moment, rubbing her temple. Her
voice becomes audible as she mutters under her breath.

                    MATILDA
          She doesn't even feel the way we
          do. So why does it feel like I'm
          losing... someone?

She shakes her head again, picking up the pen with renewed
determination. Her voice continues as she writes, more
audible now, filled with a mix of wonder and apprehension.

                    MATILDA (CONT'D)
          How could anyone return to normal
          after this? She's shown me things,
          truths about our universe, about
          ourselves, that make everything I
          thought I knew seem so... small.
          And yet, she trusted me. She chose
          me to share this with.

She stops writing and stares at the page. Her voice-over
becomes softer, almost uncertain.

                    MATILDA (V.O.)
          Why me? Why did she trust me, of
          all people?

She leans back against the wall, looking at the stars
outside. Her face hardens slightly with quiet resolve. She
picks up the pen again, speaking aloud as she writes.

                    MATILDA
          Whatever happens, I have to see
          this through. Not just for the
          military. For myself.

She exhales, setting the notepad on the nightstand. Her voice-over returns, calm but resolute.

> MATILDA (V.O.)
> If Airl is right, and each of us creates our own reality, then I have to decide what mine will be. And I have to live with that choice.

She looks out the window again, her gaze fixed on the infinite expanse of stars. The soft hum of the base outside fades as her expression grows distant yet firm, grappling with the weight of the decision ahead.

EXT. SPACE - VIEW OF THE MILKY WAY GALAXY

The galaxy's vast expanse sparkles with countless stars. A silent, infinite ocean of light. The voice of Airl the Alien seeps in.

> ALIEN (V.O.)
> Although The Domain will not hesitate to destroy any active vestiges of the 'Old Empire' operations wherever they are discovered, this is not our primary mission in this galaxy.

EXT. THE MOON - DOMAIN BASE OPERATIONS

A massive, sleek base spreads across the lunar surface. Its design is seamless, otherworldly, with glowing structures of unearthly metals. Domain spacecraft come and go, moving in choreographed silence. The voice of Airl the Alien flows...

> ALIEN (V.O.)
> I am sure that the 'Old Empire' mind control mechanisms can be deactivated and destroyed eventually. However, it is not possible to estimate how long this will take, as we do not understand the extent of this operation at this time.

INT. DOMAIN SPACECRAFT - COMMAND BRIDGE

Domain officers, in "doll bodies" of various designs, monitor holographic displays filled with alien symbols and diagrams.

One screen shows a map of Earth's solar system overlaid with pulsating energy grids. The Alien's voice comes through clearly.

>   ALIEN (V.O.)
> We do know that the 'Old Empire'
> force screen is vast enough to
> cover this end of the galaxy, at
> least. Each force generator and
> trapping device is very difficult
> to detect, locate, and destroy.

EXT. ASTEROID BELT - DOMAIN OUTPOST

Small, crystalline structures glint on the surface of asteroids. Domain spacecraft dock and undock, the station bustling with activity. Airl's voice seems introspective.

>   ALIEN (V.O.)
> It is not the current mission of
> The Domain Expeditionary Force to
> commit resources to this endeavor.
> The eventual destruction of these
> devices may make it possible for
> your memory to be restored, simply
> by not having it erased after each
> lifetime.

EXT. EARTH - VIEW FROM SPACE

Earth rotates quietly in the distance, vibrant with life. The faint glow of atmospheric shields shimmers like a web around the planet. Airl's pointed voice is heard.

>   ALIEN (V.O.)
> Fortunately, the memory of an IS-BE
> cannot be permanently erased. Many
> other active space civilizations
> maintain various nefarious
> operations in this area, not the
> least of which is dumping unwanted
> IS-BEs on Earth.

INT. DOMAIN SPACECRAFT - STRATEGIC OPERATIONS ROOM

A high-ranking Domain officer gestures to a star map. Points of interest blink red, showing "Old Empire" remnants. Other officers, in different doll bodies, nod in acknowledgment. The voice of Airl the Alien continues.

                    ALIEN (V.O.)
          None of these craft are hostile or
          in violent opposition to The Domain
          Forces. They know better than to
          challenge us!

EXT. DOMAIN SPACECRAFT FLEET - NEAR EARTH

An enormous fleet of Domain spacecraft hovers silently above
Earth's orbit. Their metallic hulls glisten as they form an
impenetrable perimeter. Airl's voice is strikingly powerful.

                    ALIEN (V.O.)
          For the most part, The Domain
          ignores Earth and its inhabitants,
          except to ensure that the resources
          of the planet itself are not
          permanently spoiled. This sector
          of the galaxy was annexed by The
          Domain and is the possession of The
          Domain, to do with or dispose of as
          it deems best.

EXT. EARTH'S SURFACE - DESERT LANDSCAPE

A faint shimmer in the sky reveals an invisible spacecraft
stationed above the barren desert. Airl's voice expounds...

                    ALIEN (V.O.)
          The moon of Earth and the asteroid
          belt have become a permanent base
          of operations for The Domain
          Forces. Needless to say, any
          attempt by humans or others to
          interfere in the activities of The
          Domain in this solar system will be
          terminated swiftly.

INT. DOMAIN SPACECRAFT - COMMAND BRIDGE

A holographic display shows Earth, its moon, and the asteroid
belt highlighted. A series of blinking signals show
movements of human-made satellites and craft. The Domain
officers dismiss them with a wave of a hand, as if dealing
with mere gnats. The voice of Airl is heard.

                    ALIEN (V.O.)
          This is not a serious concern, as I
          mentioned earlier, since homo
          sapiens cannot operate in open
          space.

EXT. SPACE - DOMAIN SPACECRAFT FLEET

The Domain fleet begins a slow and silent dispersal, moving into strategic positions around Earth and its moon. The scene fades into the vastness of space, the galaxy glowing faintly in the distance. The seemingly distant voice of Airl is heard.

> ALIEN (V.O.)
> The Domain's presence will remain.
> The operation is secure.

The screen fades to black. The weight of Airl's words lingers.

INT. ROSWELL ARMY AIR FORCE BASE - INTERVIEW ROOM - DAY

The room is silent except for the faint hum of the recording equipment. Matilda sits across from Airl the Alien, her notepad untouched in her lap. Her eyes are locked with Airl's, the silent connection between them palpable.

> ALIEN (V.O.)
> (calm but urgent)
> Of course, we will continue with the next steps of The Domain Expansion Plan, which has remained on schedule for billions of years. Over the next 5,000 years, there will be increasing traffic and activity of The Domain Forces as we progress toward the center of this galaxy and beyond, to spread our civilization through the universe.

Matilda's breathing deepens. She can feel the weight of Airl's words pressing against her mind.

> ALIEN (V.O.)
> If humanity is to survive, it must cooperate to find effective solutions to the difficult conditions of your existence on Earth. Humanity must rise above its human form and discover where they are, that they are IS-BEs, and who they are as IS-BEs, to transcend the notion that they are merely biological bodies.

Matilda's fingers tighten around the notepad.

> MATILDA (V.O.)
> And if we fail? What happens if
> humanity doesn't—can't—transcend?

Airl's gaze softens, but her response is unwavering.

> ALIEN (V.O.)
> Once these realizations have been
> made, it may be possible to escape
> your current imprisonment.
> Otherwise, there will be no future
> for the IS-BEs on Earth. Your
> civilization, as it exists, will
> perish. Your potential will vanish
> into oblivion.

Matilda swallows hard, the words cutting through her resolve.

> ALIEN (V.O.)
> Although no active battles or wars
> are being waged between The Domain
> and the 'Old Empire', there still
> exist the covert actions of the
> 'Old Empire' taken against Earth
> through their thought control
> operation. When one knows these
> activities exist, the effects can
> be observed clearly.

A flicker of confusion crosses Matilda's face.

> MATILDA (V.O.)
> Thought control? How can that even
> be possible on such a large scale?

> ALIEN (V.O.)
> The most obvious examples can be
> seen as incidents of sudden,
> inexplicable behavior. Consider a
> very recent instance. Three days
> before the Japanese attack on Pearl
> Harbor, someone in authority
> ordered all the ships in Pearl
> Harbor to go into port and secure
> for inspection.

Matilda's eyes narrow, trying to reconcile the historical account with what she's hearing.

> ALIEN (V.O.)
> The ships were ordered to take all
> the ammunition out of their
> magazines and store it below.
> (MORE)

                    ALIEN (V.O.) (CONT'D)
          On the afternoon before the attack,
          all of the admirals and generals
          were attending parties, even though
          two Japanese aircraft carriers were
          discovered standing right off Pearl
          Harbor.

Matilda sits back, stunned.

                    MATILDA (V.O.)
          You're saying... that was
          intentional? Manipulated?

                    ALIEN (V.O.)
          The obvious action to take would
          have been to contact Pearl Harbor
          by telephone to warn them of the
          danger, to put the ammunition back,
          and to order the ships out of port
          into the open sea. But that action
          was not taken.

Matilda's hands tremble as she presses the notepad to her lap.

                    MATILDA (V.O.)
          How many more of these 'thought
          control' operations have there
          been?

                    ALIEN (V.O.)
          Many. But recognizing them is the
          first step toward understanding the
          covert influence of the 'Old
          Empire' and freeing yourselves from
          it.

The room feels heavy with unspoken truths. Matilda exhales, her determination renewed as she straightens her posture and prepares for the next question.

The hum of the recording equipment fades as their telepathic conversation continues.

INT. ROSWELL ARMY AIR FORCE BASE - ROOM - DAY

The rhythmic clattering of a stenotype machine comes to a stop. The STENOGRAPHER, a composed woman in her mid-thirties, removes the fresh transcript, neatly stacks it, and stands. She walks across the room to Colonel William H. Blanchard, who is seated at a desk, his expression stern but expectant.

The stenographer hands him the transcript.

                   STENOGRAPHER
        Here is the latest, Colonel.

Blanchard nods, takes the document, and begins scanning it with furrowed brows. His jaw tightens, and his breathing slows as he reads deeper. He suddenly stops; his face clouded with unease.

He reads aloud from the transcript, his voice tinged with disbelief.

                 WILLIAM H. BLANCHARD
        "About six hours before the
        Japanese attack began, a U.S. Navy
        ship sank a small Japanese
        submarine right outside the harbor.
        Instead of contacting Pearl Harbor
        by telephone to report the
        incident, a warning message was put
        into top-secret code, which took
        about two hours to encode, and then
        it took another two hours to
        decode."

Blanchard's hand trembles slightly as he flips to the next page. His voice grows louder, tinged with anger and confusion.

                 WILLIAM H. BLANCHARD (CONT'D)
        "The word of warning to Pearl
        Harbor did not arrive until 10:00
        AM Pearl Harbor time, Sunday -- two
        hours after the Japanese attack
        destroyed the U.S. Fleet."

He looks up, staring at the stenographer, though the question isn't truly meant for her.

                 WILLIAM H. BLANCHARD (CONT'D)
          (half to himself)
        How do things like this happen?

He reads further, shaking his head, almost as if in disbelief.

					WILLIAM H. BLANCHARD (CONT'D)
				"If the men who were responsible
				for these obviously disastrous
				errors were stood up and asked
				bluntly to justify their actions
				and intentions, you would find out
				that they were quite sincere in
				their jobs. Ordinarily, they do
				the very best they can do for
				people and nations."

Blanchard stands abruptly, pacing the room, his boots thudding against the floor.

					WILLIAM H. BLANCHARD (CONT'D)
				"But this... this isn't just human
				error. It's something else.
				Something... unseen."

He reads the final line aloud, his voice dropping to a near whisper, as though the words themselves are heavy.

					WILLIAM H. BLANCHARD (CONT'D)
				"All of a sudden, from some
				completely unknown and undetectable
				source enters these wild,
				unexplainable situations that just
				'can't exist'."

Blanchard lowers the paper, his grip on it tight. He looks out the window for a moment, the weight of the revelations sinking in.

The stenographer watches silently, sensing the gravity of the moment.

					STENOGRAPHER
				    (softly)
				Is there anything else, Colonel?

Blanchard turns back to her, his face stern but troubled.

					WILLIAM H. BLANCHARD
				No. That will be all for now.

The stenographer nods and exits, leaving Blanchard alone with the transcript. He stares down at the document, the lines replaying in his mind. Slowly, he sinks back into his chair, the enormity of the implications pressing down on him.

INT. ROSWELL ARMY AIR FORCE BASE - INTERVIEW ROOM - DAY

Matilda sits across from Airl, her notepad untouched on the table. Their eyes are locked in intense focus, the energy of the telepathic connection humming in the still air. The camera's red tally light blinks steadily in the background, the only movement in the room.

                    ALIEN (V.O.)
            (calm yet laced with a
              subtle bitterness)
     The "Old Empire" thought control
     operation is run by a small group
     of old "baboons" with very small
     minds. Their games are insidious,
     cruel. They have no purpose, no
     goal, other than to control and
     destroy IS-BEs who could otherwise
     manage themselves perfectly well if
     left alone.

Matilda's breath catches, and she shifts slightly in her chair, processing the enormity of the statement.

                    MATILDA (V.O.)
            (thoughts tinged with
              disbelief)
     If what you're saying is true, then
     humanity... we've been puppets,
     haven't we?

                    ALIEN (V.O.)
     Yes. These artificially created
     incidents, these wars, these cycles
     of oppression, are forced upon your
     race by the operators of the mind
     control prison system. They
     empower madmen to run your
     governments, mirroring their
     commands through covert thought
     manipulation. Why not keep the
     inmates fighting amongst
     themselves? Why not?

Matilda looks down, her fingers tightening on the edge of the table.

                    MATILDA (V.O.)
            (struggling with the
              weight of the revelation)
     But why? What purpose does this
     serve?

                    ALIEN (V.O.)
              (somber tone)
         The prison guards have no higher
         purpose. It is their game, their
         entertainment. The suffering,
         confusion, and pain of IS-BEs on
         Earth feed their insidious need to
         control. It is the only "purpose"
         they have. The men who run your
         criminal governments are their
         reflections, shadows of their
         influence.

Matilda's gaze lifts to meet Airl's once more, her expression
a mix of sorrow and determination.

                    MATILDA (V.O.)
         But this can't go on forever, can
         it? Surely, something can be done
         to stop this... cycle?

                    ALIEN (V.O.)
              (soft yet resolute)
         The cycle will continue as long as
         IS-BEs on Earth remain unaware of
         who and what they truly are. They
         live a series of consecutive lives,
         over and over. The same IS-BEs who
         built and witnessed the rise and
         fall of civilizations in India,
         China, Mesopotamia, Greece, and
         Rome now inhabit bodies in America,
         France, Russia, and beyond. Each
         lifetime begins anew in pain,
         misery, and mystery.

Matilda leans back in her chair, the words settling heavily
into her mind. She closes her eyes for a moment, overwhelmed
by the implications.

                    MATILDA (V.O.)
              (thoughts turning to hope)
         Then perhaps
         knowledge—awareness—could break
         this cycle? If we could remember,
         if we could teach others...

                    ALIEN (V.O.)
              (trace of encouragement)
         Awareness is the first step. The
         memory of IS-BEs cannot be
         permanently erased. It lies
         dormant, waiting. But awakening is
         no easy path.
                         (MORE)

                    ALIEN (V.O.) (CONT'D)
          It requires courage, strength, and
          an unwavering desire to be free.

Matilda nods slowly, her resolve hardening. She opens her
eyes, meeting Airl's unflinching gaze.

The connection between them deepens, the weight of the
conversation settling into the air. A faint hum of
determination seems to pass silently between them.

EXT. EARTH'S ANCIENT LANDSCAPE - NIGHT

We see an expansive view of Earth's distant past and a
sweeping view of the lush, untamed wilderness, illuminated by
a sky filled with stars far brighter than today. In the
distance, shadowy figures gather around primitive fires,
their silhouettes flickering against the glow.

                    ALIEN (V.O.)
              (calm and resonant)
          Some IS-BEs have been transported
          to Earth more recently than others.
          They wander, lost in the haze of
          their confinement, with no memory
          of the lives they once lived among
          the stars.

EXT. ANCIENT LEMURIA - DAY

We see a sprawling city of towering crystalline structures,
perched on cliffs overlooking a vast ocean. IS-BEs, in
ethereal humanoid forms, move gracefully through the streets,
exuding energy and light. This utopia brims with a sense of
harmony and purpose.

                    ALIEN (V.O.)
          Others have been here since the
          first days of Lemuria, their
          brilliance dulled over millennia by
          the relentless cycle of amnesia and
          entrapment.

EXT. EARTH - VARIOUS CIVILIZATIONS

Babylon: The ziggurat rises against a desert backdrop.
Priests perform rituals while ordinary people toil.

Rome: Gladiators battle in the Colosseum as the crowd roars.

India: Intricate temples teem with devotees, their faces
alight with faith.

China: The Great Wall snakes through the mountains, soldiers patrolling its length.

> ALIEN (V.O.)
> The same IS-BEs who witnessed the rise and fall of civilizations in Babylon, Greece, and Rome now inhabit bodies in your modern world. Their true selves hidden; their memories locked away.

EXT. EARTH - MODERN METROPOLIS - NIGHT

A bustling cityscape of towering skyscrapers and glowing neon lights. People rush through crowded streets, faces illuminated by the cold glow of smartphones.

> ALIEN (V.O.)
> In every lifetime, they begin anew, trapped in the illusions of pain, misery, and mystery. They wander without answers, perpetually reborn into a cycle that they cannot escape.

I/E. SPACE - THE DOMAIN'S STATION - NIGHT

We see a massive, sleek spacecraft hovering silently above Earth. The Domain officers study holographic displays, their faces marked with determination.

> ALIEN (V.O.)
> Because The Domain has three thousand of their own IS-BEs in captivity on Earth, we have a vested interest in breaking this cycle. This problem has never been encountered or effectively solved before, as far as we know.

INT. DOMAIN STATION - COMMAND ROOM

A team of IS-BEs, housed in their advanced doll bodies, gather around a circular console. Holograms display Earth's landscapes and energy fields. They exchange nods and gestures, their focus unwavering.

> ALIEN (V.O.)
> We will continue our efforts to free those IS-BEs when and where it is possible.
> (MORE)

                    ALIEN (V.O.) (CONT'D)
          But to do so requires time,
          unprecedented technology, and an
          unyielding diligence.

EXT. EARTH - STARLIT SKY

We see the Earth's surface, rising into the endless night
sky. Stars stretch across the cosmos like a jeweled
tapestry.

                    ALIEN (V.O.)
          Until that day comes, the IS-BEs of
          Earth remain prisoners of an
          ancient design, their light
          confined to the shadows of their
          own minds, yearning to break free.

The scene fades to black, leaving only the stars.

I/E. ROSWELL ARMY AIR FORCE BASE - COMMANDING OFFICER'S
OFFICE - DAY

The sound of heavy boots echoes down the hallway as FOUR
HEAVILY ARMED MILITARY POLICEMEN escort Matilda through the
base. Their presence is intimidating, their rifles ready.

The door to the COMMANDING OFFICER'S OFFICE opens, revealing
a large, makeshift conference room. A long table dominates
the space, surrounded by chairs filled with stern and
distinguished faces. The air is thick with authority and
importance.

Matilda hesitates at the threshold, aware of the gravity of
the moment. The men in the room turn their attention toward
Matilda, and an AIDE gestures for Matilda to take a seat at
the table. Matilda swallows hard, her heartbeat quickening.

ANGLE ON: THE CONFERENCE ROOM TABLE

Seated around the table are ARMY AIR FORCE SECRETARY
SYMINGTON, GENERAL NATHAN TWINING, GENERAL JIMMY DOOLITTLE,
GENERAL VANDENBERG, and GENERAL NORSTAD. Their uniforms
gleam with medals, their expressions a mix of curiosity and
gravity.

Among them sits a familiar face that takes Matilda by
surprise: CHARLES LINDBERGH, calm and composed, with an air
of quiet authority.

Matilda sits down, her hands resting tightly on her lap. Her gaze darts around the room, recognizing several dignitaries she had seen before in "the gallery." Others are unfamiliar, likely aides or intelligence agents, observing in silence.

                    SECRETARY SYMINGTON
             (leaning forward slightly)
    Don't be nervous. You're not in
    any trouble.

                    MATILDA
             (nodding, attempting
              composure)
    Thank you, sir.

                    SECRETARY SYMINGTON
    We've reviewed your transcripts
    extensively. You've done an
    exceptional job interpreting Airl's
    communications. This is an
    unprecedented moment in human
    history, and your role is
    critically important.

                    MATILDA
             (taken aback but humbled)
    I didn't realize it was viewed that
    way, sir. I've just been focused
    on... doing my part.

                    SECRETARY SYMINGTON
             (gesturing to Lindbergh)
    Mr. Lindbergh is here as a
    consultant to the Chief of Staff of
    the U.S. Air Force. He and the
    generals have prepared a list of
    questions for Airl. We need to
    determine if she would be willing
    to provide more information,
    particularly about military
    security and the construction of
    the craft.

                    MATILDA
             (hesitant)
    I understand, but Airl has been
    very clear about her position.
    She's already communicated
    everything she's willing and
    permitted to share.

The generals exchange glances. General Twining speaks up, his voice firm but not unkind.

                    GENERAL TWINING
          We still need you to ask her again.
          It's imperative. If her answer
          remains "no," then we'd like her to
          review the transcripts for
          accuracy.

                    MATILDA
               (thoughtful, choosing
                words carefully)
          Airl can read English fluently.
          I'm confident she'll verify the
          accuracy, but I'll ask her.
          However, I must reiterate: she does
          not trust the intentions of the men
          in the gallery.

                    SECRETARY SYMINGTON
               (nodding)
          Understood. But her verification
          of the transcripts could be vital.
          We'd like her to write any
          necessary corrections directly on
          the documents while we observe.

                    MATILDA
               (resolute)
          I'll follow your orders, sir.

The weight of the room presses down on Matilda as she takes the stack of TRANSCRIPTS handed over by an aide. She glances at the pages, the words of her conversations with Airl staring back at her.

Matilda's expression hardens with quiet resolve. She knows that she must fulfill her duty, even as doubt gnaws at the edges of her mind.

Matilda rises from her chair, transcripts in hand, the burden of responsibility heavier than ever.

INT. ROSWELL ARMY AIR FORCE BASE - HALLWAY OUTSIDE INTERVIEW ROOM - DAY

The clatter of boots echoes in the hallway as Matilda approaches the INTERVIEW ROOM. An envelope of TRANSCRIPTS is tucked neatly inside the breast pocket of Matilda's uniform jacket. Her face is a mask of focus, though her mind races with uncertainty about how this interaction will unfold.

INT. ROSWELL ARMY AIR FORCE BASE - INTERVIEW ROOM - DAY

The room feels smaller, the weight of unseen eyes pressing through the one-way glass window. Airl the Alien sits, calm and watchful, her gaze a steady anchor. Matilda takes her usual seat, the envelope feeling heavier now.

Matilda carefully pulls out the envelope and places it on the table between them.

>   MATILDA (V.O.)
>   (hesitant but direct)
>   The Secretary has requested that
>   you review these transcripts and
>   confirm their accuracy. If they
>   are correct, they have asked you to
>   sign the cover page.

>   ALIEN (V.O.)
>   (telepathically, measured)
>   If you have read them and they are
>   accurate in your own estimation,
>   there is no need for me to review
>   them also. The translations are
>   correct. You can tell your
>   commander that you have faithfully
>   conveyed a record of our
>   communication.

>   MATILDA (V.O.)
>   (reassuring)
>   I have read them. They are exact
>   recordings of our conversations.
>   Will you sign the cover page then?

>   ALIEN (V.O.)
>   (firm but unyielding)
>   No, I will not.

>   MATILDA (V.O.)
>   (confused)
>   May I ask why not?

>   ALIEN (V.O.)
>   If your commander does not trust
>   his own staff to make an honest and
>   accurate report to him, what
>   confidence will my signature on the
>   page give him? Why will he trust
>   an ink mark on a page made by an
>   officer of The Domain if he does
>   not trust his own loyal staff?

Matilda sits back, stunned by the simplicity and precision of Airl's logic. Matilda's lips press together in frustration and helplessness. She nods slightly, acknowledging Airl's point.

> MATILDA (V.O.)
> (quietly)
> Thank you. I'll ask my superiors for further instructions.

Matilda places the envelope back into her breast pocket and rises from her chair.

SFX: THE DOOR SLAMS OPEN

Five HEAVILY ARMED MILITARY POLICE storm into the room, their weapons drawn. Matilda's breath catches in her throat as a man in a WHITE LAB COAT wheels in a cart holding a box-like machine covered with dials.

Airl's expression remains calm, though her gaze sharpens. She doesn't resist as two MPs grab her arms and press her into the chair. Another MP steps forward, rifle leveled at Airl's head, no more than six inches away.

Matilda attempts to stand, but two MPs force her back into the chair, their iron-like grips pressing down on her shoulders.

> MATILDA
> (audibly, panicked)
> What are you doing? Stop this! Please!

The man in the white lab coat places a circular HEADBAND over Airl's head. His movements are precise and mechanical. He turns to the machine and adjusts a knob.

> MAN IN LAB COAT
> (shouting)
> Clear!

The MPs release Airl as her body stiffens and shudders violently. Matilda's heart pounds as she watches, feeling helpless.

Airl's body jerks and convulses. After about 15 seconds, the man turns the knob again, and Airl slumps back into the chair, lifeless. The process repeats several times, each cycle a horrifying tableau.

> MATILDA
> (screaming)
> Stop it! You're killing her!

Two men in WHITE LAB COATS enter the room, examining Airl briefly. They confer in low, clinical tones, their words unintelligible to Matilda. One of the men waves toward the one-way glass window.

SFX: DOOR OPENS

A GURNEY is wheeled in. Two attendants lift Airl's limp body onto it, strapping her down securely before wheeling her out.

Matilda slumped in her chair, the MPs still holding her down. Matilda's breath is ragged, her mind reeling with disbelief and fury. Tears stream down her eyes as she watches Airl disappear through the door.

Silence settles over the space, heavy and suffocating. The MPs release Matilda and file out, leaving her alone in the now-empty room. The envelope of transcripts feels like a weight in her pocket, a bitter reminder of her powerlessness.

EXT. ROSWELL ARMY AIR FORCE BASE - INTERVIEW ROOM - HALLWAY

The heavy door to the interview room swings open abruptly. Matilda, pale and visibly shaken, is ushered out by two-armed MILITARY POLICE officers. Her steps are hurried, her eyes darting back toward the room she just left, her mind racing with unanswered questions.

The hallway feels cold and sterile. The echo of the MPs' boots against the polished floor reverberates through the space, mingling with the distant hum of machinery.

One of the MPs speaks firmly.

> MP #1
> Keep moving, ma'am.

> MATILDA
> (softly, almost to
> herself)
> What are they doing to her?

The MP doesn't respond, his face a mask of duty. Matilda's gaze lingers on the door they've left behind, her expression a mix of confusion and dread.

EXT. ROSWELL ARMY AIR FORCE BASE - DAY

The MPs lead Matilda briskly across the base under the watchful eyes of several passing soldiers.

The bright sunlight feels almost jarring against the weight of the moment. Matilda shields her eyes briefly, her mind still consumed by the events in the interview room.

I/E. ROSWELL ARMY AIR FORCE BASE - BARRACKS - CONTINUOUS

The door to the barracks creaks open as the MPs guide Matilda inside. The space is sparse and utilitarian, its only adornments the bunk beds lined against the walls and a solitary desk in the corner.

                    MP #2
You'll stay here until further notice.

                    MATILDA
        (stepping inside, turning
         back)
Why? What's happening? I need answers.

                    MP #1
        (avoiding her gaze)
Orders, ma'am. That's all we know.

They close the door firmly, locking it with an audible CLICK. Matilda stands in the center of the room, staring at the door for a long moment.

Matilda sits on her bunk, her arms folded tightly across her chest. There's a knock at the door, it startles her.

                    MATILDA
        (quietly to herself)
Now what?

She stands and opens the door. General Twining enters, followed by DR. WILCOX, a stern-looking man in a white lab coat. Two MPs stand just behind them.

                    GENERAL TWINING
Sergeant MacElroy, this is Dr. Wilcox. We need you to accompany us immediately.

Matilda hesitates, her gaze shifting between the General and the doctor, but she nods reluctantly.

                    MATILDA
Understood, sir.

She steps out of the barracks, followed closely by General Twining, Dr. Wilcox, and the MPs.

INT. ROSWELL ARMY AIR FORCE BASE - CORRIDOR - NIGHT

The group walks briskly through a maze of hallways, their footsteps echoing in the sterile silence. Matilda's unease grows with every turn.

INT. ROSWELL ARMY AIR FORCE BASE - SMALL ROOM - NIGHT

Matilda enters the room to find Airl lying motionless on a gurney. Airl's small, still body is connected to various machines, including an EEG monitor and a vital signs monitor, which emits an occasional soft beep. Several DOCTORS in white lab coats stand nearby, murmuring among themselves.

General Twining steps forward, turning to face Matilda.

                    GENERAL TWINING
        Sergeant, The Domain represents a
        significant military threat to the
        United States. We could not risk
        allowing Airl to depart and report
        what she observed here. Decisive
        action was necessary. Do you
        understand why this had to be done?

Matilda stiffens, suppressing the anger rising in her chest.

                    MATILDA
        I understand, sir.

But her tone is clipped, her words hollow. She does not meet the General's eyes.

Dr. Wilcox gestures toward Airl.

                    DR. WILCOX
        Sergeant, please approach the
        gurney.

Matilda steps hesitantly toward Airl. Her gaze scans the motionless form. She cannot tell if Airl is alive or dead.

                    DR. WILCOX (CONT'D)
        We administered a series of mild
        electroshocks to subdue her
        temporarily. This will give us
        time to evaluate the situation. I
        need you to attempt communication,
        telepathically.

Matilda's jaw tightens, but she complies, leaning in closer to Airl.

She concentrates, her brow furrowing deeply as she tries to establish a connection. Minutes pass in heavy silence.

Finally, Matilda steps back, shaking her head.

> MATILDA
> I can't sense her. I don't think she's... present anymore.

Dr. Wilcox exchanges a concerned glance with the other doctors.

> MATILDA (CONT'D)
> (voice rising)
> I think you must have killed her.

Dr. Wilcox adjusts his glasses, his voice steady but defensive.

> DR. WILCOX
> That remains to be seen. We'll continue monitoring her condition. You'll be asked to try again later.

Matilda clenches her fists but says nothing. Her eyes linger on Airl's lifeless form as the doctors begin recording data from the machines.

INT. ROSWELL ARMY AIR FORCE BASE - CORRIDOR - NIGHT

The MPs escort Matilda back to the barracks. Her steps are heavy, her mind racing with worry and rage.

INT. ROSWELL ARMY AIR FORCE BASE - BARRACKS - NIGHT

The door shuts behind Matilda with a metallic clang. She sits heavily on her bunk, staring blankly at the floor. The weight of betrayal and helplessness settles over her like a suffocating shroud.

INT. ROSWELL ARMY AIR FORCE BASE - INTERVIEW ROOM - MORNING

Matilda sits stiffly in a plain office chair, her eyes scanning the room. The overstuffed chair where Airl once sat has been replaced by a utilitarian desk and several office chairs. Four MPs stand near the door, their presence a constant reminder of her guarded status.

Matilda fidgets slightly, glancing at the empty space where Airl's presence once filled the room.

After a few minutes, the door opens, and Dr. Wilcox enters, followed by a man in a plain business suit. The man carries a black case and looks at Matilda with a neutral expression.

> DR. WILCOX
> Good morning, Sergeant. This is Mr. John Reid. He's been flown in from Chicago at the request of your superiors.

> JOHN REID
> (placing the case on the desk)
> Pleasure to meet you, Sergeant.

Matilda nods, her brow furrowing in confusion.

> MATILDA
> What's this about?

Dr. Wilcox crosses his arms, his tone calm but condescending.

> DR. WILCOX
> Mr. Reid is here to administer a polygraph test. It's a routine procedure, for your protection, of course.

Matilda's surprise is immediate.

> MATILDA
> A lie detector test? You think I've lied?

> DR. WILCOX
> (raising a hand)
> This isn't about mistrust, Sergeant. It's about ensuring the accuracy of the transcripts. Since the alien declined to verify them herself, we need to rely on your testimony. This test will help validate your credibility.

Matilda's eyes narrow, but she says nothing.

> JOHN REID
> (gesturing to the chair)
> Please, sit back. This will take some time.

Reluctantly, Matilda adjusts her position as Reid begins unpacking the machine.

                    JOHN REID (CONT'D)
          I'll be strapping a few monitoring
          devices to measure physiological
          changes. Nothing invasive, I
          assure you.

He wraps a rubber tube around her chest, securing it firmly.
Next, he attaches a blood pressure cuff to her arm and places
electrodes on her fingers.

                    JOHN REID (CONT'D)
          This machine will track your
          responses to our questions. The
          graphs will tell us if there's any
          deviation that suggests dishonesty.

Matilda stiffens but remains silent.

                    DR. WILCOX
          This is a scientific process,
          Sergeant. Nothing personal.

Reid switches on the machine. The rhythmic hum fills the
room as he loads a roll of graph paper beside the device.

                    JOHN REID
          Let's begin with some baseline
          questions.

Reid's tone is methodical, and the questions come steadily.

                    JOHN REID (CONT'D)
          What is your name?

                    MATILDA
          Matilda O'Donnell.

                    JOHN REID
          What is your date of birth?

                    MATILDA
          June 12th, 1924.

                    JOHN REID
          Your age?

                    MATILDA
          Twenty-three.

The questions continue, straightforward at first, but
gradually become more pointed.

                    JOHN REID
          Are you able to communicate by
          telepathy?

                    MATILDA
          No. I've never been able to do
          this with anyone except Airl.

                    JOHN REID
          Were any of the statements you made
          to the stenographer falsified?

                    MATILDA
          No.

                    JOHN REID
          Have you intentionally or
          unintentionally imagined or
          fabricated any of the communication
          you claimed to have had with the
          alien?

                    MATILDA
          No, of course not.

Dr. Wilcox leans forward, studying the graph as it prints
steadily.

                    DR. WILCOX
          Do you believe everything the alien
          communicated to you?

                    MATILDA
          Yes.

                    JOHN REID
          Would you tell the same stories to
          your parish priest in a Catholic
          church confessional?

Matilda's eyes flash with indignation.

                    MATILDA
          Yes.

The questions continue for over an hour. Matilda remains
composed, though her jaw tightens with each insinuation.

INT. ROSWELL ARMY AIR FORCE BASE - INTERVIEW ROOM - LATER

The machine finally hums to a stop. Reid begins collecting
the graphs, rolling them up meticulously.

JOHN REID
That will be all for now.

Matilda exhales slowly, her hands gripping the edges of the chair. Dr. Wilcox straightens, offering a placating smile.

DR. WILCOX
Thank you, Sergeant. We'll review the results.

Matilda rises, her posture rigid as the MPs step forward to escort her back.

MATILDA
(coldly)
I hope your machine enjoyed itself.

Without waiting for a response, she strides out of the room, her footsteps echoing in the tense silence.

INT. ROSWELL ARMY AIR FORCE BASE - HALLWAY - DAY

Matilda walks with purpose down the long, sterile hallway, flanked by two MPs on either side. Their boots click in unison against the polished floor, the sound echoing in the empty space.

Her face is a mask of frustration, her hands balled into fists at her sides. The events of the polygraph test swirl in her mind, a mixture of indignation and exhaustion weighing heavily on her shoulders.

INT. ROSWELL ARMY AIR FORCE BASE - BARRACKS - DAY

The door to the barracks opens. One of the MPs steps aside, gesturing for Matilda to enter. She hesitates for a moment, her eyes narrowing as she looks back at them.

MATILDA
You can stand outside. I won't be running off anywhere.

The MPs exchange glances but remain silent as Matilda steps inside. The door shuts firmly behind her, the sound of the lock sliding into place reverberating through the quiet room.

Matilda exhales sharply, her shoulders slumping as she crosses to her bunk. She sits heavily, her hands pressed against her temples, massaging away the lingering tension.

Her eyes drift to the small, cluttered desk in the corner. The transcripts from her sessions with Airl lie stacked neatly, a stark reminder of the weight she carries. She leans forward, staring at them intently, as though willing the pages to offer her answers.

INT. ROSWELL ARMY AIR FORCE BASE - BARRACKS - LATER

Matilda stands at the window, gazing out at the base. Beyond the fences, the desert stretches out endlessly, the sun casting long shadows over the barren landscape.

Her reflection stares back at her in the glass, a silent witness to the turmoil within.

MATILDA
(quietly, to herself)
What am I doing here?

She turns away from the window and moves to her desk. Sitting down, she flips open a notebook and begins to write, her pen moving quickly across the page.

INT. ROSWELL ARMY AIR FORCE BASE - OUTSIDE THE BARRACKS - DAY

The two MPs stand stoically outside the door, their rifles slung over their shoulders. One glances at his watch, while the other looks up at the clear blue sky.

A muffled sound of scribbling and the occasional heavy sigh can be heard from within the room.

INT. ROSWELL ARMY AIR FORCE BASE - BARRACKS - DAY

Matilda finishes writing, placing the notebook down with a sigh. She rests her head in her hands, her fingers running through her hair.

The weight of the day settles over her like a shroud. Despite the chaos surrounding her, a flicker of determination glimmers in her eyes.

She whispers softly, almost inaudibly.

MATILDA
I have to see this through.

Matilda closes her eyes, steeling herself for what lies ahead.

INT. ROSWELL ARMY AIR FORCE BASE - INTERVIEW ROOM - AFTERNOON

Matilda steps into the room, her expression neutral but her eyes sharp and wary. The familiar chair and desk from prior sessions have been replaced by a hospital gurney. The sterile smell of antiseptic lingers in the air.

Dr. Wilcox stands near the gurney, clipboard in hand. Beside him is a staff nurse, organizing vials and syringes on a rolling cart. They both look up as Matilda enters.

> DR. WILCOX
> Ah, Sergeant O'Donnell. Thank you for coming back this afternoon. Please, have a seat—well, in this case, lie down.

Matilda raises an eyebrow, hesitating for a moment before stepping closer to the gurney.

> MATILDA
> (steady voice)
> A gurney? What's the occasion, Doctor?

Dr. Wilcox glances at the nurse, then back to Matilda.

> DR. WILCOX
> We've been asked to repeat the same questions you answered during the polygraph test. This time, however, we'll administer a small dose of sodium pentothal.

Matilda's professional demeanor falters slightly.

> MATILDA
> Truth serum?

> DR. WILCOX
> Yes. You're familiar with it, I assume, given your background?

Matilda nods, stepping closer and inspecting the syringe on the nurse's cart.

> MATILDA
> I've seen it used as an anesthetic. It's potent.

> DR. WILCOX
> That's correct. But I assure you, we'll use a very controlled dose. This is purely procedural.
> (MORE)

                    DR. WILCOX (CONT'D)
               You've already been cooperative,
               and no one here doubts your
               honesty.

Matilda's gaze lingers on the syringe. Then, with a sigh, she climbs onto the gurney, lying back stiffly.

                    MATILDA
                 (quietly)
               I've got nothing to hide.

The nurse adjusts the gurney's angle while Dr. Wilcox preps the syringe.

MOMENTS LATER...

The room feels heavy with silence. Matilda lies still, her breathing slow and steady as the serum begins to take effect. Dr. Wilcox positions himself at her side, clipboard in hand.

                    DR. WILCOX
               Alright, Sergeant O'Donnell, we're
               going to begin. Just answer the
               questions as clearly and honestly
               as you can.

Matilda's eyelids flutter slightly, her head lolling to one side.

                    MATILDA
                 (slightly slurred)
               Go ahead, Doctor.

Dr. Wilcox nods to the nurse, who jots down notes.

                    DR. WILCOX
               What is your name?

                    MATILDA
               Matilda O'Donnell.

                    DR. WILCOX
               What is your date of birth?

                    MATILDA
               June 12th... 1924.

The questions continue, mirroring the polygraph test from earlier. Matilda's voice is calm but detached, her words spilling out automatically under the drug's influence.

                    DR. WILCOX
               Do you believe everything the alien
               communicated to you?

MATILDA
Yes... every word.

DR. WILCOX
Did you fabricate or imagine any of
the communication you claimed to
have with Airl?

MATILDA
No... I couldn't even if I wanted
to.

Dr. Wilcox exchanges a brief glance with the nurse, who scribbles quickly on the clipboard.

DR. WILCOX
Do you consider yourself a gullible
person?

MATILDA
No. But I'm not... blind, either.

Dr. Wilcox allows himself a small smile before continuing.

LATER...

The session concludes, and the nurse begins unhooking the monitoring equipment from Matilda's arm and chest. She's groggy but cooperative as the MPs enter the room to escort her out.

As she's helped off the gurney, Matilda looks at Dr. Wilcox with bleary eyes.

MATILDA (CONT'D)
(softly)
Are we done, Doctor?

DR. WILCOX
Yes, Sergeant. You can rest now.

The MPs support her on either side as she stumbles slightly.

INT. ROSWELL ARMY AIR FORCE BASE - BARRACKS - NIGHT

Matilda lies on her bunk, finally alone. Her body is heavy with exhaustion, but her mind feels strangely light, as though the drug's haze had momentarily lifted her burdens.

For the first time in days, her breathing slows, her muscles relax, and she drifts into a peaceful, uninterrupted sleep.

INT. TOWNHOME - LIVING ROOM - DAY

INSERT CARD: 2007 MEATH, IRELAND

Soft sunlight filters through the lace curtains of Matilda O'Donnell MacElroy's modest townhome. At 83 years old, her frail frame is seated in a worn but comfortable armchair, surrounded by a lifetime of memories. Across from her sits LAWRENCE R. SPENCER, 61, a writer with a notebook and a recorder on the table between them. He watches her attentively, sensing the gravity of the moment.

On the coffee table lies a large, weathered envelope, its edges frayed from decades of handling. Matilda rests her hand on it, her fingers trembling slightly.

              MATILDA
    Lawrence, you're the first person
    to see these transcripts since I
    left Roswell.

Lawrence leans forward, his eyes locking with hers.

              LAWRENCE
    I don't take this lightly, Matilda.
    I know what it means for you to
    share this with me.

Matilda nods, a hint of a smile crossing her lips.

              MATILDA
    I don't have much time left. My
    body may be frail, but my spirit is
    as strong as ever. I need you to
    help me tell the truth. The world
    deserves to know what happened in
    1947.

She slides the envelope across the table toward him. Lawrence hesitates for a moment, then carefully picks it up, as though holding a sacred artifact.

              MATILDA (CONT'D)
    Inside are the transcripts from my
    interviews with Airl. I kept them
    hidden all these years. The
    military, the government... they
    didn't want anyone to know. But
    Airl trusted me, and I owe it to
    her to share what I know.

Lawrence opens the envelope and pulls out a thick stack of typewritten pages, yellowed with age. He glances over the first page, his brow furrowing.

                    LAWRENCE
          And you're sure this is safe?
          Sharing this now?

Matilda chuckles softly, a sound tinged with both resignation
and defiance.

                    MATILDA
          What can they do to me now,
          Lawrence? They can't silence me
          anymore.

She pauses, her gaze distant, as if peering into the past.

                    MATILDA (CONT'D)
          I've lived with this secret for
          sixty years. I've seen the world
          change in ways I never imagined,
          but the truth... the truth hasn't
          changed. Airl's words, her
          insights—they're more important now
          than ever.

Lawrence sets the pages down, leaning back in his chair, his
expression a mix of awe and determination.

                    LAWRENCE
          I'll do it, Matilda. I'll write
          your story—the world's story.

Matilda smiles, her eyes glistening with gratitude.

                    MATILDA
          Thank you, Lawrence. Remember,
          this isn't just my story. It's
          Airl's story, too. It's humanity's
          story.

She leans back in her chair, a sense of peace washing over
her.

                    MATILDA (CONT'D)
          It's time for the world to wake up.

Matilda leans back in the armchair, and a sense of resolve
covers her face. She now feels content, believing she can
leave this life with no regrets.

                                                  FADE OUT.

THE END.

www.ingramcontent.com/pod-product-compliance
Lightning Source LLC
Chambersburg PA
CBHW081216170426
43198CB00017B/2628